A Quiet Dawdle THROUGH LIFE

Jim

by

James *and* Else Mellor

Grosvenor House
Publishing Limited

All rights reserved
Copyright © James Mellor, 2015

The right of James Mellor to be identified as the author of this
work has been asserted in accordance with Section 78
of the Copyright, Designs and Patents Act 1988

The book cover picture is copyright to James Mellor

This book is published by
Grosvenor House Publishing Ltd
28-30 High Street, Guildford, Surrey, GU1 3EL.
www.grosvenorhousepublishing.co.uk

This book is sold subject to the conditions that it shall not, by way of
trade or otherwise, be lent, resold, hired out or otherwise circulated
without the author's or publisher's prior consent in any form of binding or
cover other than that in which it is published and
without a similar condition including this condition being imposed
on the subsequent purchaser.

A CIP record for this book
is available from the British Library

ISBN 978-1-78148-961-1

Dedication

To my family in Britain, I hope you will enjoy reading about my life, Jim Mellor.

To my family in Trinidad, Norway and Britain, I hope you will be fascinated by Jim's early life, our adventures together and then retirement to the Hebrides, Else Mellor.

I would like to give my thanks to the sewage profession for a lifetime of vastly interesting and rewarding employment.

Introduction

Dad was in the Royal Navy, his grounding being in engineering. Mum worked in a cotton mill as a girl and learned to speak the language of the cotton mill girls where the noise of the mill defeated any attempt to speak normally. Instead, they mouthed the words with exaggerated movement of their lips.

I grew up in a small village in Derbyshire, Dad being away in the Royal Navy. The war started when I was two years old. I have memories of the distinct noise of bombs dropping, krupp, krupp, on the nearby small town, hiding under a table with Mum and the upset of my auntie whose husband never came home from army service in the far east.

I had the wonderful Derbyshire countryside for my playground and learned to fish, tickle trout, shoot and generally enjoy country life in all its riches. School was a necessity rather than an enjoyment and one school report said, "could do better."

With advice from My Dad I applied for and was accepted for a job at a sewage works in Buxton. This gave rise to many raucous comments from my friends. However night school study, leading to a certificate as an Associate Member of the Institute of Water Pollution Control, soon put my feet firmly on the ladder of promotion to Stockport and then Shrewsbury to an amazingly interesting profession of sewage purification.

I found it no hardship to read many books on a variety of topics and quickly acquired a very substantial library. In due course, I started writing articles initially to do with my work, my first being entitled, 'Sewage Sludge for Rich Black Soil,' for which I was paid the handsome sum of £12.

Over the years I have written articles relating to my work, hobbies, interests and travels, some of which are included in this book. Writing articles, catering for weddings, funerals and other joyous occasions afforded me the luxury of building my own vessel *Ospray*.

As in the old adage, 'Derbyshire born and Derbyshire bred, strong in th'arm and wick in th'ead,' whilst claiming to be neither, I was certainly born in Derbyshire. My work and family life in

Shropshire saw four boys growing up on a farm, my first wife Ruth working as a nurse and enjoying my hobbies of breeding horses, fishing and shooting and building a steel copy of the *Spray*. My retirement years were mostly in the Highlands with my second wife Else, following our yearlong circuit of the north Atlantic and sharing our hobbies and interests on the Isle of Seil.

As my sight has deteriorated substantially and I can no longer read, which was one of my greatest pleasures, jolly music does help to while away some hours and Else fortunately enjoys reading aloud on topics of mutual interest e.g. whaling and the American Indians. Both of these topics are now lower on out list of favourites as we have learned so much more about them. Knowing what happened in the past and todays radical change of concept has readjusted our views regarding what constitutes cruelty, which has thankfully altered to a huge extent. After my two strokes, my mobility is greatly reduced but I now have a Tramper, a four-wheel drive mobility scooter, which takes me mostly wherever I want to go. So Else, our dogs, Kate, Grouse, Gypsy and our pup Glen can go 'where others may fear to tread.'

Acknowledgements

Thank you to Stuart and Ann Reid for proof reading. For their invaluable help, worthy comments and huge encouragement, to them we tender our heartfelt thanks.

Thank you to Robert Cameron for introducing me to stalking in the Highlands and to Harry Fowler, now deceased, to the fishing in Argyll. For their jolly companionship on many happy days stalking and fishing.

Thanks to Else for her boundless enthusiasm, reading, typing and taking more and more part in the actual writing of this book. Else accomplished this feat with never a cross word between us. She was a capable assistant when I wrote my last book and will no doubt be active in her own genre in time.

Over the years, thank you to Ruth and my sons Robert, Mark and Jonathan, unfortunately Andrew is deceased, for the help freely given, for many and various tasks and enjoyable times we have spent together.

About the Authors

James Mellor was born in Buxton, Derbyshire, where he was educated at Buxton College and Mile End Grammar School. He worked as a chemist and biologist in the sewage profession in Buxton and Stockport living with his first wife Ruth. They moved to Shrewsbury where he was initially Assistant Manager and chemist and was later promoted to Manager of Severn Trent Water Authority. He had four boys with Ruth and living on a farm gave space for the boys to experience country life at its best. He enjoyed keeping and breeding horses, fishing and writing. James met Else in the mid 1980's, decided to voyage in the boat that he built with his sons in a barn on the farm, and having survived a yearlong voyage, decided as they had much in common, that they wanted to get married.

Else Mellor, nee Jardine, was born in Point-a-Pierre, Trinidad, educated in Trinidad and Barbados, then travelled to Norway, where her mother was from, to do a nursing course. She then travelled to England and studied to become a Chartered Physiotherapist, married and worked in orthopaedics at Oswestry, Shropshire. Years later when she was divorced and met Jim, she applied for and got a sabbatical of a year off to go voyaging across the Atlantic and to visit her home and family in Trinidad. On their return, both felt that they could continue voyaging at sea as it was a very happy and satisfying time. Else was to return to work and stayed at the Orthopaedic until 1998 when she took early retirement, as Jim had heart surgery and they were planning a move to Scotland.

Together, Jim and Else lived for a few years in Shropshire, then spent many holidays searching for the right spot to call home, before moving to Argyll in 1999 where they still live on the island of Seil with their four spaniels.

A Quiet Dawdle Around The Atlantic is the book that James wrote about building and sailing his beloved *Ospray*, a copy of Slocum's *Spray*, the first vessel to sail around the world single-handed.

Chapter 1

My Formative Years

I spent my formative years living in the High Peak district of Derbyshire. My father had spent the War years in the Royal Navy, which he left after being offered a Commission. Dad refused this tempting offer, thinking that mother had bravely struggled through the War years bringing up we boys, while Dad was at sea in the Mediterranean, with his ship often being under enemy fire. I remember vividly Mother's distress when the hymn 'For those in peril on the sea' was played on the wireless. When Dad came out of the Navy, he took us for a holiday of a lifetime to Torquay. The train journey took us through Herefordshire and I saw these amazingly different cattle. It certainly felt like a strange new land. At the hotel our family were waited on at the table by a smartly dressed waiter, respectful and aloof, as in the manner of such people at the time (their profession). I was vastly impressed especially when being called Sir as a child. This was when I started to like sprouts and coffee. Being a child, I was given small portions that were never enough.

Another sad memory was of my Auntie Louie (Anne Louise Oldham) Mother's sister, who received a telegram to say that her husband, Uncle Louis (Louis Vincent Oldham) was missing in action in the Far East, Burma. He never came home. She never found out if or how he died. I remember finding her in floods of tears, which she tried to hide, but I knew what it was all about. I think that they had not long been married when he went off to war. On the records, he was a gunner in 1943 when he died, as we discovered recently.

In those early days I can remember having a bath in front of the fire, a cosy feeling. The tin bath hung up in the kitchen. I also remember hearing bombs landing in Manchester, 'crump, crump.'

Mother and I did hide under the table when the bombs hit New Mills about two miles away.

Sometimes Mother and I would go to visit her three old aunts and often I would be sent out doors to "go and pick some raspberries" so that they could gossip without little ears being about. On one occasion I was very confused. Mother said in general chat, "Oh, you know whom I am talking about, she married a Fox!" This conjured up many a mental vision of a wedding with Mr Fox standing at the altar, smartly dressed and given away only by his bushy tail! I went to one of my aunts, Auntie Hilda, to stay when Mum gave birth to Bryan. One incident that took a long time to forgive was when one day I was hiding under my bed when Auntie Hilda came into the room. I grabbed her leg from my hiding place but was very soon out from under and down the stairs with a severe telling off. I secretly thought that Uncle Eric was quietly amused. Their daughter, Dorothy, must have been about five or six years older than I and I remember going to meet her when she arrived on the train. I was most surprised when the young folk that we passed addressed her with great respect as Miss Taylor, a rarity in those days. They lived in Hindlow, which only consisted of a row of a few houses surrounded by moorland and a huge quarry. Uncle Eric worked on the nearby railway.

On weekends I went up to Jodrell Meadows and was allowed to go with Uncle John but mostly Uncle Fred, Dad's brothers, in the lorry. It was an old fashioned model, a J-Type Bedford with a pointed bonnet, very noisy, especially when it rained on the cab roof as there was no lining. There was also no heating. It smelled of oil and petrol in the cab. It may also have been a tipper truck. They were coal merchants but would carry anything else, perhaps stone and aggregate for roads from the quarries in the Buxton area. At the yard in Whaley Bridge where the trucks and coal were stored, the men as well as driving had to do their own maintenance on the trucks probably, on the weekends. Again freezing cold, except for the little office at the side of the building, which had a coal fire which, when lit, was lovely and cosy. Upstairs above the building was a loft full of things to explore.

I remember seeing all of the mink traps. Granddad used to have mink in one of the buildings but then one of the Baxter children let a cage out. This led to the mink being sold. My brother Bob told me a story about Fred, the Stores Man, who worked for J D Mellor, Dad's firm, going in the lorry helping with a delivery and complaining about the freezing cold. When they arrived at their destination, he found out that a rope had been caught in the door and thereby was the reason for him feeling frozen. Fred was known to go home for lunch where his wife would have a pair of warmed socks waiting for him, so this tale was told a few times.

I felt a distinct sense of cosiness and camaraderie. Uncle Fred often talked about the 'perils' of crossing Shap Fell. There was at that time a certain awe reserved for crossing bleak wide-open spaces, which Shap Fell, then was. Uncle John's house was adjacent to Granddad's farm and buildings. He would talk about going up the 'clough', a wooded clough near the farm building, tales of 'derring do,' about rabbiting, something akin to someone discussing a tiger hunt. At Granddad's house there was a grandfather clock. I was told that Granddad had carried it on his back eleven miles over the moorland from Flash to Whaley Bridge. I remember where it was in the house and the sound of it. An incident that happened relating to this clock was when I had been shooting rabbits in the clough, part of which belonged to Granddad. A policeman saw the gun when I was walking from the farm about half a mile from the house. I was terrified that I had possibly caused a problem for Granddad who was a very law abiding person. I ran into Granddad's house with the policeman, a short distance behind, following on his bicycle. The offending article was hidden behind the grandfather clock but on opening the door to the policeman Granddad said nothing, as there was confusion as to which garden I had entered. As nothing was said, Granddad didn't have to tell a lie. The clock is passed down from grandfather to eldest grandson, so I now have it and it will go to my eldest grandson George. It has been in my possession for many years.

When I was about ten, Geoff Knibb and I would go onto Sam Evans' farm, less than a mile from home, where we built a 'cabin'.

This was merely a few poles cut from the nearby 'Tanglewood' that was a mass of rhododendron bushes and other small trees. The poles supported an old railway tarpaulin. At the back end of the 'cabin,' I had dug out of the bank a space big enough to hold a wood fire. No expense spared! Ray Mears eat your heart out! Seating was for us on the border of luxury and consisted of two short logs, one each for Geoff and myself. At the 'cabin' our meals consisted of brown trout tickled from the brook, rabbits snared from the fields, the occasional wood pigeon shot with an air rifle, mushrooms gathered from the fields and my porridge was best left undescribed!

With a good fire burning in the dugout inglenook our nights were considered by some to be cosy if a little smokey, (some considered it very smokey). But we hardy souls were quite content. Geoff's and my parents vowed that we smelled like old tramps, decidedly woodsy, and in some need of a good bath and a change of clothes!

Tickling trout is an art acquired only by much practice. One feels under a partly submerged rock until one touches the underside of a trout. The trout is manoeuvred gently into a position when it can be grasped and pulled out onto the bank whence it can be swiftly dispatched. If one is planning to catch more fish, a stick with a fork on one end is needed, so that the fish may be threaded onto the stick through the gills and thus carried home. If one moves further down river, fish should not be left uncovered on the bank as crows have amazing eyesight and are very partial to trout. On the subject of fishing, Mum came across a suspect tin while clearing out my bedroom one day. She opened the old tin, her curiosity getting the better of her and was met by a buzzing swarm of bluebottles. I was definitely not in her good books! My brother Michael was often in bad books as well. One incident occurred when mother was doing the washing and was putting a sheet through the mangle only to find that Michael had also put some cinders in with the sheet!

It was many years after when I revisited the big wood not quarter of a mile from home, that I realised it was less than five acres in extent and next to it was the little wood of one acre.

We delighted in climbing the trees to discuss any matters that we thought were of great importance and therefore out of earshot.

Dad had various engineering jobs but eventually bought a newsagents shop in Hazel Grove near Stockport. I remember from the paper round days that I hated Thursdays. The paper bag was very heavy with the magazine 'Woman's Own.' One Thursday the rain was bucketing down. As the flap on the paper bag was lifted at every point of delivery, so the papers got naturally a little bit wet. A Scotsman called Mr Mc Fadgen, (I had a crush on his daughter) came into the newsagents shop and complained to my Father. He was in a furious temper about his wet newspaper and said they were "Ripped to hell!"

After passing my 11-plus exams, Dad put me down for going to Buxton College as a preference. No doubt because he was a Buxtonian, hailing from that neck of the woods. Buxton College was a grand old school comprising of about a third boarder and the rest dayboys of which I was one. As I didn't like football I was able to choose cross-country running for sports and enjoyed Corbar Woods the huge expanse of woodland near to the school. At this time I went to the Devonshire Royal Hospital once a week for physiotherapy, electrical treatments, to strengthen my right leg.

I met John Richies when I transferred to Mile End School who also became a paperboy and remains today a life long friend.

About a year later Dad had sold the newsagents shop and gone back to engineering. Being, I suspect, unable to cope with small talk and gossipy chitchat expected of a shopkeeper. We moved to No 322 Moorland Road halfway between Hazel Grove and Stockport, where I moved from Buxton College to Mile End Grammar School. Here I met Colin Crees.

I knew Geoff from age six when I lived in Furness Vale; he lived about half a mile away. He was drawn strongly to the farming community of the area. He adopted the North Country way of speaking. His parents were quite well spoken, possibly evacuated to Furness Vale because of the war in the City, which city I don't know. We went to different schools but camped and tickled or fished for trout in the local streams, often returning home with sopping wet shirt sleeves despite being rolled up and often with mostly wet shirts. Our Mums must have had a hard time trying to keep us looking half tidy!

Having moved to Hazel Grove I spent most of my weekends at Furness Vale and I remember Geoff and I finding a dead deer somewhere on the hill behind the 'Murder Stone.' We skinned the beast, it being an extremely cold day. This was the first animal of any size that we had skinned so had to proceed as we thought best. On the way home, it started to rain heavily, so we stretched the skin over our shoulders. We were still five to seven miles away from home where we arrived a few hours after our normal teatime. Both our parents questioned the wisdom of our actions but apparently Geoff found himself in extremely hot water and was grounded. I have no doubt that his choice of companion came into question.

The first deer I ever shot was an escapee from Lyme Park on Dad's farm and it was killed by a brain shot. It was dragged back to the farm and prepared in the cellar where it was hung up from a beam.

The Murder Stone stands on the Buxton old road on the way from Whaley Bridge to Disley in Derbyshire. A man called William Wood, a weaver, had been to a market day in Manchester to sell some of his cloth. It is thought that he stopped at an Inn for refreshments and some ne'er-do-wells must have seen that he had on his person a bundle of money and surreptitiously followed him. So on the way from Eyam to Whaley Bridge, Wood, about thirty years old and a family man was viciously murdered, on a desolate stretch of moorland, his skull being crushed by a stone. The murderers then buried Wood in a shallow grave on the side of the road. Two men, Edmund Pott and John Mellor, found the body and as they were passing in their cart, they brought the body to The Cock Inn at Whaley Bridge. Two of the murderers were caught, one was never found. Dale was executed, Taylor tried to hang himself but died later, Platt was never seen again.

I had been told that my few 'O' levels would guarantee me a place in the apprenticeship of the major engineering firms in the nearby town of Stockport.

MY FORMATIVE YEARS

If you asked a little boy what he would like to be when he grew up, his answer would be likely to range from the slightly bizarre, such as a ringmaster in a circus with his astounding powers over snarling black-maned lions, whose avowed intent seemed to be to slay and devour the impudent ringmaster, then probably for afters a few of the audience as well.

Another popular choice would include Engine Drivers. The sheer thrill of being in charge of 1000 tons of a snorting monster belching smoke while tearing along at speeds in excess of 80 mph seems intoxicating in the extreme.

Another favourite might be a Fireman. It seems that the thought of being seen clinging to a slim ladder at unimaginable heights, squirting water in a valiant attempt to extinguish a ravenous fire, which threatened the safety and even the lives, of lord knows how many damsels in distress.

In contrast to these glorious and valiant occupations, an advert for a job on a sewage works, one would be unlikely to get killed in the rush! And yet as will be gradually revealed, the job had hidden depths and possibilities. So when an advert appeared 'Junior Chemist required at Stockport Sewage Disposal Works,' naturally I sought my Dad's advice expecting him to advise the engineering apprenticeships. Dad thought long and hard, then he surprised me by suggesting that I try for the Junior Chemist job. I did so and was successful. Dad's reasoning was that the engineering jobs involved stiff competition for years whereas the Junior Chemist's job depended only on my endeavours.

A formidable looking Borough Surveyor interviewed me at the Town Hall. After interviewing the other candidates I was sent for again and sternly offered the job. He said that if I did well, I would be left alone to get on with the job. If I did not do well, I should soon hear from him again. I feared death more than this so tried hard not to be brought to his attention.

Chapter 2

Learning The Job From The Bottom Up

1955 – 1959 I was Laboratory Assistant, Borough of Stockport. I began attending college for one day and two nights per week with the aim of obtaining a National Certificate in chemistry. At the end of which I could attempt the home based course for the AMIWPC (Associate Member of the Institute of Water Pollution Control).

Surrounding the sewage works, there were several hundred acres of farmland. Part of this was used for sludge disposal. Spreading or pumping sludge onto the land accomplished this. Then after a period of months this was ploughed, and if sufficiently dry, it would be ploughed in and possibly a crop sown in the extremely rich soil. I remember a crop of mangolds of prodigious size! Mangel-wurzels, a variety of beet, were often used for fodder.

Also on a small field next to the works, a crop of oats was sown which when ripening, attracted hordes of pigeons. I told the farmhands that I had an old muzzle-loading shotgun. A single barrel 11-bore, for which I had a supply of black powder. Words were spoken in the right ears and I was given permission, on condition that my laboratory work was kept up to scratch, to slip out of the lab and take an occasional blast at the predators. I once killed eleven birds with one shot, giving some to the shift men and taking the rest home! This gun was the start of an intense interest in and a collection of black powder weapons.

When I joined the sewage works staff as a junior chemist, there were the remnants of the farm and equipment from when the area was more extensively farmed. There were two shire horses and two elderly men who were referred to as ostlers and who looked after the horses and used them for the smaller farming jobs still performed. I have no idea what the financial arrangements were. I do not recall the presence of a tractor. The two men seemed very rural in character and I suspect they were there as a result of a deal with the previous landowners.

After the oats were harvested to feed the horses, the field had to be ploughed. This was then done with horses, as there were still drains deep in the soil, which may be damaged by the weight of a tractor. I asked to help when I had finished in the lab.

Imagine my delight when this was granted! I had handled horses before but usually singly and smaller than these two great shires. I took hold of the harness of the inside horse while one of the ostlers steered the plough and made a fair job of following the previous plough line until we reached the end of the plough when the horses had been trained to turn and walk back to the start of the plough on unploughed ground. This meant that the horse would have to cross over the placing of his feet. He did this and because I was holding the head collar close to me with a bent arm, placed a hoof, the size of a dinner plate, squarely on my foot, which, I thought, was crushed. The old ostler, who was only a few paces away, told me sternly. "Hold the head collar with a straight arm, when you turn the horse." My crushed foot recovered after a week or two with a lesson well learned the hard way! When leading a horse, which may be turned, hold the lead collar at arm's length! Here endeth the first lesson.

The event gave the men many a chuckle and me a blush! I shall never forget handling these gentle giants. I was allowed to on several occasions, each one memorable and treasured immensely!

I had been at the usual Saturday afternoon 'pigeon' shoot. I mentioned my growing interest in black powder guns to one of the farmers on the shoot. He said that he had an old black powder weapon that had stood in the corner of his parlour for many, many years. He said it was red rusty but he thought it was still sound. I fumbled in my pocket to find I had 30 shillings only. To my amazement he said, "That will do." You can imagine my zest in attacking the gun with all the ultra fine emery paper and wire wool until the gun looked as if it were made the day before.

During this period another great plus emerged. This was the three monthly visit to the sewage works of the trainee pupils of Poise House, a training school for nurses and allied professions. These were nearly all girls. Part of their education was considered to be a visit to a sewage works. Part of my job was to show these young ladies round and give them a talk on the health and hygiene aspects. This included showing them the various organisms, which are part of the purification process. I would show the girls some of the organisms such as paramecium, vorticella and amoeba through the microscope.

Some of the girls were extremely attractive, so you may be sure I swotted up on the talk for the girls and donned my smartest white coat for these visits. I cultivated a mild but effective friendship with the lecturer who always accompanied the girls and of course knew their names and social status such as, 'going out with a six foot rugger player' or, more promising, 'the girl with the dark hair, her name is Sadie and she is Irish, she stays in most nights.' And so on. I had many a pleasant night out from this productive source.

I was part of a skiffle group with Colin, Geoff and others, something that I miss still being able to do. Geoff was a welcome participant having some musical knowledge and was often able to voice an opinion on the best key to play some of our songs. We would play a variety of instruments e.g. washboard, guitars, spoons, the occasional banjo or ukulele, mouth organs and all of us would sing, well or badly. We would visit a pub that would let us in and receive the odd pint in appreciation. I don't remember being paid any money. We might travel on a bus, no mean feat with a tea chest base, and would often walk the two or three miles home after. Some pubs would not allow us in, as they did not appreciate our music. A few of my friends still sing in choirs and we can all still pick up an instrument and make music and have a good time!

Despite these welcome attractions I passed the AMIWPC exam and was told at the time that I was the youngest to pass. My boss, Mr Holt, who was party to anything that went on in the Institution, would only say whilst warming his behind in front of

LEARNING THE JOB FROM THE BOTTOM UP

the lab fire and closing his eyes in defence against the smoke from his Craven-A, "You might be hearing some good news in the next week or two." The 'good news' duly arrived with the realization that I could now start applying for jobs. However I was in no hurry. In this profession like many others, there was what was known as 'plum jobs.' In the meantime I was quite happy.

One of the shift men was named Edward. He was very proud of the fine fare his wife had packed for his lunch. One day in order to display this to the wider world, Edward stood in the doorway of the shift house looking out over the Howarth Units. At that precise moment a lump of foam blew from the Howarth units (which consisted of many paddles like that seen on a paddle steamer set in channels many yards long). The chunk of foam, the size of a large loaf landed on his prized lunch and instantly dissolved, ruining his feast.

Now Edward was exceedingly cynical about 'scientists' and that with regard to the samples that they were instructed to take every hour. I noticed one day, that one bottle had slightly more fluid in it and had a green tinge to it. Edward had once been recorded as saying that we couldn't tell the difference if he peed in the bottle. A quick test confirmed my suspicions. Edward was testing us out! I reported to Edward that I had sent part of yesterday's sample to the public analyst, as there were signs of a serious outbreak of VD. Edward blanched visibly and was very quiet for days. Jibes about scientists dried up completely.

Frank was the gardener for the sewage works. His greenhouse was situated behind the lab and the Manager's office. Frank's job was to grow ornamental flowers for the several large beds around the works. We persuaded Frank to allow us to sow a couple of large seed trays with tobacco seeds. When the plants were a few inches high (about the height of a pencil) they were planted, just behind Mr Holt, the Manager's, office window. I began to feel mildly alarmed when the plants reached four feet tall. No one said anything! The plants grew mightily and eventually reached a height of over six foot, cutting out the view and much of the light from Mr Holt's window. Obviously we did any work required during our dinner hour. Mr Holt never said a word. A fact that we attributed to his pride. Eventually the plants were harvested and the leaves, some of them over four foot long, hung in Frank's greenhouse until cured and a lovely copper brown. The leaves were anointed with a secret mixture before being tightly rolled up and ready for the pipe. Although being unfairly described as being like smoking Arab's underpants but not quite so good! It was not all bad.

One of my colleagues was called Alec Spotswood, who was also a pipe smoker. He had some rather peculiar interests. He walked the boundaries of Stockport as they had existed in times past and then again in times more recent. Alec always wore Veldtschoen and persuaded me to try them, which I did and found them very comfortable. Although they were expensive to buy initially, they could be sent away and given a full repair at a low cost thus lasting almost indefinitely. Following my move to Shrewsbury, we continued to meet at annual conferences and remained good friends. He was my partner in crime in our tobacco growing enterprise. Sadly, he has passed away but we still keep in touch with his wife, Margaret.

Rats were not an uncommon sight on the plant as the farm crops were grown near the sewage disposal machinery. One day a big rat was killed, a touch larger than the average. I arranged it in a life like posture on the doorstep of the lab and Manager's Office. Apparently our boss, Mr Holt, very nearly jumped out of his skin – but also pretended not to be upset or frightened by it.

I had put my latest batch of gunpowder to dry in an oven which was kept at what I thought was a very modest temperature. Apparently it wasn't modest enough, for I arrived at work next morning to find a large black scorch mark on the ceiling. Great haste was used to erase the large black burn, only just in time to avoid Mr Holt's arrival at work. He never noticed. As usual Mr Holt was warming his backside by the fire, eyes closed against the smoke of his first Craven-A of the day.

Eventually, one of the 'plum jobs' came on the market. Although it was maybe only a plum job for a few of whom I was one, I always had a great fondness for Buxton.

1959 – 1961, I was Manager and Chemist, Borough of Buxton. I was newly married to Ruth who was a fever nurse at

LEARNING THE JOB FROM THE BOTTOM UP

Cherry Tree Hospital and who would easily find work at one of the Buxton Hospitals. And who was not put off by the lowly name of No 1 Gas Works Cottages, the name being slightly softened by the second line of the address being Ashwood Dale! Our first son Robert was born at Corber Nursing Home in Buxton.

No 1 Gas Works Cottages lay snugly between the Gasworks and the Sewage Works. Hardly the address of a social climber! And because of its position it was often a good wind that blew no ill!

It was a cosy cottage with an outside loo, which was situated in the back yard diametrically opposite to the back door some ten yards away. One winter's night, my wife Ruth popped across the yard for her pre-bedtime tinkle. She had just settled down when there was the most spine-chilling shriek. The loo door burst open and with further shrieks which, like Peel's 'View Halloo' would have 'wakened the dead.' Ruth crossed the yard in a series of gigantic bounds, with her nether garment round her ankles dictating her novel but inelegant means of locomotion. This precluded the taking of strides.

Apparently a fleeting thought occurred to pull her nether garment up, till a second thought occurred, that this might bring the rat into close contact with her body. This was instantly voted emphatically no! Ruth's choice of locomotion was inelegant but undoubtedly a mile eater which apparently suited her just fine, as a mile was the very minimum distance she wished to be from the rat, which she described with her hands as being roughly the size of a sabre-toothed tiger.

Elegance? Who the hell gives a fig about elegance? When you have just had a rat run over your feet while you were having a tinkle! Even if, in retrospect, the creature was maybe not quite as big as a sabre-toothed tiger! And women have such bizarre ideas regarding where a frightened rat may try to hide!

Meanwhile the Gas Works gang, who were alerted by the screams, had witnessed the whole event from their eyrie at the top of the Gas Works building which towered above our house. Their howls of mirth did nothing to soothe Ruth's injured dignity but instead torched her temper to exploding point. A change of address was included in the topics of conversation. Eventually, to my relief, a terrier was decided upon! The breed was unimportant but the vital trait was the one commonly found in terriers. The ardent desire to kill something! Especially a rat.

We were soon given a terrier of the Manchester variety by Ruth's mother. Her name was Ginnie, an appropriate name, and her bite being like that of a gin trap. Quick to grip and slow to let go! As you may imagine, one of Ginnie's first tasks was a nightly inspection of the loo, which she took on with unbounded eagerness, which was a sure sign of lingering rat scent that served to retain Ginnie's enthusiasm at a high level.

The occupants of one of the other two cottages, No 2, next door to us were Arthur Plant and his wife. Arthur was fond of a joke and a tall tale, full of accurate detail. One such tale came after I had shown him our grandfather clock. He said, "I used to have a grandfather clock. I was taking it to that little clock repairer just up that little lane off Spring Gardens. Just as I was going round the corner, I bumped into an old chap and knocked him sprottling. As he picked himself up he said angrily, why the hell don't you buy a wristwatch!"

Most Wednesday nights, we would cycle up to Jim and Bella Dempster's house, family on Dad's side, in Upper Burbage, just below the edge of the moor. This was where Jim had once been employed as a shepherd. Jim had a sheepdog, which had been taught that a man should always remove his hat when entering a house. Jim would say to the dog, "What should a good boy do?" The dog would immediately spring lightly up and remove the offending headgear.

It was a hard pull on the tandem to visit the Dempsters but an easy ride back, down the hill all the way. We would arrive home to find Ginnie snoring on the hearthrug in front of the fire. However, the rocking chair was still rocking merrily which gave the lie to Ginnie's slumbering!

As one may imagine, there were times when a strong stomach was an advantage in this job. The screens were one point where this could occur. The screens were where the incoming sewage passed through a set of steel bars, placed at equidistant spacing,

LEARNING THE JOB FROM THE BOTTOM UP

to sieve out anything not wanted to proceed through the works. A mechanical rake, a sturdy steel machine that though extremely strong, occasionally broke down, cleaned these screens. When this happened, the cause had to be determined. This usually meant that a man had to don waders, and with the machine safely locked off, enter the channel, and search the channel and the screens for the cause of the blockage. This could be a broken part of the machinery or an unusual object entering the sewers. This would initially be achieved by using a hand held rake. If this was unsuccessful, a hand search, for which gloves were unsuitable, was necessary. Remember this would take place by a man in his waders standing over knee deep in crude sewage often searching for say, a broken bolt up to an inch in diameter, slightly rusty. Those with a fertile imagination may by now have leaped ahead of me and considered what other objects, which may be a perfectly normal constituent of crude sewage! One's thoughts need not be super fertile to imagine a few possibilities. Under water or in sewage, it is difficult to assess the weight or hardness of an object. Are you with me yet? To the few innocents who may not be, let me explain. We are searching for possibly a broken, rusty bolt, possibly ¾ inch diameter, in a torrent of crude sewage! I will leave the rest to your imagination! I'll bet you scrub your hands before you eat your tea!

The appearance of false teeth on the screens was not uncommon. Usually as a result of drinking well but not too wisely. Occasionally an enquiry was received about such a loss. Accordingly, the staff was instructed to save such objects for a short period. Such an enquiry was received one day and the querying gentleman invited down to the sewage works. The gentleman duly turned up and was visibly surprised to be shown a plank shelf of wood on which were displayed a grinning row of around twenty sets of gnashers! The gent soon spied a set, which seemed familiar and before I could intervene, he grabbed them and stuffed them in his mouth, although they had only been quickly rinsed under a tap. Declaring his pleasure at being reunited with an old friend, the gent thanked us profusely and went on his way rejoicing. If I had the chance, I would have advised him to soak the dentures in mild disinfectant. Heaven knows what fellow travellers the dentures had encountered and rubbed against on their voyage to the sewage works since being launched by their previous owner.

Buxton, as the highest town in England, had earned itself the jibe of having 'six months winter and six months cold weather!' I always considered that Buxtonians had a sort of a glow of confidence. Whether this was because of the tang of the air or despite it, I was never sure, but it was there.

Years ago when I was at Buxton College, I was often in detention. Thursday was the night for detention. The college was almost two miles from the railway station. The master in charge had worked out a fiendish refinement. He would release me with devilish cunning after eleven minutes. This gave me just enough time to run to the station where I would arrive in a muck sweat to be dragged into the carriage by the other lads.

Most of the boys went through their time at Buxton College without having been caned. However, I was caned three times. I can't remember why but I'm sure it was for something 'reasonably trivial.' The procedure was when one was sent for, to be ushered into the Head Master's study, Mr Bolton-King, known as BK, with his instruction to bend down and face the window. One was given normally three strokes of the cane. The second time I knew my fate. At the first stroke, instead of being a 'thwack,' there was a soft 'womph,' the second sounded no different and I knew that I had overdone the padding and that wily BK was not to be outwitted. It wasn't very long before I was sent for, another trivial offence, without warning and to report instantly, to the Head Master's study. This time, the whacking went as expected and was quite painful as it should have been. BK was always dramatically dressed in a suit with a black gown, tall, slim and austere. His smiles were rare. No grudges held.

The four compartments of the train reserved for us were labelled Scholars, possibly more in hope than in expectation. Occasionally, the Scholars compartments were part of a corridor portion of the train. This meant that mixing could, and did, occur between boys and girls. Being in the Peak District, our journey involved travelling through two long tunnels. Bulbs could be, and sometimes were, removed from their sockets. What occurred during these blackouts shall probably remain behind closed doors but I was not aware of a single complaint being made by the Cavendish girls and most definitely not from the boys!

There was a problem with the Gas Works Manager's house, which was situated about one hundred yards from our house. The Manager's wife came home and was welcomed by the sight of sewage cascading down the stairs. Not a pretty sight! The carpets were ruined and the house had to be evacuated while the mess was cleaned up. The culprit was eventually found to be a fault in the internal plumbing of the house. Being situated in a steep sided Derbyshire valley, that of the Derbyshire Wye, the sewage treatment plant had to be designed and placed with great care.

The primary works which included screens, primary settling tanks and sludge treatment facilities were placed together just below Gas Works Cottages. The secondary treatment bacteria beds took place a mile or two down the Wye valley. The sludge from the primary settling tanks was treated with slaked lime then pumped through powerful hydraulic presses, and then the pressed sludge was eagerly taken away by a local farmer as a valuable soil conditioner because of the lime.

To run this works I was allowed three and a half men! They were a splendid bunch of whom I grew very fond. The half a man worked half his time on the highways department and the other half for me on the sewage treatment. This tight staffing meant that if a man were off either sick or on leave, I would have to fill the gap. I did not mind this as it meant learning the job from the bottom up!

My office was directly above the mess room and every morning a shout would come up the stairs, "Tea up boss!" I would go downstairs and take my tea with the men and enjoy their jolly chatter and leg pulling.

The foreman's name was Joe Legge, a man in his sixties who had been a blacksmith. He had built himself a forge and would make or repair any iron or steel object broken or needed on the plant. He taught me many valuable things including the exact colour required for heating metal. For example, bright cherry red in a dimmed room. That is why blacksmith's workshops were rarely brightly lit, dimness was essential to discern colour properly. Little did I know that I would use this knowledge later in life when I built my steel copy of *Ospray* and forged many of her fittings which saved me a great deal of money. Joe Legge was worth his weight in gold. Hard working, skilful, loyal and unfailingly polite. I thought the world of him and still treasure my memories of this grand old man, and this after fifty years!

I forgot to mention the occupant of No 3 cottage, next to Arthur Plant and his wife. She was a nice old lady by the name of Mrs Featherstone. She was, I thought, very aptly named, as she was a fluttery old bird of a lady who kept herself very much to herself.

The second and or tertiary part of the plant, the bacteria beds, were positioned a couple of miles down Ashwood Dale, which required a daily bike ride for routine attention. This was long before the provision of vehicles for such trifles! At Buxton, I had a small but adequate laboratory well equipped for basic analysis including a microscope that I used to assess the health of the bacteria beds. It could be seen at a glance whether there was a healthy balance of organisms. Meanwhile Ruth resigned from her job as staff nurse at the nearest hospital some few miles away and to which she cycled each day on our tandem. She had become pregnant with our first child who was to be named Robert.

On one of our holidays we visited Scotland on a tandem. No mean feat cycling up the Rest and Be Thankful I might add. But I was reminded by John Richies and his wife, who were also on the cycle tour with us, that I said at some time, "I could easily live here!" And we stayed one very rainy night in a barn belonging to a Mellor! And this was very close to the Isle of Seil in Argyll. More about this later.

Mum and Dad on a picnic

Chapter 3

Balmy Shropshire

My next job resulted from an advert for 'Assistant Manager and Chemist, Borough of Shrewsbury.' I was genuinely sorry to leave Buxton and its crew of splendid, loyal and hardworking fellows who I take my hat off to!

When I first moved to Shrewsbury, a young married man with one child, we lived at No 4 Allerton Road. My second son Andrew was born here and then we moved to No 322 Monkmoor Road where Mark was born. While still at this address, our last son Jonathan was born at the new Copthorne hospital. Ruth worked as a nurse at Monkmoor Hospital just a short walk away. I think my boys must have been accident-prone as I seemed to be always attending the hospital due to some mishap or other and I was subsequently asked if I would like a season ticket to Casualty!

One day Rob had been knocked down on the road while cycling. A neighbour informed me that he was covered in blood and in a bad way, which did nothing to steady my nerves. The boys fell off horses, fell out of trees, Rob stepped on a plank full of nails, so went to casualty with welly and plank in situ! Rob always loved to play with snakes, often adders, and would catch them with a shoelace.

And some of the funny things said in childhood. I remember telling my Mum, Amy, "Gand day mammy, up jessit." And Andrew saying to Rob, "Stop watchin at me bum." Andrew would never accept a broken biscuit only wanting a whole one, firmly turning his nose up at something even slightly broken. Taking Jonnie to school one day, I told him, "Don't be late home, your Ma's making possum stew." This no doubt caused him much embarrassment but he also soon became vegetarian!

BALMY SHROPSHIRE

1961 – 1969 I was Assistant Manager and Chemist, Borough of Shrewsbury.
1969 – 1974 I was Manager Borough of Shrewsbury.
1974 – 1987 I was Area Reclamation Controller Severn Trent Water Authority. (Reclamation is a fancy word for sewage treatment).

I was delighted to find that the sewage farm also included a herd of some five hundred pigs, a legacy from the war years. Part of this arrangement was a swill collection round, which included a small lorry with sides which would let down to allow bins of swill collected to be loaded, a driver and the driver's mate. Their job was to collect the swill from commercial premises such as restaurants, cafes and shops, a few individual households and everywhere else e.g. the hospital, which may produce waste food. A useful service which saved a great deal of waste.

This was brought to the farm and poured into huge steel vats, which were then boiled for a legal minimum time to ensure proper sterilization. The vats had integral paddles or mixers. I may say the smell of the boiling swill was extremely appetising. When this had cooled sufficiently it was fed to the pigs in glazed earthenware troughs. There were few but certain things that pigs would not touch. One of these oddly enough was oranges. After the pigs had licked the troughs shiny clean, there would be the occasional orange licked bright. The noise the pigs made at feeding time was indescribable screaming until their turn came. The swill contained some luxury goods including fresh salmon and fancy cream cakes and other delicacies from freezers which had broken down and the contents of which had to be discarded. Sometimes hundredweights of luxury goods were boiled and fed to the pigs. I often thought "Lucky old pigs."

I was later told that Mark and his friend Ginger who were in the gang would try to ride a sow pig for 15 seconds. The pig would go absolutely mad. Then there was Boris the boar. The boys would try to walk to his bedroom door and back to the trough without running. Boris had bitten Jack the pig man several times, who had been nicknamed by the boys as Grumpy Jack. I am sure this also related to the boys misbehaving on the farm and being chased by Jack!

Inevitably some pillock failed to boil his swill properly and instead of a punitive fine and tighter controls the arrangement was stopped resulting in the loss of a fine use for a valuable product and the loss of a job for two good men and the loss of a valued service which eventually resulted in the curtailment of a thriving pig breeding business! All because of a neglectful procedure hundreds of miles away.

It was also the end of our ratting days. Jessie, a mongrel collie dog, was an excellent ratter. The only good rat was a dead rat! There were huge holes in the concrete granary floor where the grain and the potatoes were stored probably for the pigswill. When one turned the lights on where the tanks were in the pigswill room, the rats and cockroaches would scatter in every direction. On occasions, a few friends, all armed with sticks, would help on a rat hunt in an effort to keep the numbers down. I once picked up a stunned rat by its tail and flung it hastily. The rat unfortunately hit one of the helpers square on the open front of his shirt. I will not attempt to repeat the language! Another method of killing rats was to lead a hose from an exhaust pipe of a vehicle down into the holes. Often the rats would be partly dozy from the fumes and easily dispatched. I have known as many as thirty rats to be killed by this method. The holes, which had been fumigated, remained free of rats for sometime.

Sewage Sludge For Rich Black Soil

This was my first of many articles, so please excuse its many failings. Hopefully I got a little bit better as time went on! Written before decimalisation.

Sewage sludge is valuable organic manure. My local authority receives many enquiries from gardeners who are looking for an alternative to farmyard manure, which is either costly or unobtainable. Here are a few facts. The most suitable sludge for horticultural use is one that has been subjected to a process of controlled rotting down. This takes place at temperatures up to 100 degrees

Fahrenheit. Known as digested sludge, it is then partially dried, leaving a material that is safe and pleasant to handle.

The moisture content of the sludge varies according to prevailing weather conditions and the method of drying. Some authorities dry the sludge to around 12% moisture, pulverise it and offer it under a trade name. Mainly, however, the sludge is available from a storage heap with a moisture content in the region of 50%. As farmyard manure is often over 75% moisture this means that for a given weight of manure 'as bought' you are getting twice the amount of solid matter. It is important to bear this in mind when making comparisons.

Now for some vital statistics.

The following is a table showing the main plant nutrients as contained in digested sludge and farmyard manure.

	%Dry Matter	% of Dry Matter Organic Matter	N	P_2O_5	K_2O
D.S.	50	60	2.5	2.2	0.5
F.Y.M.	25	65	2.2	1.6	1.3

It will be seen that for some crops, it will be necessary to supplement the sludge with potash. Being almost black when moist' sewage sludge will darken the soil, increasing the heat absorption. Rich in humus, it will retain moisture for long periods and promote vigorous growth, yet keep the soil 'open'.

Methods of application. Sludge may be applied to the soil in any of the ways suitable for farmyard manure. In the case of pulverised sludge, this may be scattered on the surface and hoed in. Pulverised sludge is particularly good for lawns and is much used on golf courses where it is rolled in to provide a dense, springy turf.

How much does it cost? From many authorities semi-dry sludge may be had for the collection or for a few shillings a ton. Some authorities can arrange delivery but, of course, normally make a charge. Gardeners often collect their own material, a few sack-loads at a time, in a van or the boot of a car. The pulverised variety is frequently sold ready bagged at prices ranging from 2/6d to 5/-d per cwt. Or loose at 30/-d to 40/-d per ton, which at approximately 12% moisture represents quite good value.

I know several gardeners who prefer sewage sludge to farmyard manure. Their names appear on the prize lists at local shows and the rich black soil in their gardens is the subject of much envy. Why not make a short phone call to the Sewage Works Manager of your local council? He will be pleased to provide information regarding the type of material available and its cost.

I was asked to supply manure on many occasions. Almost everyone asked for farmyard manure but I couldn't suppress a chortle when I was asked for farmhouse manure. It does make one wonder about the state of their house!

Dad came to visit the works, keen to show interest in my new job. He parked his first ever-new car, of which he was inordinately proud, near the main building. Behind this building was a set of six storm tanks used in periods of particularly high flows (as the name suggests). Quite often a layer of scum that to the casual observer closely resembled concrete would coat these tanks. Dad's dog, a Weimaraner, was let out of the car. Up to this point the dog's sense of adventure being boundless, he leapt into this 'concrete,' only realising his mistake when he disappeared beneath the surface. He exited the storm tanks without wasting anytime as you can imagine, making for the refuge of Dad's new car that had been left open. In typical doggie fashion, his immediate aim was to rid himself of this most unpleasant coating, which he achieved by several violent doggie shakes, successful in redecorating Dad's new car with this nasty and unwelcome thick, greasy, vile apparel. Mum was always known for having a queasy stomach and was severely overcome by a violent attack of nausea all the way home to Poynton sixty miles away!

By this time the area for which I was responsible had been extended due in part to a major reorganisation. My area of responsibility was extended appreciably and now included many works, which incorporated often, a large area for possible extension often looking many years ahead. These areas had to be kept tidy and not overgrown so were usually mowed by a man with a small reciprocating mower. I often watched a man trudging up and down behind his mower and thought that there must be a better way of achieving this end. So I began asking round the men for ideas. We had some grand fellows who had been or were involved in farming and several suggestions were received which when considered and discussed boiled down to a mobile sheep grazing unit which could be transported from works to works as required.

The idea worked like a dream. None of the dreaded things occurred. Unforeseen benefits happened. Quite a few neighbours appreciated our way of thinking and would ring us up to say something like, "Mr Mellor, there is a sheep on Works D and I don't think she is very well. She was limping this morning." "Thank you very much Mrs Jones. I will get someone to check her." This was wonderful and resulted in many bonds being forged with many neighbours. This was splendid and valuable. It worked well for several years.

One of the most interesting aspects of our sheep farming enterprise was the study of the many different breeds and the considerable difference in the suitability of certain breeds to thrive on different types of soil. This meant much reading and research. We were extremely fortunate in having several men with wide experience in this field. One of them was Trevor Potter who lived up in the hills. He was in some ways as rough as a bear's bum but if you dug deep enough you would find lumps of 24 carat gold and he knew sheep as an old hillman would. If he thought you were wrong he would let you know without too much choice of words. However if he thought you were right he would back you to the hilt and a bit further. His choice of words was capable of refinement but underneath lay a deep intelligence. I found this in several individuals and a fair part of my enjoyment of my job was to perceive this and make full use of it. I consider myself a lucky man! Except when I met a nitpicking auditor.

One day I had a visitor from the Audit department. He said, "How many lambs does a sheep have?" I replied that it could be one, two or three. "How is this recorded?" "As they are born or soon after," I replied. "Is it possible for a mistake to be made?"

"Not really! The guys are very reliable and trustworthy." This was apparently translated as slightly possible. A short time later I discovered that 'a decision had been made to discontinue the farming of sheep.' I never did find out the full details but I came close to resigning. Such things can happen. To some, the word honesty is suspect. How pathetic!

Another day I had a visitor from the Black Country (Birmingham area). He wanted to take samples from a widespread area on the sewage farm. He was about to set off on this little trek, dressed in smart suit and polished black shoes. I said there had been several days of wet weather and a certain amount of sogginess could be expected. Would he like to borrow a pair of wellingtons? He politely refused, as he was quite sure that he would be O.K. However, on his return several hours later, plastered up to and sometimes above the knee, he looked ruefully at his city clothes and said, "It kind of creeps up on you don't it?" In a strong Brummie accent.

Andy Mumford started working with me in August 1964, a Shrewsbury lad. He was my right hand man. He remembered that the new building work was completed in 1974 when Severn Trent Water Authority was formed. Andy and I worked well together and I became good friends with him and his wife Gill.

A Light Hearted Look At Sewage Disposal – A Talk given in 1979 and 1981

Have you all finished eating? Because I am going to talk about sewage. You may well laugh. It may be sewage to you but it is my bread and butter.

I have been in sewage – metaphorically speaking – for twenty-two years and I began my career in this rather unusual profession in Stockport at the Cheadle Health Works. This department came under the eagle eye of Mr Schofield and I am sorry and glad that he cannot be with us today. I am sorry because I should have very much welcomed the opportunity for a chat after all these years. However, Mr Schofield's absence will enable me to relate without blushing too furiously a few incidents that took place in his domain.

Now one does not normally grow up with a burning desire to work on a sewage works. Not like one does to be a Jet Pilot or an Engine Driver, or almost anything, but just consider for a moment, life and death, without drains.

The Severn Trent Water Authority was formed from various constituent local authorities in order to bring the responsibilities for the complete water cycle under one organisation. The theory behind this move being that it should be possible to exercise, with greater facility, a more firm control over our water resources and their proper distribution and eventual reclamation, than when these functions were divided amongst many bodies. Thus was the idea of a comprehensive Water Authority born. The Authority to be responsible for the abstraction, supply and distribution of clean water and the maintenance of all rivers, reservoirs and boreholes. Then the eventual reclamation and recycling of these waters after use. This involves the purification of a watercourse without causing pollution.

This is where I come in. It is my job, sometimes a privilege and sometimes a curse, to look after the sewage treatment and pumping installations in the west of Shropshire. There are 170 installations, big, little and tiny. What a strange job you may say. Dabbling in sewage for a living. Not everyone's cup of tea. I entered the profession as a Laboratory Assistant in Stockport.

At first glance the work certainly does seem to be somewhat lacking the tang of romance or the spice of adventure. In their place are the inevitable connotations of ribaldry. Living is an earthy affair and people love to make earthy jokes about jobs like mine. Which is as it should be. Nevertheless this is work in which a person can easily become thoroughly immersed.

My work includes the application of chemical and biological principles to the technique of sewage purification, the maintenance of a flourishing team spirit in the men under my control, most important, and dealing with complaints from the public. Now everyone has an absolute right to complain if he thinks he is not receiving good value for a service, which costs him money. My approach to a complaint is to try to interest him or her in our work and explain the cause and nature of the problem and what we are trying to do towards its solution. We do have problems and always will have but in order that these may be seen in their proper perspective it is necessary sometimes to consider, for a moment, life (and death) without drains.

The humble water closet, efficient drains and sewage works may not be the stuff of heroic prose and romantic verse but, until they became part of our lives, scourges more terrible than all the wars, than all the depredations of tyrants and oppressors afflicted countless generations. Our ancestors dragged out their often brief lives in comfortless indignity whilst Typhus, Bubonic Plague, Typhoid and Cholera stalked the land unchecked, taking lives on a scale almost beyond belief. Diseases being the sharp scythes of the Grim Reaper.

Before the Industrial Revolution sewage disposal was largely a matter of individual responsibility. Carts collected refuse from the streets. Middens lay dotted about the towns, covered in flies and swarming with rats. Towns sprang up, always near water. The sewer was an open channel to the river that provided a natural vehicle for carrying away the rubbish but was rather unfortunate for the people living downstream.

It is interesting and entertaining to trace a finger down the course of history and catalogue some of the events that led to our present system of sewage purification. In this dirty old world of the past the connection between dirt and disease was not clearly understood. Indeed, an English proverb of the late Middle Ages advised, "Wash the hands often, the feet seldom and the hair never." Death acknowledged no class distinction and sometimes came dramatically.

Picture the scene, in 1183, during a feast at Erfurt, eight ruling princes and many noblemen died when, with a resounding crash, the floor of the great hall broke and deposited the guests in a vast cess-pool underneath.

1427 6th year of Henry VI. First Act was passed appointing a Commissioner for sewers.
1531 23rd year of Henry VIII. Act amended. Six Commissioners in every district to use 'cunning, wit and power to prevent and rectify annoyances caused by improper disposal of waste.'

BALMY SHROPSHIRE

1552   A certain Mr Shakespeare fined 12 pence by Lord Mayor of Stratford on Avon for making a dung heap in Henley Street. Again six years later for not keeping his gutters clean.

About this time came another great concession to sanitary reform. Good Queen Elizabeth I had a bathroom installed at Windsor Castle. A courtier reported that "Queen Elizabeth bathed herself therein once a month whether she required it or not." Shortly afterwards her godson, Sir John Harrington, designed a flushing toilet. (200 years in advance of John Doulton). Elizabeth with her usual appreciation of genius had one installed at Richmond Palace. The mechanics of the thing must have been quite complicated, because it was found necessary to place at the side of it a copy of Sir John's book of instructions on how to use it. Nevertheless, we are told that the seating accommodation was almost up to today's standards.

There was very little legislation on sanitary improvements for some two hundred years except for local Acts of Victoria's reign. London was too near to the seat of Parliament to be a typical town. In order to illustrate more clearly the progress in sanitary reform, I have decided to look at some of the developments that took place in Glasgow.

Glasgow had several interesting features that make it ideal for a study of this nature. Situated on a valuable salmon river, which was also a major means of transport and played a vital part in the economy of the town. A rapidly growing town, in thirty years from 1800 to 1830 the population increased from 77,000 to 200,000.

In the year 1781 health and hygiene took a great step forward when a proclamation was issued, stating empathically that 'the throwing of nastiness out of the window is expressly forbidden.'

1790   First sewer was laid, conveying waste to river.
1793   Water closets reinvented by John Doulton, began to catch on.
1794   Salmon fishing almost worthless.
          Until 1830 the only drinking water came from thirty wells, dangerously impregnated with sewage, which had seeped in from the middens around the town.

1847   Irish Potato Famine. Thousands sought a living and found a grave. Why? An irate citizen demanded to know was the death rate in Glasgow four times that of Edinburgh? Average age of death in U.K. was twenty-nine, Glasgow was seventeen, the average age of well to do in Glasgow was forty-three and the poor was sixteen. Too many potatoes? The annual death rate was one in eleven.

1866   Progress, it was established that bowel discharges were the means by which Cholera and Typhoid spread.

1871   Sanitary reform spurred to further the effort when the Prince of Wales and Lord Chesterfield contracted fever. It was discovered that below the Royal Closet was a cesspit that had not been cleaned for six years, great fear of another Cholera epidemic. Advice on how to avoid it came very appropriately from the Privy Council. Commission. Pump to River Graff.

1878   Royal Commission, 2nd report. Recommended that an attempt be made to purify sewage instead of merely disposing of it. Many ideas were volunteered. Companies were formed. One writer valued sewage at 8/4d per person per year based on ammoniacal content and the price of guano from Peru.

From 1880's progressive members of the community became exasperated by the inertia of the Town Council over the nauseous state of the river. One correspondent wrote "The shores of Sodom's pestilential sea. Would that the river could be led by a devious course around the Council Chambers." One forward thinking individual sent in extensive plans showing how he proposed to divide the river in half so that the tide would flow up one half and down the other, "sweeping all refuse away." Glasgow Corporation admitted there was offensive pollution, but said it did not endanger health. In a book of Clyde Ballads, "No salmon hast thou in thy jet black waters save what is adhering to the tins."

    A railway company undertook to reroute sewers to Dalmarnoch where Alsing, a gent of Danish extraction, using chemical precipitation, designed a sewage works. Sewage purification was on its way. Meanwhile, in various places in Europe, halting steps forward were being taken although there were many outposts of resistance. Oxford and Cambridge Universities were amongst these oddly enough and one learned Cambridge Don, supporting his opposition to a proposition to install baths said "Why, these young men are with us only eight weeks at a time!"

Venice was described by an English traveller as, "The Stinkpot of Europe." Paris was described as being "Fair above and foul below" and the poet Coleridge was moved to verse when writing about Cologne.

> In Köln, a town of monks and bones,
> And pavements fang'd with murderous stones,
> And rags, and hags, and hideous wenches;
> I counted two and twenty stenches,
> All well defined and several stinks!
> Yet Nymphs that reign o'er sewers and sinks
> The river Rhine, it is well known,
> Doth wash your city of Cologne;
> But tell me, Nymphs! What power divine
> Shall henceforth wash the river Rhine?

One cannot help but speculate as to whether the invention of Eau de Cologne was not mothered by dire necessity.

Britain was at this time, and probably still is, leading the world in the battle against pollution. Victoria's reign had brought considerable legislation on sanitary reform and once the nature of the problem was fully realised, the immense inventive vigour typical of this period was unleashed and the problems began to crumble under the weight. On hundreds of sewage works throughout the country, but mainly in the North, thousands of experiments were being carried out with feverish enthusiasm by chemists and engineers, often using the most Heath Robinson equipment. Thus was the cult of the Artful Dodger born. Perhaps the most useful contribution of all to the technology of sewage purification. Several basic systems were developed for the treatment of domestic sewage, each with their own advantages.

Dad and Mum with mare and foal, Ruth and Robert looking on

Jim with Velvet and her foal

Chapter 4

Tales About Some Of My Friends And Family

In the wilds of Derbyshire, the biblical way of speaking lingered much longer than in the rest of the realm. Many especially older men used thee and thou routinely. I remember a conversation with such a fellow, Geoff. "Dost thee know what I seed t'other day?" "What dids't thee see?" "I seed a hinjun wi a turbine on his yed!"

Also I remember an occasion when I was travelling in one of Geoff Knibb's American cars. I think it was a Pontiac. It had an enormous front seat on which sat Geoff as driver with me on the left side and my young son Robert in the middle. Rob was fascinated by the baffling array of instruments and dials and wanted to know the purpose of each and every one. Fast and furious came the endless queries. "What does that dial do Uncle Geoff?" Geoff with great patience replied, "That is for measuring how many amps the engine is making." "What does that lever do Uncle Geoff?" "Oh that switches the windscreen wipers on." And so on and on. "What will happen if I pull that red lever Uncle Geoff?" "Your eye will turn black and swell up." "Will it Uncle Geoff?"

Geoff and I were on holiday in Anglesey with our families. We were camping on a farm. Like good campers we were abiding by the scouts guide 'Be Prepared', so we had with us a good strong spade. Unfortunately the spade was not as strong as we thought and we broke it when digging our hole for the final disposal of our toilet waste. There were no other campers from whom we could borrow one so we decided to carry the brimming pail down the steep rocky path to the sea. It was a lonely spot so we intended to dump the waste in a little cove and cover it up with sand. I was in front down the steep path when I stumbled and dropped my end of the spades broken handle on which hung the brimming pail from which poured a torrent of toilet waste. My corduroy trousers were covered but never recovered despite several valiant attempts at washing. I could never get rid of the smell that included a slug of creosote as a disinfectant. Whether it served as such only the ravens could tell but it did serve to render me less welcome in Geoff's car. Even with my trousers banished to the roof rack. My brand new dark brown cords were never the same again. Although their colour slightly camouflaged the mixture but did little to mask the smell of the pail's contents. The tiny addition of creosote seemed to accentuate the aroma of the other contents.

Geoff was, or became, a very skilled mechanic. His patience and lack of clockwatching were phenomenal. At one stage, I was slightly bothered about an engine that I had installed in my newly built boat, as she was due to be lifted into the water. On seeking Geoff's advice, he was summoned with Joyce, staying with us in our camper van at the harbour. His reaction was typical of the man. He hunkered down, looked and listened to the engine. After what seemed to be a long time, probably no more that an hour, Geoff made one or two, what seemed to be minor adjustments, but which were apparently all that was required. The difference in the sound of the engine was distinctly sweeter even to my insensitive ears. This was prior to our Atlantic Trip. Ian and Beryl then stayed to help put her in the water, it being our turn to be lifted in at Port Penrhyn.

I met Colin Crees and John Richies when I changed school from Buxton College to Mile End Grammar School near Stockport. I was attending a history lesson and found myself sitting alongside Col. Now the history master, a very decent guy, had a most boring voice and he was droning on as was his custom about some minor details of some topic of history. Out of sheer boredom on this seemingly endless topic, I found myself delving into my pocket in search of some distraction. My fingers encountered a couple of fishing floats which I withdrew from my pocket to see if they needed any attention which might distract me for even a fleeting moment. My next-door neighbour Colin inclined his head and said, "Oh, do a bit of fishing do you?" Thus began a friendship that has lasted over sixty years and many an angling expedition, even to the Arctic Circle!

Colin was called up for National Service and moved to Rhyll. One fishing trip of note, Colin and I were on a pier fishing. Colin left and I stayed on a bit longer as the bites were still fairly frequent. After a while the bites ceased fairly suddenly, the moon came out from behind a cloud and revealed that I was fishing on pure sand and had been for some time! I sheepishly hastened to join Col just in time for the last pint.

My great passion at this time, which I inherited from my Granddad and my Dad, for about twelve years, was buying unbroken horses off the hill. Being unbroken, they had no bad habits. Some that I selected were cob-like horses, thick set, often with some Arab in their breeding which gave them a finer aspect. Several of the Severn Trent employees were horsey people and helped. I would partially break them and then sell them on at the various horse sales.

I was able to rent several paddocks from the Water Authority. After pig keeping was terminated there were often several pens usable for keeping a horse for a spell especially at winter. They all used to know their stable in the piggery if it was a cold winter and were snug in their 8 foot by 10 foot pens. This was also very useful for times when I was beginning to handle a horse. When a horse was first put into a pen they were sometimes very wild and this was obviously an opportunity to begin the handling process. Great care was required with some horses not to frighten them into jumping over the wall of the pen as this could have easily caused serious injuries to the horse or myself. Sitting in the corner of the pen never looking at the horse with a book and a few treats in my pocket would often reassure them so that they became accustomed to human company. They would then pluck up enough courage to have a good sniff. Giving them the occasional titbit from my pocket began the gentling process. I can still sense the degree of gentleness increasing, with softly spoken words, gently talking and something nice to eat. After a few nights it often became possible to breathe gently into their nostrils, which seemed to cement the beginning of a relationship.

One of the men who helped was Trevor Potter who thought it was right to buy the horses straight off the hill and said "Thaim as rough as a bears arse but they 'anna be mucked about."

It was common knowledge among horse people that you should never walk up behind a horse either in a stable or outside without introducing yourself verbally and quietly so as to make the horses not feel threatened or surprised. I remember forgetting this golden rule when I walked into a stable in the dark having other things on my mind. I heard the unmistakeable sound of a large and hairy hoof passing my ear at a fair rate of knots. I never made this mistake again. This was a possibly fatal mistake, which should happen ideally never but certainly very rarely.

With one horse that I was beginning to exercise, a partly broken horse, evidently partly broken was insufficient, the horse suddenly decided that another part of the field was more to his liking and took off at high speed towing me in its wake through a field full of nettles and thistles. This was a rare occurrence and I determined from now on that it would be even rarer, only funny when it happens to someone else.

I had a Clydesdale cross mare called Velvet. The foal was born with a rare condition and diagnosed by the vet who said that it would not live for more that 24 to 48 hours. I stayed in the barn that night to keep her company and eventually fell asleep by the side of the mare. Next morning I awoke to find my head between her two massive front feet and her muzzle inches away from my face. Her foal had died.

My boys rode the horses bareback or with a saddle and their friends were vetted to make sure that they were safe and competent and would treat the horses gently and with respect. However, most of the visitors to the paddocks to see the horses were girls. I gave them strict instructions as to what they could and must do so as not to undo the gentling process. Horses are very quick to winkle out any weak spots that can be exploited or put to good use. I did not want the girls to be injured by kicks or bites. To handle the horses a regular pattern is often used so that the next moves are predictable and the actions repetitive. The person must know what they are about to do and the horse will also know what they should be doing.

Our horses varied. Amber was a big stubborn Welsh cob who would bite your bum when tightening the girth strap and she only wanted to eat. She had a very thick neck and one day Mark could not get her to lift her head from the grass so he decided to slide down her neck. Only to find that on reaching her ears, she put up her head and sent him spinning into orbit. That manoeuvre was never tried again.

Suillamon, the name taken from the Neil Diamond song, was a half Arab chestnut mare. She was brilliant to ride, so very sensitive that she reacted to the shift of body weight beautifully. Yasmin was another mare that was very easy to ride. Mark did a lot of training with Inca, lunging her and 'backed' her while I led her round. He rode her bare back for the first time, and then saddled her up and she was steady. She did not really need 'breaking.' A while later, she developed a milky eye and would often shy if frightened and threw Mark a few times. She was so good-natured that Mark did not want anyone else to ride her in case she was spooked. Sabre was a big chestnut stallion, a cob Arab cross with a lot of attitude. Rob, Chris Wootton and Mark would ride him. He would also try to jump the fence to get at the mares in the other paddock, especially when being ridden. He would also bite. Mark was once kicked by Sabre when he was throwing stones at the geese. He was kicked on his hairline and woke up being nursed by his Mum, before being taken to Casualty using the season ticket!

Seventy Five Years On, A Winter's Tale, based on facts from the Saddlers Year Book and Desk Diary 1909 – written in 1984

Outside in the January night, the drifting snow muffled the sounds of the huddled flock in the yard. An occasional flurry rattled the windows in the old house; a log tumbled from the fire in a cascade of sparks causing the sleeping spaniels to explode in a flurry of flapping ears. Three pairs of brown eyes peering from sleep rumpled faces cast suspicious glances at the fire then me, thinking perhaps that this was another of my ill conceived japes. However they soon flopped down drowsily on the hearth again, noses on toses, to resume their snores. My innocence was evident for I was far away.

I was in a land where motorcars were forbidden to travel faster than twenty miles per hour. The land of Britain in the year 1909. A land where the motorcar was still an intruder in the kingdom of the horse.

Open on my knee was a tattered mouse-chewed copy of 'Saddlers Diary and Desk Book' for 1909. The book contains a mass of general information, such as the salaries of all government ministers, of which more later, many bold advertisements proclaiming the virtues of products for the countryman, the obvious emphasis on fine leather. The striking impression is that of pride. Pride of workmanship, pride of product, and most of all pride in Britain.

It comes as no surprise to find Lane Bros. of South Lambeth, whilst advertising a range of products devoted to the welfare and beautification of leather, sneaking in a motor car polish with the 'motto,' 'keep up with the times,' but reminding customers that their harness dressing is 'much superior to foreign imitations,' well naturally!

Another British firm, The Flexible Shaft Co., who manufactured the celebrated Chicago Horse Clippers and guaranteed the drive mechanism for twenty years, all for 32/6d, showed a supreme example of confidence. Warrilows of Chippenham advertised good quality double-barrelled shotguns with top lever action and fine Damascus barrels for a trade price of 52/6d. Cartridges were 5/9d a box, about 28p. A gun for the price of ten boxes of cartridges! A craftsman would need to work about eight hours to buy a box of cartridges in 1909. Today he would work less than one hour.

The same year, a craftsman saddler earned 9d per hour and would be expected to work a sixty hour week, bringing in £5 5s 0d.

Or about £112 for a year's work. Piecework rate for making one best quality plain side-saddle 'with pocket' was £1 5s 6d. A best plain hunting saddle was charged at £1 3s 0d; a pair of stirrup leathers12d and one head collar 'lined and stitched three rows at ten stitches to the inch, with round throat lash' could be made for 4/6d.

In sharp contrast to these prices we find that the salary of the Lord Chancellor was a staggering £10,000 per year, whilst the Prime Minister received but a paltry £5,000 as did the Lord of the Treasury. Strange. But wait a minute, we see that the above two offices were embodied in one and the same person, Sir H Campbell-Bannerman. The Lord Lieutenant of Ireland's allowance was a mind boggling £20,000 whilst the Under Secretary for the Colonies was struggling along on £1,500. His name? Winston L S Churchill.

Income Tax was a standard one shilling in the pound whilst Estate duty ran from 1% for legacies up to £500 to a maximum of 10% for anyone whose father was considerate enough to depart leaving more than £1,000,000.

In a population of 41,000,000 there were one hundred and seventy-two packs of foxhounds, one hundred and twenty-eight packs of harriers and seventy-two of beagles.

To be eligible for jury service one had to dwell in a house with fifteen or more windows. I wonder, did they have a window inspector to ensure fair play?

At the post office one could send a letter for a penny, a telegram for a halfpenny a word, or even take out life insurance, for either sex. Emancipation was on its way!

Licences of all sorts were issued. The cost of these relative to a man's wage then and now provides food for thought. Remember our saddler craftsman was considered to be earning good money at £2 5s 0d per week. Carriages and motorcars licences were fixed equally, 15/-, for a small size and two guineas for larger ones. A game licence cost £3 0s 0d. This would represent about 150% of the average man's weekly pay. Equivalent today, not far short of £200. Dog licences were 7/6d except in Ireland where it was 2/6d for the first dog and 2/- per dog thereafter. When 6d would buy several pints of Guinness you can be sure there would be a wangle somewhere. Working dogs were exempt, as now.

A licence for a manservant cost 15/-. Female servants were tax free, a very convincing argument for his lordship to explain to her ladyship, the reason for his choice of some gorgeous young thing. "One must consider the finances m'dear." Supposing his lordship was a tax dodger! "Now listen here Godfrey, if you should ever answer the door to a policeman, I want you to wear this long black dress and this nice little cap!" A day at the races could be fraught with peril. "Excuse me sir," says Mr Plod. "Would this be your man who is driving you and could I see his licence please?"

Decimalisation found grumbles from many of us but back in 1909 the quaint but ambiguous system of measurement must have brought many a headache. Innkeepers and brewers had a rough time of it. A gill could be a half pint in one country and a quarter in the next. A barrel of beer could be either thirty-two gallons or thirty-four gallons or thirty-six gallons depending on where you were at the time. A hogshead of ale was a standard fifty-four gallons. However, in order to avoid over-simplification, a hogshead of wine held sixty-three gallons.

If drink measures were confusing, the system of wool measurement seems contrived to drive a wool merchant round the bend.

7 pounds	=	1 clove
2 cloves	=	1 stone
2 stones	=	1 tod
6 $1/3$ tods	=	1 wey
2 weys	=	1 sack
12 sacks	=	1 last

Come to think of it, sheep men to this day employ a bewildering variety of terms. Anyone under the impression that sheep begin life as lambs and then, assuming they escape the mint sauce, progress to either ewes or rams is in for one big surprise. There are wethers, tegs, hoggerels and wedders, hogs, shearlings, gimmers and thieves, wews and sheeders to name but a few. However a gimmer on one hill may not be a gimmer on the next.

Maybe we haven't changed all that much. Thank goodness they can't decimalise names.

Which reminds me, I must take the dogs out before bedtime and have a last look at those woolly things in the yard!

This next article I wrote soon after I became diabetic in the 1980's. *Oat Cuisine*

Oats are making a comeback and about time too! There is a centuries old tradition in Scotland, where oats were once a staple part of the diet, that porridge is good for the heart and eyes. The decline in the domestic use of oats can be related to the drastic increase in heart disease in which Scotland is now almost top of the world league.

Oatmeal is known to be rich in Inositol, one of the B complex vitamins. Guess which organs of the body are richest in Inositol? Surprise, surprise! The heart and the eyes.

Long before the discovery of the B group vitamins, it was known that oats had valuable medicinal and tonic properties. In Potters Cyclopaedia of Botanical Drugs, an ancient tome of herbal remedies, oats are prescribed as nerve tonic and stimulant, an important restorative in nervous prostration and exhaustion. Seems to exert a very beneficial action upon the heart muscles, on the urinary tract and on the reproductory organs.

The B vitamins, for most of which oats constitute an excellent source, are now known to be essential for clear skin, sound nerves and good digestion. Vital also for healthy hair and eyes and a strong heart and circulatory system.

The table below shows a comparison between oatmeal and 100% wheat meal.

	THIAMINE	RIBOFLAVIN	NICOTINIC ACID	B.6	FOLIC ACID	PANTOTHENIC ACID	BIOTIN	PANGAMIC ACID	VIT. E	CHOLINE	INOSITOL
	←─ The energy vitamins ─→			Anti Depressant	Anti Anaemic	←─ Anti-Stress ─→		Reduces effects of diabetes & benefits circulatory system	Healthy Heart & Goood Circulation	Healthy Nerves	Healthy Eyes & Heart
	mg	mg	mg	mg	mg	mg	mg	mg	mg	mg	mg
Oatmeal	0.55	0.14	4.1	0.75	60	0.9	20	106	0.8	240	320
100% Wholemeal	0.46	0.08	8.1	0.50	57	0.8	7	8	1.0	155	190
Plain White Flour	0.33	0.02	2.0	0.15	22	0.3	1	1	Trace	120	150

Oats are more sustaining than other cereals and supply such an abundance of energy that horse owners recognise the danger of feeding large quantities to animals unless they are in hard training or work. The surplus of energy, without outlet, makes a horse very hard to handle and he is said to be 'feeling his oats.'

Small wonder that a racehorse owner will scour the country for the very finest of oats. Oats that are plump and shiny and will rattle and not rustle when poured from hand to hand. He will heft them, for oats should feel heavy in the hand. He will sniff them to ensure there is no taint from mustiness or rats. He will bite a few grains across to ensure that they break clean and even, then crush a handful beneath his boot to expose the flour that should appear startling white.

These rituals are traditionally conducted in silence, save for the odd non-committal grunt. If the sample passes each test to his satisfaction our horsemen will grudgingly concede that they 'might just do for the hens,' then brace himself for the price because he knows that he will have to feel deep into his breeches pocket to pay for a couple of tons of this corn.

Oats are acknowledged to be the finest of all feeds for horses. Indeed all livestock seems to show a distinctive bloom when oats are a substantial part of the diet. Why should we be any different? To be ruthlessly honest, I am inordinately fond of oats. I always have been and I hope I always will.

Imagine my delight when, two years ago, feeling a little forlorn and hard-done-by after being diagnosed as a diabetic, I read that recent discoveries by an American doctor had confirmed another 'old wives tale' that oats were distinctly beneficial to diabetics!

It is now considered that pangamic acid, (oatmeal has twelve times that of wheat meal), not only lowers the blood sugar but improves the blood supply to all parts of the body, thus reducing the risk of arterio-sclerosis and gangrene of the lower limbs.

Needing no further excuse I immediately set about finding and devising recipes that included the oat. Some of which, in the furtherance of science and goodwill to all persons I am now prepared to divulge. I should warn you though, unless you are of strong mind and temperament read no further, for these recipes are habit forming and may lead to addiction! This would have dire consequences, meteoric rise in the price of oats, street corner porridge peddlers and Mafia involvement. We don't want that do we?

Broatfast: 1 small cupful oat flakes
1 sliced banana
1 tablespoonful raisins
1 cupful milk or lemon yoghurt.

An iron will is required not to mix a second bowlful. Be firm with yourself.

I bake all my own bread. It takes five minutes to mix and is a shade easier that falling off a log.

Oatbread: 1½ kg wholemeal flour
2 cupfuls medium oatmeal
3 sachets dried yeast
1 dessertspoon salt
1¾ pints water at blood heat.

Mix all dry ingredients. Add water, mix again adding a little extra flour if too sticky. Knead well to a soft dough. Cut into four pieces and place in oiled tins in a warm place for one hour or until doubled in size then bake for one hour at 325F.

This bread is so deliciously fragrant and nutty that one slice tends to lead to another. If you think enough of someone to send a loaf as a present, send it by Securicor or it will never arrive!

Another favourite of mine has been handed down in my family for generations. I must be an utter fool to part with the secret without thought of personal gain, but what the heck! This goes particularly well with turkey and cranberry sauce.

Oatmeal stuffing or Skirlie (in Scotland):

Mix ½ lb medium cut oatmeal with milk in a loaf tin until a stiff paste is formed. Half of a finely diced white onion can be an additional ingredient. Season generously with freshly ground black pepper and salt to taste. Add a couple knobs of butter on top and a smidgen of grated garlic if desired. Cover with foil then bake for the last hour with the turkey.

Christmas dinner will never be the same again, but in these days of self-indulgence why not throw caution to the winds and try it with the chicken next Sunday?

Before frying trout, herring or mackerel, dip them in flour, egg and then oatmeal instead of breadcrumbs. The one makes a good meal, the other a feast!

And lastly, add some porridge oats to your crumble mix. Rhubarb, apple or other fruit crumble will definitely be the family's favourite dessert.

Chapter 5

Hobbies And Interests Of The Watery Kind

A group of us, John R, Geoff K, brothers Mike and Bob and many others, up to twelve of us, would go on annual deep-sea fishing trips to Whitby or Anglesey. Once when we were going to Yorkshire, we called to pick Geoff up, who appeared with black marks all over his face from under the bonnet where he had been replacing a defunct engine. Dismissing the surprise shown on our faces, he said that he would be no more that twenty minutes to finish installing it. We would have a howl of a day with lots of banter.

We often came back with over 100lbs of fish. As you might imagine there were many tall tales and mishaps of one sort or another. The time that brother Bryan came, he was either sat on the bucket or with his head in the bucket. He didn't join us that often. On another day, towards midday, Bob decided he felt a bit peckish and opened his flask to have some nice hot soup that his wife Mary had specially made for him. When pouring it out his brother Mike commented, "That looks a bit like gorilla snot Bob." That was the end of Bob's pea soup and those aboard boat that were feeling a bit icky were soon calling for Huey and Ralph!

Bob reminded me that on one fishing trip I had brought a whole, very ripe Stilton. They were all so hungry at the time that a single spoon was shared, despite the dirty fishy hands of the starving fishermen! It could be that same evening when driving home penniless, that Bob, Mike and I shared a tin of cold baked beans!

On one occasion, towards the end of an excellent fishing day, I was given money by all of the individuals and was about to hand it over to the master of the fishing boat. A gust of wind came and 'whoosh' all of the money was whisked out of my hand and disappeared out to sea. Bob commented on my tight fist and that it must have been a hurricane! Most of the lads chipped in and thankfully we were still able to pay our way.

Colin and I were in the habit of fishing many different locations, one of them being the estuary of the river Clwyd.

This led to the article *Flounders In Fast Water*

It was while staying with a friend on the North Welsh Coast that he and I discovered a most effective, and I think unusual, method of catching flounders on tidal stretches of river estuaries.

The month was September. The weather was, for a change, fine; what I like to think of as typical September weather, fresh and tingling in the early part of the day, and later on, becoming warm and as mellow as old ale. The walk across the saltings was exhilarating. The crisp, salty tang on the breeze, the daybreak sound of piping birds, and the brittle rattle of reeds on wellington boots all combined to make one bubble over with exuberance. The shingle and mud banks, recently exposed by the receding tide, as fresh as when the world had just been born.

Colin led me to a pool about a mile from the sea in which he often sought flounders. We fished the pool for about two hours, ledgering with lobworm and talking three or four flounders the size of jam pot covers. This hectic sport began to pall so Colin and I strolled down the bank to where the river became swift to run down a long shingly glide to the pool below. There, Colin told me, sea trout could sometimes be seen making their ascent of the river, and estuarine brown trout had their abode. Although the way to the river was over an expanse of treacherous glistening mud, the thought of darting trout led us to wallow through the sucking slime, to arrive with aching legs on the shingly bed of the river, where our muddy boots sent a thick trail down the river.

Having replaced the ledger tackle with a swan shot and No 6 hook, I baited up with lobworm and cast across the rippling stream. The bait was whisked downstream in an arc and I could feel the shot trundling along the pebbly bottom. As the bait entered the mud there was a pluck and a rush upstream, then slack line. I still think the lost fish was a sea trout. Heart thumping, I cast again, lead trundling along, another sharp pluck as the muddy trail was encountered, missed. After missing several more good bites I lowered the tip of the rod at the next tug, one, two, strike, a fish was thumping at the end of the line. After a really good tussle, I brought the fish into the shallows and netted a flounder as big as a dinner plate.

Colin came up to examine the catch and expressed surprise at finding a flounder in such fast water. He also had been having good pulls but missing them as I had done. I told him, in my most patronizing manner, about the delayed strike business. Several minutes later he had a fish on, another good flounder. On the light tackle we were using i.e. light spinning rod, 4 lb line, these fish provided most excellent sport, taking several minutes to net in the fast water. It was, as Colin said, like trying to pull a dustbin lid up a waterfall. Fishing up the glide we had six good flounders in less than an hour, besides several smaller ones that we released.

We returned the next day and caught fourteen good fish. The next day eighteen. Each day that week we became a little more expert at timing the strikes and at skipping lightly over the mud without sinking in, returning each afternoon with a heavy bag of fish. Each evening we dined on flounder and towards the end of the week our right eyes had moved to the left side of our heads. Colin and I achieved that week a long desired objective, we silenced the guns of bantering families and sent a box of fish home.

A little ditty relating to Wales: –

Oh the bees along the Gower,
As they flit from flower to flower,
They are gathering of the pollen (pronounced pothlen),
As they do up in Llangollen (pronounced Llangothlen)!

Following one of my articles published in Trout and Salmon many years ago, I received an enquiry from a gentleman. He invited me to fish his stretch of water and to teach him the finer points of worming. This led to a most enjoyable few days

And another fishing article, *Do Not Decry The Garden Fly*

Worming for salmon is simple. All you have to do is to thread a nice big bullet up the line, impale four or five lobworms on a large hook, then cast across the pool and swing round with the current. You may, if you wish, just lob the whole shooting match out into a likely spot, open up a can of beer, light up your pipe and await results. And that is about all there is to know about the subject. Well, isn't it?

It is, according to many a fine book on salmon fishing which, although chiefly devoted to fly fishing, may cheerfully allocate a couple of chapters to spinning and even fishing the prawn, yet either scorn to mention worming at all or relegate the topic to a few grudging paragraphs. Slightly embarrassed at having mentioned a method to be used if you absolutely must, when spates preclude the fishing of the fly.

Quite plainly this is selling short a noble sport and one may as well refer to Yehudi Menuhin as a busker. Worming at its finest demands a degree of sensitivity of touch, a delicacy in casting and an interpretation of those subtle nuances of water lore, which are the marks of the maestro. The method is capable of artistry, which is a worthy rival to the use of the fly.

The cat, I imagine, is now well and truly among the pigeons. However it is high time the record was put straight. We brothers of the angle should not denigrate another's sport without good reason. Whatever our preferences, there are many rivers which, for most of their lengths, are totally unsuitable for fly-fishing. There are few rivers which are totally lacking in pools where this is so. My own favourite stream is a cascade of torrents and deep dark pools rushing through water-riven gorges in a thickly wooded Welsh valley.

A climber's rope is a part of the tackle and the thunder of the water drowns a companion's shout for the net.

Broad lowland rivers I have also frequented and the peaty burns of the Hebrides. Each must be fished according to its character and the water must be read with all the cunning and wit at your command. Twenty-five years of worming for salmon finds me still learning but I have developed a few preferences and arrived at some conclusions by way of tackle and tactics. Let us start at the business end. There are two popular myths often propounded in print regarding bait for my lord salmon. The first is that the lobworm, or dew worm, is the bait par excellence and the second is that one needs a great bunch of them.

Although it is dangerous to be dogmatic about such subjective matters as bait, I have no hesitation in stating that ordinary garden worms are streets ahead. Especially those lovely hard pink ones that are to be found amongst the nettle roots. What better excuse for having a garden full of nettles!

Anyway, you will also save yourself the excruciating backache that comes with collecting lobworms by torchlight. You will also save yourself the agonizingly funny looks one receives from late night dog walkers on the village green, and the reputation of being two pence short of a shilling for mushrooming in March!

The size of bait depends on the state of the water, the size of the river and the time of the season, but even in early spring when rivers and fish are apt to run big, two good sized worms will not be scorned by a twenty pounder.

Salmon are not particularly hook shy and at this time of year a No 1 or No 2 will not be too big. To ensure penetration the worms should not mask the hook. I use a little device which I am positive has improved my catch to offer ratio. This is a small piece of red India-rubber tubing cut and threaded above the hook. The worms remain attractive for much longer and I fancy that the bright red 'eye' of colour also plays its part.

A fact seldom recognised is that in worming as in fly-fishing the size of the bait should diminish as the season progresses and the water warms up. From June onwards a single worm on a No 6 hook is ample and if sea trout are running I use the small red worms, beloved of trout but also taken avidly by salmon so long as they are scoured in moss and not straight from the muck heap. This also makes for lively worms, which is all-important. A limp worm is a poor offering for the king of fish, or even the prince, and is likely to be disdained.

Fish seem to react unfavourably to the smell of certain people's fingers. I rub my fingers frequently on moss or ferns and often use a little eucalyptus oil, which, although strong smelling, seems either to attract fish or remove any human scent. I suspect the latter. Either way I am certain that it has a beneficial effect.

It pays to be fussy about hooks. I will go to some lengths to procure my ideal hooks that are short shanked, tapered on the eye, of fine wire and ultra sharp. If you can draw the point across your thumbnail without a scratch then it is too dull.

A salmon has a very hard mouth and that sudden, dreaded slackness of line signalling a lost fish, upon whose size you may only speculate, will give ample time to reflect on such matters.

The line need be no more that 10 lb breaking strain (B.S.) in larger rivers and 6 lb B.S. in the stream especially when sea trout are expected, as they are notably shyer than cousin salmon. A swivel and a 2 to 3 ft trace about 10% lighter than the main line should terminate the line. This is primarily to reduce the amount of line lost on snags. A few yards of line can render a good lie unfishable for a season and is a danger to wildlife.

Rods for worming should have a soft but firm action going right into the butt. I prefer an 11 ft Richard Walker style carp rod for early fishing on big rivers. For smaller rivers and summer use I make up my own rods from 10 ft wet fly blanks.

Now we come to a topic on which I hold positive (but admittedly very personal) views. I happen to think that there is nothing, but nothing, so simple, so effective and so delightful to use for worming as a centre pin reel with a side casting facility. Alvey marketed by Auger Accessories Ltd. manufacture a large range. I use a lovely little three-inch model for sea trout and grilse and a four-inch for salmon. The various drags available are unnecessary, with a fingertip on the drum one can react to every leap and plunge.

Weighting should be achieved by soft swan shot pinched on below the swivel. This should be just sufficient to trundle the worms near the bottom. The bait should be kept moving and should never be anchored by the shot. It follows that the shotting will need to be adjusted from pool to pool and often several times in the same pool. This may seem a fiddle but be assured that it pays.

Contrary to popular view, worming is a mobile sport and I consider that more than half an hour in any but a large pool is wasteful of effort. Better to try the next pool, then if time allows fish the best pools again later. Salmon have definite taking times that vary and are difficult to predict. A stretch, which was fished thoroughly three hours before, may suddenly yield several fish in rapid succession, and then go dour again.

Technique varies to the character of the river. On large lowland rivers some knowledge of the water is most essential as many stretches are devoid of fish. If the position of the lie is known or a fish is seen to show several times in the same place, position yourself upstream and, ideally, so that the fish lies at approximately forty-five degrees from your stance. The worms should be cast well above the lie and somewhat further out. The idea is for the worms to trundle along the bottom towards his majesty then, at the end of the swing, flick tantalizingly past his nose thereby sending him into a frenzy of territorial aggression.

Let us assume a fish has just showed. A glimpse of a huge mother-of-pearl back in a classic head and tail rise that often denotes a taker. The liveliest pinkest worm is selected with trembling fingers from the cloth bag pinned to your jacket. The distance and angle is gauged with an appraising glance, worthy of Ray Reardon, and the worm plops into the water four yards above the last ripple. Finger on line you crouch like a heron, tense with concentration. The shot sends constant messages up the line to your stylus of a finger for interpretation. A bump on a rock, a wave to and fro on a frond of weed. Then your heart jumps. A gentle but very definite pull. You drop the rod point and flick the reel handle to give a few turns of slack. The catenary of line straightens and you lean back to set the hook. Rock solid resistance, then the rod arches and kicks. Your heart thumps abominably. The battle is on!

On smaller streams, holding pools are often more easily recognisable, although on my favourite Welsh river, after fifteen years, I still catch fish from water which I had previously thought not worth fishing.

The golden rule is, if you cannot see the bottom, fish it. Obviously some stretches will be more appealing than others but appearances can be deceptive. Do not spend too long in one place. I know pools, which, deep, dark and mysterious are full of promise, yet have yielded never a fish. Small rivers demand a difference in approach. Especially if sea trout run the river. Despite the thunder and roar of the rapids, or a waist high fringe of reeds, Red Indian style hunting is a must. This is, in my book, la crème de la crème of all fishing. Softly, softly making use of every tree and rock as cover, the worm is flicked upstream, under the shadow of the far bank or in the riffle of a submerged rock. Accuracy of casting and shotting is paramount. Six inches laterally or vertically is the difference between dismal failure and that mind-blowing moment when a bar of silver explodes from the torrent.

There is no doubt, worming is an art form; sadly misunderstood, worthy of an honourable place in game fishing techniques. Mind you, I will concede one point to the fly enthusiast. It is a pity that the Good Lord did not see fit to imbue the humble worm with the beauty of a 'Silver Doctor' or a 'Jock Scott', so that I might wear one in my hat or sit up on a winter's night creating their image beneath the angle poise lamp.

Dribs and Drabs of Weather Lore

> When the wind is in the North,
> The prudent angler goes not forth.
> When the wind is in the East,
> The fickle fishes bite the least.
> When the wind is in the South,
> It blows the bait in the fish's mouth.
> But when the wind is in the West,
> That's when the fish do bite the best.

I have found this saying almost always true.

My scornful brother Bob, when I asked him to confirm the details of one of our outings, he reminded me of an example of one of his lines in sarcasm about my tackle. My trusty old seagull engine was not always quite so trusty. Following one of the engine's troublesome days I said, "Hope it doesn't let us down today." Bob replied, "Why, won't it hold bottom?" He also commented on my toolkit of one adjustable spanner and a handful of different coins!

Another occasion, I was mackerel fishing, and apparently narrowly missed a boat in a race that led to the story of Captain Ahab.

Captain Ahab, M.R.C.D.S.

Toothache can ruin anything. And nothing is more liable to bring on an attack of toothache than a stiff north-easter coming over the gunwale.

Having suffered untold miseries at sea during the past season I decided to take the old molars into dock for an extensive survey and refit. Besides, you try explaining that half bottle of Captain Morgan has gone on medicinal purposes. People just will not believe you!

The appointment made, I strolled casually along to the dentist, my teeth chattering like halliards on an aluminium mast. After a stiff haul up three flights of stairs, I was ushered straight into the surgery where I collapsed with exhaustion, or did my knees fail me, into THE chair. Allowing just sufficient time for me to study with terror a glittering array of exceedingly painful looking instruments, the dentist hove into sight on the starboard beam. "Morning!" he grunted without enthusiasm. I turned with a weak smile, which I hoped would engender immediate friendship between us. He started and a gleam of recognition showed in his eyes. "I say, aren't you the chap who obliged me to take a port tack at Aberdaron last August?" I immediately clothed him in yachting cap and oilskins. My heart sank like a plummet as I remembered an exchange of blistering nautical expressions as his twenty odd foot of yacht swept past my little tub with only feet to spare. Until then his boat had been leading in the Bell Trophy

HOBBIES AND INTERESTS OF THE WATERY KIND

Race. "You nearly ran me down," I began, then I realised with growing horror the position I was in. Being a bit short of valour at that precise moment I did a quick change to discretion. "I'm afraid it was all my fault," I admitted humbly, "I was doing a spot of mackerel fishing and my boat drifted from behind the point onto the course." "Doesn't matter, worse things happen at sea," he growled, looking as if I was responsible for sinking the Q.E.2.

I was not allowed to reply for at that moment I was told to open wide. Hanging a small bilge pump over my lower jaw he proceeded to poke at my teeth with a miniature boathook. "One there you'll have to lose I'm afraid. Another a bit dicey. Might have to drill down to the nerve canal and root fill." I took a rough bearing on the door in case this should be necessary whilst the boating dentist began to load an enormous hypodermic syringe. "Ever been aboard a whaler?" he queried, brandishing the syringe. I shook my head vigorously and said "Ngaa." "Always fancied a go at whaling," he mused.

For a moment he took on the appearance of a vengeance crazed Captain Ahab poised in the bows in pursuit of Moby Dick. I felt like a very small whale wallowing helplessly with open mouth waiting for the thrust of the harpoon. However, the blow, when it came, was relatively painless as was the rest of the treatment. To my intense relief it was found unnecessary to drill down to the nerve canal. I didn't fancy that somehow!

Afterwards we had quite an amicable chat, the dentist and I, during which the rogue disclosed that he had, in fact, won the race but couldn't resist giving me a few moments of mental agony in view of the suspense he had suffered as a result of my carelessness. He then invited me to crew for him in an important race early in the forthcoming season. Sweating profusely with relief I thanked him and made for the door. "See you May 7th Captain Ahab," I blurted, and fled down the three flights of stairs.

Jim looking at the river – are the fish on their way up?

Jim sea fishing with Jason

Chapter 6

Snapshots And Brief Musings

I have had many dogs but began to breed English Springer spaniels when we lived at Monkmoor Farm. As well as having cats named Topper, Skinny cat, Fat cat and Marmalade, we had Freeman, Hardy and Willis the geese. One of the geese had a broken leg, which I plastered and in due course healed. Amongst the dogs there was Jason, Janie, Misty, Mishka and Ciao. More of these characters at another time. I did not show the spaniels as I bred them for 'picking up' when shooting. I was never attracted to show dogs as they are often larger than ideal. I prefer a medium sized dog, large enough to carry a cock pheasant, full of intelligence and even wit. I had liver and white spaniels mostly and then changed to black and white in the 1990's. I find that by breeding a black and white to a liver and white the brown colouring is then a deep rich chocolate colour. I wonder if the black and white spaniels are more intelligent or quick witted and have a greater sense of humour? They seem to play or can occupy themselves with play more often.

Both Jason and Misty would climb the ladder onto and off *Ospray* when she was being built in the barn. The boys would put Jason on Velvet's back; he would also sit in Rob's motorbike sidecar or on the tank of Andy's motorbike. Misty was a horror for killing hens and was never really cured of this no matter how much or how strong the mustard in her mouth. At Christmas, when the tree had been decorated, we often found both Misty and Mishka, as if in a trance, stalking under the bottom of the tree. We also found the carpet littered with silver paper from the chocolate decorations next morning! Jason was known to pilfer stilton if it were left in his reach, so when he was buried at the bottom of the garden, alongside him was a partridge and a large slice of stilton.

When training the dogs I believe in the importance of gentleness with their handling. I prefer to keep the dog indoors rather than in a kennel as each gets to know the other better. Temper ruins a dog. Once the whistle to return is obeyed, commands and hand signals of sit, come and heel are learned then the dog is well on his way in obedience lessons. The fun then starts with a dummy wrapped in rabbit fur, going out in the car to access longer walks with wonderful smells and water. Socialising with other dogs and walking on the lead, preferably without pulling, all taking time and a great deal of patience and understanding on both sides. I believe in a whippy stick to get the dog to initially walk to heel, a sharp tap and it knows not to pull.

Colin's son Mike is also a keen fisherman. On one occasion, he was employed as a ghillie in the Outer Hebrides, the Uists. Geoff, Else and I sailed up to South Uist, rented a car and set off to find Mike to do a bit of trout fishing. All I can remember from that expedition was a long walk through heather scrub, avoiding flooded areas, to the river and catching no fish but catching many bites from the hordes of midges erupting from the heather which attacked us without mercy. We did not stay long. We repaired to the midge-less sanctuary of the hotel bar for sustenance both liquid and solid and thence to our boat anchored in the bay. We pitied Mike amongst all of those ravenous midges during daylight and living in a tiny caravan secured with a multitude of ropes against the buffeting winds.

Hitchhikers have become more rare these days, as there is more money and more cars about. But now that we live in the Highlands having your own little car is essential and we do see the odd person to give a lift to.

Thumbs Up! Hitch Hiking from All Angles

Are you the bedraggled roadside figure, standing dismally in pouring rain with thumbs raised and spirits low?

Cars flash by with drivers basking snugly in the fug of their purring heaters, radios belting out Top of the Pops, whilst on you the chilling rain pours drearily down. Having been a hitcher and now a driver, I feel well qualified to comment on this most common of backpackers' problems.

If you are young and female read no further. The only accessories you are likely to need to solve your transport troubles are a tight sweater, a pair of short shorts and a black belt in karate. However, if you are unmistakeably masculine you will have to make a little more effort. Drivers usually pick up a hitchhiker for one of three reasons. The other two are compassion or to relieve the monotony of a long journey by some stimulating conversation, which is usually the only price you are expected to pay for a nice warm ride out of all that nasty weather.

All too often this is where the hitcher fails sadly to deliver the goods, relapsing into a stupefied doze the moment the warmth from the heater begins to seep into his bones. Or, perhaps, reliving in stony silence some hairy moment from yesterday when he was clinging to some lofty crag and the rope slipped.

So greet your prospective chauffeurs with a warm smile, giving hope of a lively chat, yea even though one thousand cars have driven past thee! This is a feat of endurance, which will tax the stamina of all but the stoutest hearts, but they will reap their rewards.

Another major reason for failure despite the most appealing grins, is if your pack is large and abristle with ironmongery such as ice axes, crampons, pots and pans etc. You may well look like part of the British Expeditionary Force to Everest but you won't get many lifts. After forking out perhaps five thousand pounds on his pride and joy a man is not going to be too frantic to have his luxurious upholstery ripped to shreds and smeared with soot from the bottom of a kettle.

Lastly, I know only too well how the rigours of outdoor life are often not conducive to a dapper appearance, but before embarking on the homeward journey a few minutes spent on a wash and brush up will give you a flying start on the guy down the road displaying a wild and unkempt appearance with smoke-blackened face and mud caked boots.

Being a driver now I still enjoy giving lifts to hitch hikers but having been the victim of all the characters depicted, I am becoming a little choosey. So take care and good thumbing.

The Britisher (This account is of a personal experience.)

Before me in the Chemist's shop stood an old gentleman with wiry grey hair. We were waiting for our prescriptions to be prepared. The old boy's faded clothes had been freshly pressed and diligently but inexpertly patched. Ancient and cracked boots shone with a gleam that denoted much vigour but little wax. His small but erect bearing expressed a fierce independence, probably borne of service in two world wars I guessed. Presently a pretty girl in white overall emerged from the dispensary holding out a large bottle of white medicine.

"Here you are Mr Benson," she smiled, "don't drink it all at once." Our old comrade reached for his bottle, "Danka," he growled. The girls brown eyes twinkled. "Why, Mr Benson, I see you are bi-lingual." The old chap bristled with indignation. "Course I'm not," he snorted, "Bloody British I am, born and bred." Wasn't he just!

The Canine Mariner

"Women as sailing companions are just fine, but you simply can't beat the real thing", confided Sam, with a furtive glance over his shoulder. Rattles and clanks from the galley allayed his fears. He patted the head of a large and rangy dog of mixed descent that rejoiced in the name of Badger due to a white stripe running down his forehead. Badger gazed at Sam with steadfast and devoted eyes. "Look at him", said Sam earnestly, "On my merest whim he would depart for the Antarctic on tonight's tide. Couple of tins of doggy meat, a few bikkies and we should be a well-founded ship, wouldn't we old son"? Badger thumped the cockpit floor with his tail and smiled a doggy smile of assent.

Sam was quick to point out that he was not the first sailor to appreciate this astounding canine quality of unquestioning loyalty. "Take Tristan Jones", he said, "Can you imagine any woman putting up with two years in the ice living on corned beef and peanuts? Well old Nelson did. No grumbles from him and he with only one eye and three legs, in fact, I've often wondered how he..." Sam paused to listen for sounds from the galley before continuing. "Makes me shudder to think." He raised his voice to a shrewish whine. "I knew we shouldn't have come here in the first place. Mother will be worried out of her mind and if I ever see another tin of corned beef I shall scream." Sam grimaced at the thought, then leaned across the cockpit. Amber lights shone through the outstretched bottle from the sun setting down the estuary where the curlews called.

The heady smell of malt was in my nostrils as I reflected on the sea dogs I had known, and I had to concede that Sam had a point. First there was Jason, a swashbuckling spaniel if ever there was one, a canine buccaneer, who even at thirteen will crawl a million miles through broken glass to set foot on a boat. Although nicknamed Jase the Base by all his friends, for reasons I prefer not to go into, Jason came from a blue blooded ancestry of gundogs and was duly initiated into the rites of his tribe.

He made his debut into boating one warm sunny afternoon when he was allowed to come fishing. Sport was slack. Drowsy from hours peering into the green depths for signs of action, Jason noticed that we were drifting slowly up to an island. On the cliffs swarmed myriads of sea birds. "Well I'll go to the foot of our stairs", thought Jason. He cast an admiring and conspirational glance over his shoulder. Clearly he had under estimated his master's devilish cunning. This was all part of a masterly plan; any minute now we should bring out the twelve bores and loose a few salvoes into the massed flocks. The boat would be filled with booty and his lordship would be hero of the day with many spectacular retrieves. His disgusted incredulity as we quietly rowed away would have made a cat laugh!

Later, during the building of *Ospray*, our steel copy of the *Spray*, Jason, not to miss out on anything, would insist on watching the welding. Fearing for his eyesight, we fitted him with a pair of welding goggles. Sometimes though he would wander off and we should hear a thump and a yelp as he ran into something hard. When the hull was finished, Jason took to climbing up the twelve feet of near vertical ladder, followed by his daughter Misty Blue. The pair of them would then drive us mad clicking round the deck and peering into the portholes before wandering off down the ladder in search of other diversions.

Now climbing up a ladder may be a small feat for small feet but headlong progress downwards is bordering on the suicidal. However, as may be expected, he fell off one day and struck a gong like blow to a piece of scrap metal with his cranium, which acted as a temporary deterrent.

On *Ospray's* maiden voyage, Jason, after many leg-crossing hours at sea recognised the spruce mast for what it was, a tree! He made a brave sight sliding down the deck on three legs as the boat heeled to a puff of wind. "Of course, you do need the right sort of dog," mused Sam, breaking into my reverie and tinkling more liquor into my glass. "It wouldn't do to sail with a yappy dog, or one who whined all day. I should probably end up baiting the pots with him."

I must confess to a bias for spaniels. They have a sense of roguish fun and a natural love of water. Also they make the most wonderful hot water bottles. Ever cheerful, they will accept torrents of abuse without taking the slightest offence. I remember Misty's return form a joyous gallop across the mud flats in pursuit of a lame seagull, fortunately not lame enough. She was plastered in black slime from head to foot and deliriously happy. She listened placidly to the screams of invective. Accusations of being 'dirty, stinking, horrible, filthy wet beast' etc. etc. were regarded as falling only slightly short of a term of endearment, to be dismissed with a wag of the tail. "Well nobody is perfect."

And yet here is old Sam who wouldn't swap his beloved Badger for all the tea in China. While less than half an hour ago Mad Mike rowed past in a six foot tender containing a seven foot Alsatian as big as a donkey, gallivanting around in the most alarming manner whilst Mike, as usual, was attempting to hold a sensible conversation with her on the best strategy for the day's sail.

Folk are liable to ask about the sanitary problems of keeping a dog on board. To tell you the truth, there really isn't any problem worth bothering about that isn't solved by a bucket of water. My dogs think that is what the scuppers are for! There are other problems of course. It isn't a good idea to do any varnishing with a dog around. I once had a Harris Tweed hatch cover through neglecting this advice. A recent study in America shows that dog owners actually live longer than normal people, or does it seem so? Apparently some 63% have lower blood pressures. It was not stated whether the survey included sailors whose 'man's best friend' had just taken a flying leap onto a newly varnished hatch cover.

Sam sniggered as he voiced the opinion that most problems with dogs on boats are in embarking, disembarking or just plain barking. He's a bit like that is Sam when he's been at the Scotch! In the early days he had a struggle carrying Badger up and down the vertical iron ladder on the dock wall until he invented a doggy harness. Badger now descends to the deck shackled to the main halyard wearing the harness and a bored expression as though in a lift. "Mind you," said Sam, "Remember that St Bernard Chris brought down? When we shoved Adam off the harbour wall I very nearly disappeared up the mast." As Sam and I wiped away the tears of mirth at the memory, Sam's wife appeared at the hatchway to announce that diner was ready. A delicious aroma greeted us as we clambered down into the snugness of the cabin. The night air was just a mite bit chill outside.

Lying back in repletion after a superb meal, I caught Sam gazing at his wife with undisguised affection. "Badger old son," I said, "You'll never make the Antarctic until you can knock up a passable apricot crumble." Sam smiled a contented smile. "Who the hell wants to go to the Antarctic anyway? Another snifter?"

I have always loved literature, collecting beautifully illustrated books and story telling. Hopefully the art of telling stories will never die out. It is an ancient and much prized art going back thousands of years, before people were able to write. Telling stories at bedtime, be they from a book or even better, made up, are a wonderful treasure trove for children to remember. One day they will pass them on to their own families. For Christmas and birthdays, I have usually tried to find interesting books, be they factual or a fairy tale, e.g. Wind in the Willows, Arabian Nights or about Dinosaurs for the children of my family and friends.

At home, there are bookshelves in most of our rooms, the subjects being on all matter of things. They range from exploration in the north e.g. Scott in the Arctic, to whaling and to the American Indians, to mention but a few. I did plan to write a book on whaling, the ending of which I planned to confess my passion in the subject but after a lifetime being interested in whaling, I think it should cease. There is nothing that we get from whales that we cannot find elsewhere. I also thought of writing about the life of the American Indians. I was feverishly interested in their culture and lifestyle. But when examined closely, they almost always demonstrated an addiction to the most fiendishly cruel practices that I found loathsome, e.g. scalping live combatants etc.

Gilbert and Sullivan were a popular attraction during my early days in Buxton. Their music and witty songs are perhaps an old fashioned taste today, but I would laugh all the way home after a performance and the songs would tickle my ribs for weeks!

A Caricature of a Face with acknowledgements to Gilbert and Sullivan The Tale of Toby Grindley and The Swan

Toby Grindley was ugly. Many men, and women too for that matter, who are less than handsome are described as 'homely'. Poor old Toby however, was in quite a different league. Had he been three feet shorter he would have been a gnome. Or a troll, like one the Norwegians have by their firesides. An essay in the grotesque. Three feet taller and he would have undoubtedly qualified as an ogre. Mothers would have used his name to persuade little boys to eat their cabbage, or stay away from the canal. It is said however that beauty is only skin deep, and it may well be the same for ugliness, for Toby Grindley never had a wrong word for anyone. Not that many folk gave him the chance, for people tend to shun the distorted amongst us out of embarrassment.

The few regulars at 'The Swan', whose tenancy had been passed on from his father, provided him with a living. Occasionally a newcomer prospecting for a game of darts would pop breezily in only to blanche visibly as Toby's forbidding countenance emerged from the gloomy shadow behind the bar into the ruddy glow of the fire. Mostly they would order a half instead of the intended pint and quickly depart. All this was a shame really for Toby was a kindly soul and worldly wise for he had completely accepted that someone must be last in the queue when Venus doles out her favours. True, he sometimes pondered whimsically on the Good Lord's sense of humour, endowing him with the name of Toby and the face of a jug.

He was astonishingly well read in a great variety of subjects, as anyone with the insight to engage him in conversation discovered, for Toby spent much time alone. His beloved companions were his books and 'Misty', his spaniel bitch who loved him with unqualified devotion, lacking as she did, our superior ability to judge a book by its cover.

The old fashioned brewery which formerly owned 'The Swan' had recently been taken over by a rapidly expanding firm which was said to be controlled by accountants rather than brewers. Toby was not therefore unduly surprised when he received a visit from a nattily dressed dynamic young man who seemed concerned about cash flows and optimising capital investment.

Several days later a stiff white envelope came under the heavy oak door of 'The Swan.' The High Peak Brewery regretted to inform Mr Grindley that a meeting of the board of directors felt unable to offer a renewal of the tenancy that expired in three months time. It seemed that 'The Swan,' as it stood, did not offer the inducements 'visual and otherwise which today's public quite rightly demand.' No decision had yet been reached on whether the premises should be sold in the interests of consolidation or to effect radical alterations. The brewery further regretted that they were unable to offer Mr Grindley an alternative tenancy, as there was no 'suitable vacancy.'

It was clear to Toby that he was out on his crumpled ear. He was very quiet for the next few days. Misty padded behind him as he went about his chores and gazed up at him with liquid brown eyes when he sometimes leaned heavily on the bar. Her face, tilted in query, was crumpled in desperate concern. An anxious whimper would be stifled by a rough hand grasping her muzzle in gentle reassurance.

The company at the bar seemed noisier than ever. The dominoes clattered and roars of triumph alternated with groans of dismay as one protagonist lays a 'bone' to which he knew the other had no answer. Guffaws shook the oak beams as old Jack, well into his sixth pint, paid for by a rare and unusually suave stranger related his favourite joke about the time when Toby won a face pulling contest without even pulling. Face creased with mirth, Jack stabbed the air with his smelly pipe. "And when he was disqualified for not putting his face straight at the end of the contest. The daft part about it was." Now helplessly slapping his thigh with his cap. "The daft part about it was, he wasn't even in the competition, and he was only looking after the bar."

Toby smiled, a little sadly, and reached to fill the empty glasses that the stranger had placed on the bar and was now looking anxiously at his watch. At that moment there was a squeal of tyres, a car door slammed and a young woman erupted into the room wearing a white angora sweater, purple jeans and unbelievably long fingernails. The stranger fluttered his fingers at her through the fug. "Halloo Chrissie." "Nigel. Darling. How absolutely wonderful to see you," gushed the long legged creature as she wiggled across the room. The dominoes stopped rattling. Chrissie kissed Nigel fervently on the cheek making little animal noises of delight. Jack dropped his pipe on the floor breaking the stem. Tar oozed onto the quarry tiles.

More doors slammed outside. The oak door swung open, the draught swirling the smoke round the beams. Two persons entered. A pale fellow in a roll neck jumper and his companion, defying the approach of sixty by long grey hair, jeans held up by a heavily carved leather belt and an abundance of gold about his tanned hands and wrists from which the cuffs of his shirt were carefully turned.

"Rollo. Jocelyn," cried Chrissie ecstatically, weaving her way round the domino table to greet the newcomers. Not a domino stirred. Algy's cigarette bore nearly an inch of ash. Rollo and

Jocelyn were enveloped each in turn by Chrissie who bestowed loud 'mmmms' on each cheek.

Old Jack had recovered from his coma and had sidled up to the bar for a refill to steady his nerves. He leaned over to whisper conspirationally in Toby's ear. "Watch out Toby, she'll hang one on you next. I recon she fancies you." Jack bared five brown pegs in a raucous cackle.

The party settled round a table whilst Rollo ordered drinks at the bar. Algy had repaired Jack's pipe with some insulation tape from Toby's toolbox. This did nothing to improve the smell that mingled with the scent of gin wafting from the tray as Rollo returned to the table. He set down the tray and struck a pose, challenging their credulity. "Believe it or believe it not mine friends, but the man does not have Angostura Bitters!" "You have got to be joking," said Jocelyn with an elaborate gesture of stunned disbelief. "Up with this we will not put." The others giggled into their gin minus Angostura Bitters. Toby flushed. Suddenly Nigel thumped his glass down and stared slowly round the room. "My word," he said reverently. "My word what," said Chrissie tartly. "This place. It is perfect!" They glanced round uttering the occasional "Ah" as various possibilities clicked into place.

Suggestions were flung in with mounting enthusiasm. Chrissie narrowed her eyes and blew a thin plume of smoke at the ceiling. "You could even do a follow through shot of the highwayman from where he gallops out of the night and parks his horse, right through the doorway, to where he settles himself before the roaring fire and shouts for his mulled ale. You couldn't do that at 'The Unicorn' with that hideous porch." "You certainly could not," said Rollo, "and the word is tethered my dear. One does not park a horse!"

Elizabeth, a mature lady in a tweed suit, now joined the group. She was quickly brought up to date with events and asked for her approval, which after some discussion, she gave. "I thought a thousand a week for a fifteen week run was a fair offer for 'The Unicorn' but this place would need less alteration so I expect we could squeeze another couple of thousand without breaking the old piggy bank," said Jocelyn. Then with a sudden burst of inspiration he inclined his head ever so slightly towards Toby who was in his eleventh minute of polishing the same glass with studied intentness. "We could even use the original barman. Just look at those features. No make up needed there!"

"You mean old Quasimodo here." Rollo smirked. "I suppose you could train him to keep his hands off the girls but one should really catch them very young." "Rollo you are despicable," giggled Chrissie. Elizabeth smiled sweetly. There was a hint of the highlands in her voice. "Well Rollo, if he's interested in none but the lassies he should be no competition for you!" Rollo flushed deeply and went into a tight-lipped silence.

"One never knows about these things," said Nigel with an air of great mystery, "but I shall make some discreet enquiries." He rose and went to the bar. When his presence did not immediately disengage Toby's attention from his task, Nigel rapped on the polished bar with a coin. Toby's eyebrows lifted in query to reveal eyes that were deep and shrewd. "Would you be so kind as to arrange for me to meet your boss?" said Nigel, not unkindly but with pronounced clarity as if to make sure he was both heard and understood. Toby shambled into the room behind the bar and emerged a few minutes later smiling affably. "The owner of the premises will be pleased to meet you a week from today, unless we let you know otherwise."

The next morning was Tuesday and market day. A keen wind shrilled through the telephone wires as Toby trudged down the street already crowded with Land Rovers and ruddy faced farmers each hoping to come out on the best end of a deal. The solicitor's office at this hour was quiet. Mr Fothergill listened, frowning into his steepled fingers as his client made his wishes known. Words of advice and more of caution were uttered. They shook hands and Mr Fothergill rang for his secretary. Toby descended the stairs leaving the small of beeswax and old books for the mingled animal smells of the cattle market opposite.

On Thursday morning Mr Fothergill telephoned to say that the brewery had rejected Toby's offer and intended to develop 'The Swan's' potential for passing trade, which had been 'shamefully neglected.'

SNAPSHOTS AND BRIEF MUSINGS

Saturday's 'High Peak Chronicle,' bore a front page spread with the headlines, 'Road Scheme Shock for Lipton. Green Plan Adopted.' Against all odds, in the light of government pressure on public spending, the most expensive option for the Lipton Bypass had been adopted. Maps and diagrams followed reminding readers of the route which swept round the fringe of Lipton leaving 'The Swan' in a little backwater of a road which led from hardly anywhere to absolutely nowhere.

At nine twenty on Monday morning the telephone rang. It was Mr Fothergill. He had a message to convey. In view of Mr Grindley's long association with them, the brewery had decided, after all, to accept his offer. Mr Fothergill was instructed to inform the High Peak Brewery that in view of the impending road scheme, Mr Grindley had decided to withdraw his offer. However a new offer was possible provided that acceptance was confirmed by noon today. Needless to say, the new offer was much less than the original. One third less in fact, at twenty four thousand pounds.

Shortly before noon Nigel strolled into 'The Swan' and made his way to the bar. "You were to have arranged a meeting with the owner." At that moment the telephone rang. Toby excused himself and returned shortly. "That would be myself sir. Can I be of any help?" Negotiations were opened. Toby was gentle but surprisingly firm. Nigel departed with a profound respect for his bargaining powers. Fifteen weeks use of the pub at one thousand pounds a week. Certain conversion works to the Inn and stables were agreed to enhance the seventeenth century atmosphere. Toby was to be landlord of his own Inn, at the going rate for a speaking part. Most of the regulars were signed up as extras on a daily fee.

A week before filming was due to start the old Inn was the scene of frantic activity. Large vans began to arrive loaded with scenery, props and equipment. One day three stock lorries pulled into the yard. Snorting and stamping were heard from within. The ramps were lowered and a bevy of small boys stood back goggled eyed as nine magnificent horses were led out of the wagons. First came six Cleveland Bays, the coach horse of old, coats burnished like a newly opened chestnut. The next pair to emerge drew a gasp from the small boys. Two great Shires, coal black with shaggy white socks, they weighed a ton each and stood almost eighteen hands high. The wagon rocked as they stamped down the ramp, snorting in the sunlight. Finally came the highwayman's steed. Black as night save for a white blaze shaped like a dagger on his forehead. His neck was an arch of sinewy strength. He often showed the whites of his eyes and Toby knew that he would bear watching for such is often a sign of bad temper in a horse.

The old stables behind the Inn, unused for eighty years, were stables again. The air was merry with the clank of buckets and the jingle of chains. Toby went each night to visit the horses and listen to that most soothing of sounds. The rhythmic munching of horses eating corn. Steady as the tick of a clock.

One night, about a week after filming had begun, Toby entered the building to find Elizabeth seated on a straw bale within the pool of light cast by the hurricane lamp. "I hope you don't mind,' she apologised, "I need to unwind after the tensions of the day," and wryly, "I can relax with animals, they're so undemanding."

Elizabeth was in the late summer of her years and even in youth had never been a beauty. Her eyes were small but wise and kind. A little like a she elephant's Toby thought, but Toby was fond of elephants, feeling perhaps some affinity with these other oddities of nature. The nocturnal visits to the stable became a ritual, soon to be accompanied by a flask of tea and a nip of malt.

About half way through the film someone let slip that it was Elizabeth's birthday. That night Toby produced a cold roast pheasant and a bottle of burgundy. The pair picked the bones, drank the wine from the bottle and laughed and chatted far into the night while the horses munched and jingled their chains.

Twelve months later a young couple answered an advert in a country magazine. 'Old Inn offers accommodation, with hearty food, log fires, oak beams. Animals welcome. Horses stabled, dogs kennelled.' As the estate car towing a small horsebox pulled through the archway into the cobbled yard, the driver smiled at his young companion, as they glimpsed the sign over the door.

THE UGLY MUGS INN
Proprietors: Toby and Elizabeth Grindley

Chapter 7

Ebrey Day Good For Fishin, But Not Ebrey Day Good To Catch Fish

Having already fished for several years, it became obvious to me that weather had a profound influence on the quality of the fishing. So I decided to study the matter more deeply and the following two articles are the results of my findings.

Fisherman's Weather – Sunshine

"So foul and fair a day I have not seen" – Macbeth

That good weather, like beauty, is in the eye of the beholder was illustrated by the noted salmon fisherman and his (non-fishing) wife who were each writing post cards in the lobby of a highland hotel. 'The weather is blissful,' wrote the lady. 'Not a cloud in the sky the whole week.' While not a yard away her man scratched away irritably. 'Weather diabolical. Sun, sun, sun. Every damned day!'

Let there be light, but not too much. There are probably as many views on ideal fishing weather as there are fishermen but rare is the game fisher whose heart leaps with joy at the sight of an unrelenting, glaring sun. Worst of all is if this is accompanied by a steady easterly breeze. This seems to produce a glassy look to the water, which I have come to associate with few fish on the bank.

Sidney Spencer in his 'Game Fishing Tactics' describes this as a 'Hard bright day. The most intractable weather circumstances we have to circumvent.' (I like the word circumvent). He confesses to not really knowing why. Various ideas have been postulated.

The theory that terminal tackle is rendered more visible in these conditions falls down in my view because on a dull day fish will often take during a bright spell. Presumably, tackle shows up equally well during a short spell of sun as a long one.

Another hypothesis is that as fish (except for some species of shark) have no eyelids, they are unable to bear, or at least dislike, strong sunlight. This in itself poses other questions. Do fish merely object to being dazzled or does strong light make them feel vulnerable? This I can understand. As an amateur diver, I know there are certain conditions when on approaching the surface after the dimness of the depths, I am dazzled and, during my brief loss of vision, I feel at risk. Monstrous conger eels with gaping jaws writhe around my feet and speedboats with thrashing propellers threaten to turn me into instant rubby-dubby. Well maybe salmon have vivid imaginations too!

Yet another theory concerning salmon is that their behaviour is programmed by their feeding habits in the deep waters off Greenland, where apparently they are always caught in the top three feet of drift nets, but only in dull weather or at night. This is because plankton disappears from the surface in bright conditions and the capelin and sand eels on which the salmon prey, follow them down. This is very intriguing but does nothing to explain the habits of trout and sea trout who spend their lives in shallow water and even the wisest of old brown trout wouldn't know a capelin if he tripped over one.

I am more inclined toward the belief that fish know full well that in bright conditions they stand less chance of being seen by remaining motionless. Plaice and other flatfish in shallow water also seem to know this and keep utterly still and invisible for hours on bright days.

> Direction.	The Sun came up upon the left,
> Out of the sea came he!
> And he alone bright and, on the right
> Went down into the sea.
> Coleridge –	The Rime of the Ancient Mariner

The direction from which strong light comes is at least as important as its intensity. On a river I fish frequently, there are two pools either side of a 'U' bend. One is known as a 'morning' pool down which the setting sun shines and the other one is known as an 'evening' pool which receives the rays of the rising sun down its length. On overcast days, both pools fish equally well throughout the day but it is rare to catch a fish in either when the sun shines down the pool. The puzzle is that this seems to apply equally to a fly near the surface, a spinner in mid water or a worm trundling along the bottom.

Hugh Falkus in his epic 'Salmon Fishing,' admits to his dislike of fishing with a low sun on his back and believes that salmon are frightened by the shadow of fly or tackle crossing the salmon's view in advance of the fly itself. Worst of all is when the long red light of sunset shines right down a pool. However, once the sun has dipped below the horizon and the glare leaves the water, things can improve dramatically and there can be a magical half hour as the bats come out and the creatures of the night begin to stir. Indeed A H Claytor, in his 'Letters to a Salmon Fishers Sons' recommends leaving the best pools until this enchanted half hour of twilight when he has often had several fish after stirring not a fin all day. His tip for taking the glitter off gut by rubbing with a rolled up alder leaf, works to an extent with nylon and looks impressively 'woodsy' if carried out with aplomb. 'An old Indian trick,' Burt Lancaster would have said.

Also good can be the half hour before sunrise and any dull period in a bright day or a bright period in a dull day. F G Alflalo, angler and zoologist, in a survey carried out at the turn of the century on over one hundred eminent fisherman for his book 'Fisherman's Weather' found this to be a commonly held view. A typical comment reads 'Bright intervals of sunshine are good for loch trout in Orkney. If generally bright a passing cloud will often make the trout take. If generally dull a glint of sun has the same effect'.

Fortunately there are many exceptions both general and specific to this supposed rule of 'lots of sun, not much fun'. When the river is high and coloured, a sunny day improves chances no end, presumably by extending visibility. The second, and for my money, the most important exception is that of the heavily wooded stream. I have not the slightest doubt that for such water, a bright day is best. There is also a special thrill when a shaft of sunlight penetrates the leaf canopy to highlight a foaming cascade or a bank of primroses. There is more to fishing than fish.

It is worthy of note that a heavily shaded pool rarely fishes well either very early or late. Some rivers, of course, are obliging enough to have both open and shady pools so in bright weather fish the open pools early and late and shaded pools between times and you can often have excellent fishing the whole day. In any case it is apparent that fish, like us, often do not read the small print in the rulebook. A J Hutton, the famous Wye fisherman, writing in 1920 tells of a 'hopeless' fishing day; "the water was clear, there was not a cloud in the sky, and it was broiling hot." He returned home with his best ever fish to date, a forty-four pounder! It could be this fickleness in fish that holds such a death grip of fascination on us. Long may it continue!

Rising Steadily

"Ebrey day good for fishin, but not ebrey day good to catch fish." This West Indian saying outlines with beautiful simplicity many a fisherman's philosophy. To what do we attribute our success? On what do we blame our failures? A full bag is due to our devilish cunning and masterly skill. An empty creel, on the other hand, is nearly always due to circumstances beyond our control. Quite often the scapegoat will be the weather.

"Have you caught anything dear?" The wise wife waiting with warmed slippers and thrice warmed supper for the hunter's homecoming avoids this query. She has known it to be received with the enthusiasm and glee reserved for donning a pair of wet waders! Instead she will ask if he has had a good day, which provides an escape route for our empty handed hero. "Marvellous, but the sun was too bright, too much wind, or too little."

We know full well that when the river roars in brown torrents carrying hencoops and dead cows, the fishing is unlikely to be dramatic. Similarly, when the water skulks from stone to stone, seeking refuge from a blazing sun, then shares in John West are under no threat. The extremes of weather have effects that we constantly strive to interpret. Their effect on fish behaviour and, indeed, on other animals, we often fail to recognize or acknowledge.

Nevertheless, biometeorology, the study of the effects of weather on animal behaviour has recently emerged as a science and is accepted as being worthy of substantial grants to Universities by august governing bodies. Studies have revealed startling weather-linked behaviour patterns. Suicides rise and fall in output from factories, examination results, etc. The research goes far beyond the more obvious effects on the soul of dreary depressing drizzle, or the old adage of hot summers leading to high birth rates the following spring.

Barometric pressure changes often go unnoticed, yet I was particularly interested to note that these often manifested themselves in behavioural patterns. Aha, thought I. Vindication at last of a pet theory. Now for many years I was a part time meteorologist. My duties with the Water Authority included the observation and recording of weather information. Rainfall, sunshine, humidity, wind speed and direction, temperature and, of course, barometric pressure.

Concerning barometers, I like the story of an English Peer. He came down to breakfast one morning and decided to consult the oracle to see if the weather was set fair for a day's sport. Delighted to find that, on the interrogatory tap, the pointer registered on the cheerful side of change, he hurried away to make his preparations. As soon as this task had been accomplished the heavens opened to release a torrential downpour. His Lordship grabbed the instrument off the wall and flung it through the open door with the suggestion. "There you fool, go and see for yourself."

Living as I did on the banks of a salmon river, quite often I had been fishing before going to work, where I took all the readings at 9am. Frequently I would go fishing instead of going to work, having a splendid arrangement with myself, being largely my own boss, about taking holidays at short notice. Very often the decision as to whether or not I could be spared for the day was made at around 9.15am in the light of the runes cast by the readings from the various instruments.

Of prime importance amongst these was the barometric pressure. I had noticed over the years a distinct correlation between this and the salmon catch. The magic figure was 30.4 inches of mercury, rising steadily. Given a reasonable river level and the wind anywhere from west to south, I would fish my shirt off my back from dawn till dusk, anticipation in every cast. With everything else right but the barometric pressure way off the mark the success rate dropped dramatically. Oddly enough the water would often lose the indefinable look of invitation and assume a hard glassiness in appearance that I came to associate with a blank day. I eventually became so confident in the BP as an indicator of the quality of fishing on the Severn that I would never speculate a day's holiday unless the pointer was near the magic 30.4.

The influence of pressure on fishing has been noticed before. I was delighted recently to acquire an old book written around the turn of the century by the late F G Aflalo, FRGS and FZS. Member of the Salmon and Trout Association and member of the Marine Biological Association. The book is entitled 'Fisherman's Weather.' The work is a referendum among 'upwards of one hundred living anglers' seeking observations on the effects of the elements on their beloved sport. The list of names reads like the pages of Debrett or Who's Who. Earls, Lords and Marquises pool opinion with Bishops and Surgeons. The list fairly bristles with the military moustaches of Generals, Colonels, Majors and Captains, their pithy comments clipped and precise. For the academic, a sprinkling of professors offer theories and hypotheses and to ensure the net was cast nationwide the editors of the angling press were counselled for their own views and their access to the fathomless public opinion in their readership.

Names, which are now legendary in angling circles, peer out from the pages. John Bickerdyke and J J Hardy. For many of these characters, whose wraiths now mingle with the mists over many a river, fishing was a way of life. A consuming passion to be pursued at every opportunity. Many were sufficiently fortunate for opportunity to be almost every day. And so they had time to observe. Time to stand and stare. On the subject of barometric pressure Colonel Davies-Cook, writing from Mold in North Wales, asserts that the local trout could foretell a change in the weather twelve to twenty-four hours before his Admiral Fitzroy barometer recorded it. His close neighbour, Major Wynn Eyton, confirms that his hatchery fish abnormally voracious in their slashing consumption of food, refused to eat when the bottom dropped out of the barometer. This he considers due to their expectancy of a glut of food coming down on the flood.

Colonel Davies-Cook continues his views, that with a falling barometer, salmon and trout may leap and appear active but will not take. For grayling fishing it is fatal, though flies may hatch and everything else appears to be perfect, writes a Mr Holt, author of a much-respected treatise on this species. Grayling he considers 'are influenced by minute weather changes more probably than any other freshwater fish.'

Sea fish are, it seems, also much influenced by atmospheric conditions, especially shoal fish such as herrings and pilchards. Mr Mathias Dunn of Mevagissy noticed this and attributed it to some special sense that was also used to navigate around headlands etc. This view was not accepted by contemporary scientific opinion but may not have been very far off the mark. A fish's lateral line is now known to be extra-ordinarily sensitive to pressure change.

A Norfolk gentleman, one Mr Hubert Hall, expresses his puzzlement at the inability of local trout to differentiate between the frequent thunderstorms, which burst in his valley, from the ones, which, though passing close, eventually burst in another watershed. The local inhabitants, the birds and animals had learned to treat one with respect and the other with indifference whilst the trout ceased to rise and leaped continuously in agitation. My own guess is that the trout, unable to see very far, reacted mostly to the fall in pressure.

Fortunately, however, there are always exceptions to the rule and the book is well spiced with nerve tingling tales of astounding catches being made in atrocious conditions. F G Aflalo gives, perhaps, the soundest advice. "The best plan, unless the day is actually too bad for enjoyment, is to take notice of the weather, but to get to the waterside as soon as possible and there tempt fortune!" See you by the river.

Eel fishing on the Severn was a very popular pastime avidly pursued by a crowd of, what I would describe as, Artful Dodgers. This can be quite an exciting pastime, especially on a thundery night that was often considered a good sign. All that is required is a supply of worms and sound nerves because practical jokes were common amongst the brethren of this ilk. I remember catching a big eel one night, a dark and stormy night, probably almost as thick as your arm. I had given him what I thought was the coup-de-grass and then I dozed off. I awoke suddenly to find that the eel had slithered down the neck of my shirt where he was an unwelcome guest to say the least. I often remember that moment with a most peculiar sense of revulsion.

    I would take one home for the pot. There was a considerable market amongst the fishmongers of the town if there had been a good night's catch. Good prices could often be commanded.

Chapter 8

Messing About In Boats

Boat Owning A Century Ago – D.I.Y. in the Victorian Era

"Nice? It's *the* thing," said the Water Rat solemnly. "Believe me my young friend, there is nothing, absolutely nothing, half so much worth doing as simply messing about in boats."

Sorry Ratty old boy but on a winter's night when the wind lashes the rain against the windowpanes, I would rather read about boats than be in one. Thus, basking in the mellow glow of a log fire and a wee dram, I was browsing through a pile of my favourite old books, Claude Worth's 'Yacht Cruising,' 'Cruising Hints' and 'Corinthian Yachtsman' by F B Cooke and Dixon Kemp's 'Manual of Yacht Sailing.' It struck me that the D.I.Y. boat owner emerged as a species about a hundred years ago. Until then, a sailor either followed the sea for a living or was rich enough to employ others to do all the work. It was unseemly for a gentleman to perform manual labour. Even the redoubtable McMullen of 'Down Channel' fame felt the need to defend himself by pointing out that 'It should not be considered ungentlemanly to wash the dishes after use,' and confessed to feeling bashful when observed scrubbing the decks in Dover harbour.

Claude Worth bemoans the dearth of published practical information, which he attributes to the notion that though a gentleman might splice a rope if he were able, it should be beneath his dignity to engage in such mechanical occupations as caulking and painting. His otherwise indulgent father refused to buy him a boat. Accordingly young Claude nearly drowned himself by putting to sea in various contraptions, which he knocked together, including an eight-foot canvas boat, 'With a younger brother and sister as ballast sailed quite well on the beam.' Dr Worth went on to become an enthusiastic D.I.Y. boat owner and no doubt his skill with tools on boat and operating table were complementary. His many innovations in the art of boat maintenance and improvement delighted him as much as sailing. He was particularly proud of a simple but effective device that he invented in 1890. This was a chain pawle in an open hawse which allows the chain to be hauled in by hand but prevents it from running out again and would be useful on many a modern boat.

The design of boats was still strongly influenced by social expectations, including, on quite small vessels, accommodation for paid hands. Dixon Kemp, who clung to the belief that 'love of sailing is one of the most striking characteristics of the English gentleman' commented on designing for yachtsmen who were accustomed to 'being surrounded by all the luxuries of the upholsterer's art, satin cretonnes, cheval glasses, Dresden china and, perhaps, a valet de chamber!' A steward was expected to go out through the fore-hatch rather than, perish the thought, pass through his master's cabin. However, times were changing. F B Cooke, who owned seventeen boats in his first twenty years sailing, was derisive about paid hands. After rowing the owner of the boat ashore on Monday morning and picking him up on Saturday afternoon, 'they are as the lilies of the field for they toil not, neither do they spin,' except for a frantic flurry of activity on Saturday mornings. He states with conviction that 'there is no work on such a yacht that cannot be efficiently performed by an amateur.'

Across the Atlantic things were a little different in the 1890's. D.I.Y. was a matter of stark necessity for survival in lonely outposts where valets de chamber were not too thick on the ground. Joshua Slocum had just been cast on the beach by the advent of steamers. He had relinquished his captaincy of the billowing clippers and turned amateur. He was about to begin a total rebuild 'from keel to truck' of the wreck of the old *Spray* which he fitted out in Spartan style and made no provision for a steward. This he accomplished in thirteen months at a cost of $553.62.

Masting and rigging, topics that have filled many a mighty tome, Slocum describes with constraint. 'Then the mast, a smart

New Hampshire spruce, was fitted and likewise all the small appurtenances for a short cruise, sails were bent, and away she flew.' Making molehills out of mountains evidently ran in the family, Joshua said of his father that he would find his way home from a desolate island if he had a jack knife and a tree!

During the 1890's, the D.I.Y. boat owner became less of a rare beast until social suicide no longer attended sailing without paid hands and was considered merely bizarre. However, the vessels of the paid hand era were of a size and complexity that were more than a match for a man and his mate (Dixon Kemp lists eighty nine blocks required to rig a ten tonner), so the awesome inventive power of the Victorians was brought to bear on the problems.

Reduction in crew dictated a reduction in sail. The Victorians had a passion for canvas and it was quite usual for a forty-footer to carry two thousand square feet in her lower sails while the eighteen-foot cruiser *Haze* carried four hundred and seventy-four feet. Patent offices were overwhelmed with an avalanche of inventions for reefing and furling gear, winches and windlasses and, of course, the outboard motor. Hard work stimulates the brain!

Topmast hands had been paid one shilling a week extra but soon after owners began to ascend the mast, large topsails took a dive in popularity and alternatives such as the jackyard topsail, which could be set from the safety of the deck, were devised with noticeable lack of delay.

From the domain of the idle rich, boat ownership spread rapidly into the ranks of professional folk. The predictable result of this was the installation of engines in yachts for there was an early train to catch on Monday morning and a living to earn, though engines were often regarded in the same light as an earth closet. To be installed out of sight, used as seldom as possible and never spoken about in polite society. Prejudices die hard however, and many years later Hilaire Belloc declared that he would 'rather die of thirst ten miles off a headland than install an auxiliary.'

"I suppose you go great voyages," said the Water Rat with growing interest. The explosion in small boat ownership in the

1890's prompted an animated exchange of ideas on seamanship, a subject that was eagerly grasped by enthusiasts the world over. Many books appeared in print. It was begun to be realised that even long distance voyaging in a small vessel well equipped and handled could be relatively safe. 'No more dangerous than fox hunting' writes F B Cooke, though whether for the fox or followers he does not say.

"I wonder you dare go to bed," said a famous mariner to the goggled-eyed landsman, "when so many of your relatives died there." The sea, however, still claimed the unwary and many an ill found ship was well foundered. On the lone night watches survival tactics for the ultimate storm occupied many a matelot's mind. The venturesome Captain Voss pinned great faith in his version of the sea anchor. Having deliberately chosen the worst type of craft he could find, he set sail on a forty thousand mile voyage to prove his point. The dug out canoe *Tilikium* measured thirty feet over all with a maximum beam of six feet and drew sixteen inches before he added on an eight-inch false keel. Rigged as a three-masted schooner she rode out sixteen great storms with waves up to forty feet high and he boasted having a hot meal every six hours throughout the voyage.

The diversity of skills and knowledge required to build a wooden vessel was formidable, yet more owners became closely involved in the construction of a yacht, gradually acquiring first the knowledge and then some of the practical skills, often under the tutelage of a kindly professional. Building costs averaged around £30 to £50 per ton according to quality and location. A yacht could last less than five years or over fifty depending on how she was built and kept up, and this is where the practical boat owner scored heavily. Maintenance began before a boat was built. Materials in a Victorian yacht had one thing in common, all were subject to rot, mildew, corrosion or weathering and even in yachts built to Lloyd's, there were instances of deck, beams and keels needing replacement in less than twelve months. In some vessels a resemblance could soon be observed to the good old axe, which had had two new heads, and three new handles but went on and on.

Selection of timbers and fastenings in terms of suitability, quality and compatibility was vital. Mahogany must not be in contact with iron, which induces rot, elm must not be used 'twixt wind and water' and should be felled south of the Humber, not from roadside and should be unseasoned. Oak must be autumn felled, seasoned for a year per inch of thickness and should be so dense that if a three inch pencil were cut from it, no bubbles could be produced on the end if one blew through it into water. Steel frames must never be used with yellow fastenings due to galvanic action, but plain iron fastenings if dipped hot into oil would often last for thirty years. And so on and so on. Come back osmosis, all is forgiven!

Small trading vessels were often sent to the West Indies for a cargo of sugar or molasses, which pickled the vessel against rot but not against the teredo worm or the gribble, which devoured the dulcet timbers with lip smacking relish if unprotected by copper.

What would our Victorian D.I.Yer, with his acres of brightwork, have thought of electric sanders, cordless drills and power screwdrivers? Worth a king's ransom? I have a sneaking feeling that many a puritanical streak would have rebelled against a life being made too easy in favour of the sharkskin and auger. However, new ways of using old materials were accepted with less prejudice. Dr Claude Worth experimented much with linseed oil. He discovered that blocks soaked for three weeks in the raw oil, then varnished after drying for three months, were impervious to weather. He treated a new lightweight tender the same way by pouring linseed oil into it until translucent and fully impregnated.

For dressing sails, his recipe is an incredibly gungy mixture of linseed oil, beeswax, Venetian red ochre and paraffin, twenty gallons of which were stewed in the wash boiler then scrubbed into both sides of a one thousand square foot sail before being hung in the garden to drip dry for several weeks. Seems like a recipe for domestic strife to me!

Victuals. 'The otter hauled himself out. "Greedy beggars," he observed, making for the provender'.

With all this work it is not surprising that the Victorian sailor was prepared to go to some trouble over his victuals. Tinned food was a last resort and large amounts of fresh and salted meats came aboard for a cruise. Claude Worth often carried over a hundred pounds of beef and pork in two crocks of brine strong enough to float a potato. Thereby hangs a tale! More to come later.

Chapter 9

Getting The Slocum Bug – Slocum, The Original Practical Boat Owner?

Captain Joshua Slocum was well known for ploughing a straight furrow across the seven seas with the keel of his beloved *Spray*. What is not so well known is that at the tender age of nine, he could plough a straight furrow across his father's rocky field driving a one-eyed horse! Later in life he demonstrated in front of astonished onlookers that he could also shoe a horse if the need arose. Self-reliance, and confidence in small boats became part of his religion. Of his own father he said what was also true of himself. 'If wrecked on a desolate island he could find his way back if he had a jack knife and could find a tree.'

Josh was descended from the Slocumbes of Taunton, Devon, who emigrated to America and bought a large parcel of land from the Chief of the Wampanoag for two shillings an acre then established the first iron foundry on the continent. The Slocums were, indeed, pioneers in every sense. The smelting works founded by Antony Slocombe was destroyed in the Indian Wars which ravaged the country but Antony escaped being scalped and lived until he was ninety-five.

In 1738 at the opening of hostilities between Great Britain and the Colonies, Joshua's branch of the family went through the fire again by being exiled as loyalists to the wilderness of Nova Scotia or 'Nova Scarcity' as it was termed with grim humour. This represented a two-century setback in colonisation for these banished people, starting virtually from scratch in carving out a living from a remote and savage country.

The exiles included many of the more cultured and far thinking of the earlier settlers and this further refinement bred the 'Bluenose', a race whose self-reliance, hardiness and versatility in practical skills is legendary and the pride of the region. Fishing, farming, building cabins, hunting, all the pioneering skills were called into play again and, of course, boat building. Everything in this distant land came and went by boat. A man might be building a farm wagon one week and a boat the next.

The feat of being the first to sail alone around the world in his stout but Spartan vessel, when many said it could not be done, has eclipsed Joshua's Slocum's amazing versatility.

Slocum has had his detractors, as men who achieve great things always have, or cloying hero worship which is almost as bad. Nevertheless, as a man of parts and a very practical boat owner Slocum, without doubt, had class. From his home on Brier Island, buffeted by the fierce Atlantic gales he saw many fine ships pass which fired a young lad's imagination. He ran away from home at the age of twelve, having been thrashed for building a model ship when he should have been earning his living making fishermen's boots in his father's shop. The model ship with yards and masts was smashed, which hurt him more than the thrashing.

Cook on a St Mary's Bay fishing schooner was his first job and he was expected to put the kettle on 'at every growl' as well as tend his hand lines. After a four-year stint in St Mary's Bay, Joshua slipped into deep water on a leaky timber droger bound for Dublin whence he took a packet for Liverpool, where he met the British Seaman and 'admired his style.'

Every minute of spare time in the next two years during voyages to China and Australia he studied navigation and seamanship until at eighteen, being promoted to second mate, he delighted at reaching the quarterdeck through the hawse pipe and not through the cabin windows.

On British ships hauling coal and grain between Cardiff, San Francisco and Liverpool he rounded the Horn twice as Chief Mate before a spell in San Francisco where in the rough and ready mushrooming town he hoped to obtain command of a ship under the American flag.

Whilst awaiting this opportunity he fell in with the salmon fishing community who gill netted on the Columbia River building and using a large number of boats. Josh designed a gill netting boat for a cannery owner, which he reckoned to be an improvement on the existing type. The cannery owner was so impressed that he bought the design on sight and had boats built from it immediately. Joshua then went into partnership with another entrepreneur building a boat, fishing the salmon for a season then selling the boat at a profit. The boat was a carvel build twenty-five footer, double ended and decked for about three feet each end. A spritsail was carried on a sixteen-foot mast. The partners then turned to hunting sea otter for its pelt, which was worth up to £350 before being traded for teas and silks in China at a 700% profit.

For a while they went to trap an unexplored region which some of his mates reported in an enthusiastic letter to be heaving with 'links and wolfmarines.' Having subsisted chiefly on bear meat the party were delighted when this hunter delivered a 'tame' goose for Christmas. When served on the festive board it was discovered to have been 'tamed' by a heavy charge of buckshot. However it was still voted an improvement on bear!

The next step in the young Slocum's career was the command of a coaster carrying grain from San Francisco to Seattle and coal on the return. Carrying grain as a deck cargo without damage required special skills and techniques in seamanship, which were quickly acquired by the keen new Captain whose abilities had been noticed by the ship-owners Merrill and Bichard. A new ship was being built for them on the shores of the breathtakingly beautiful Puget Sound. The spectacular Washington Forest with its virgin strands of towering leviathans grew down to the water's edge, big enough to yield two hundred foot planks. Sawmills with the capacity to handle them were cheek by jowl with the shipyards. A ship could be planked from stem to stern with never a butt.

Slocum's new ship was a barque of three hundred and thirty-two tons named *The Washington*. In 1870 he sailed for Sydney, Australia, with a general cargo and orders to proceed to Cook Inlet, Alaska, fully equipped to build boats and a camp for a season's gill netting for salmon. Soon after his arrival in Sydney the twenty-seven year old Josh met Virginia Walker, the twenty-one year old daughter of a well-to-do American, who after being a 'forty-niner' in California, had sought his fortune in the Australian gold fields, and apparently found it. The couple found each to the other's liking, saw no reason for messing about and less for wasting time, so pre-empted Mr Walker's ideas of a pompous ceremony by arranging a secret wedding, at which her outraged Father arrived, thundering up in a carriage pulled by sweating horses, just in time to be in at the finish. Leaving Virginia's understandably prickled family the joyous pair set sail for Alaska.

A voyage of forty-nine days brought *The Washington* to Cook Inlet where she was the first vessel to enter those uncharted waters since the Sergio Treaty when Alaska was bought from the Russians for a trifling sum. Shortly after arrival the vessel dragged her anchors in a severe gale and was driven high up the beach and lost.

Virginia's home for the following summer was a makeshift tent where she kept house for Josh whilst he and the crew seemingly undaunted by the disaster fished for salmon. Nothing daunted, the intrepid skipper and crew fished a successful season and between catching and curing the salmon it was considered no big deal to knock together a thirty-five foot boat for the hazardous return journey. The mainstay of the diet was fresh salmon and bear meat. The abundance of bears in the nearby forest nearly brought an early end to young love for the Slocums. Josh had been to an Indian village where he intended to stay the night but decided to return unexpectedly in the night. As he lifted the tent flap to enter he heard the unmistakeable click of a rifle hammer being cocked. Identifying himself 'without much delay' Josh was barely in time to escape being blown into the next world. Virginia, it seemed, had no intention of becoming a bear's breakfast. One cannot help but smile at these snippets of everyday life for Slocum. The building of the boat for most of us would be months in the planning, years in the building; the voyage through treacherous seas and the mind bending grandeur of mountains, glaciers and vast forests would be the adventure of a lifetime!

The *Constitution* and the *B Aymar*, both ship rigged, were the next vessels to come under Slocum's command. Then he agreed to build for a Mr Jackson a one hundred and fifty ton steamer for inter-island trade in the Philippines. The vessel was built at Olangapo using native and Chinese labour and materials. All planks were sawn by hand after being hauled from the mountains by water buffalo. Whilst the job was underway the practical Captain build a substantial bamboo house for his family and having regard to the flattening typhoons amazed the locals and even the Governor by staying the house with stout shrouds fore and aft and athwartships! This house on stilts at the edge of the jungle was every girl's dream come true. Centipedes and scorpions climbed up the legs of the house and all shoes and clothes had to be shaken and searched before dressing. The chickens lived in mortal dread of the huge boa constrictors that constantly preyed on them and even the odd pig that strayed within reach of the enveloping coils. Dangling by their tails from the trees the boas added a certain spice to a Sunday afternoon stroll! A swamp by the house was heaving with crocodiles whose night time roars drew hysterical natives magnetically into the morass, and death. Quite a change from the cosy Christmases on the *B Aymar* where the children hung their stockings around the butt of the mizzenmast in the stern cabin.

On launch day it was discovered that the launching way had been sabotaged by the Chinese who considered the building contract should have been theirs. Not to be foiled, an immense number of buffalo were scrounged from here, there and everywhere, hitched up to the bows and amidst a tumult of shrieks and yells the steamer was heaved ponderously over the beach and into the sea.

The ninety ton schooner *Pato* was received in part payment for the building of the steamer and had been designed by an English naval architect along the lines of the schooner yacht *Sappho* which defeated the English challenger *Livonia* in the Americas Cup. Slocum lost no time in moving his family aboard the schooner. All of them preferred to live afloat than ashore. Virginia settled her family with indecent haste, thankful to be off the reptile-infested beach. The first assignment of the *Pato* was a tricky but profitable job salvaging the rich cargo of silks, teas and camphor from a barque that had an unfortunate encounter with a coral reef some distance from Manila. The job was barely accomplished when the barque slipped off the reef into deep water. This enterprise funded the *Pato's* next voyage, which, just by way of a change, was to the Sea of Okhotsk, sheltered by the Russian peninsula of Kamchatka. The rivers of which, the Captain heard, teemed with salmon. The forests were bursting at the seams with rich fur and on the offshore banks one could hardly drop the anchor through the dense shoals of cod.

Thus inspired, Joshua and family slid the *Pato* into Hong Kong harbour to be fitted out for a cod fishing venture. A raggle taggle crew was assembled from the North Pacific flotsam of seal poachers, otter hunters etc, and with two nests of dories lashed to the deck, the *Pato* sailed for Kamchatka some two thousand and nine hundred miles away.

On arriving at the Sea of Okhotsk and being royally entertained by the Russians, it was discovered that not only did the locals feed their horses and cows on dried salmon but that the bear meat of the area was salmon flavoured. Salmon was just fine and bear was tolerable but the combination was considered to be probably an acquired taste. The scenery, however, left nothing to be desired. Awesome peaks reared glistening white from swirling clouds while along the shore hosts of sea lions barked and frolicked.

Slocum's six-year-old son, Victor, catching an enormous cod on a hand line, signalled the arrival on the fishing banks. The *Pato* was quickly brought into the wind. Anchor was dropped and the dories shot away, each laying behind them in radial fashion a two hundred fathom long line. Each day the men tended the lines whilst the Captain, his wife and family and even the cook fished from the *Pato* with hand lines, keeping careful tally of the catch as all pay was in shares. After an incredible two weeks the *Pato* sailed for British Colombia nearly three thousand miles away laden to her marks with twenty-five thousand salted cod.

Now comes another bit of Slocum enterprise. On arrival in B.C. he obtained a credit for the value of the fish at market price and paid the crew off each according to his share. Virginia was delighted to receive sixty dollars for hand lining over the rail and without delay treated herself to a brand new Singer Sewing Machine. The wily skipper in the meantime set up as a fish salesman, cut out the middle man and cleaned up right handsomely, but only after persuading the public that his darkish cod were a more wholesome food than the alum bleached cod of the local competition.

After more adventures in the Philippines, the *Pato* was sold literally for a bag of gold which Slocum flung into his wife's lap remarking, "Virginia, here's the schooner."

Slocum's fifth vessel was the four hundred ton *Amethyst* that he bought in San Francisco. She was built to 'roll downhill without hurting' for the trans-Atlantic trade and had once made the Liverpool to Boston run in seventeen days which was a record for over thirty years. She had then been converted to a whaler, hunting the sperm whale round the world, then bowhead whale in the Bering Straits before her present unromantic job of hauling coal. Slocum had her fitted out for the timber business carrying shipbuilding timber from the Philippines to China, which he did successfully for several years.

This rather cocks a snook at some of the carpings of his later critics who said that he seemed to use any old piece of wood to build and repair the *Spray*. Maybe he did but you can bet your sweet life it was a bit of good stuff for he was in and out of the timber trade all his life and knew it inside out. Even he though was known to drop the odd clanger. He once bought a gigantic rosewood tree 'on the hoof' in Bantigui which he reckoned would fetch some five thousand dollars in 'Frisco for bar tops. The giant took a team of axe men three days to fell but even when cut into lengths was too heavy to move and had to be abandoned.

Slocum's active mind could not bear to be idle for long and whilst waiting for the *Amethyst* to be converted for the timber trade he took the trans-continental railroad to Nova Scotia and, already displaying a deft hand with the pen, he secured a commission as Correspondent for the San Francisco 'Bee' in which capacity he interviewed President Hayes who was then at the helm of the 'Ship of State.' "How does she steer?" queried Slocum with a gleam in his eye. The President replied wryly, "She gripes!"

On the same trip an indignant Slocum felled with one blow a gent who was bothering a lady passenger, the morning being, as he said, fine and frosty making one feel athletic.

His puritanical background was similarly outraged when being ferried ashore in Nagasaki. The weather being unusually hot the sampan man was clad, like King Shrovetide, the monarch of Sneak Island, with 'nothing before and nothing behind and sleeves of the same.' "God damn you man. Put on some clothes," roared Captain Josh to the mystified man who it would appear did not speakee the English.

The timber trade slackened off when the Chinese began building ironclad vessels and after carrying a cargo of gunpowder to quell a revolution the adventurous '*Amethyst*' was sold. On return Captain Slocum bought shares in the most prestigious American vessel afloat. Fully rigged, two hundred thirty-three foot long and drawing twenty-eight feet, the famous *Northern Light*.

To be Captain of this vessel, a tower of billowing grandeur such as to take the breath away, could only have been regarded as the very pinnacle of a seaman's career. The stuff that dreams are made of had materialised. She was clipper built, capable of carrying four thousand tons of cargo. Even her topmost backstays were like hawsers and turned over huge brass capped deadeyes. The Captain's stateroom and apartments demonstrated the culture and refinement of the Captain and his lady. Oil paintings were hung on the walls and the furnishings included a piano. A library of more than five hundred volumes betrayed the Captain's omnivorous taste in literature, which ranged through Dickens to Gibbon and a book on limericks to Darwin. He was particularly fond of Coleridge's 'Rhyme of The Ancient Mariner.' A reporter from the New York 'Tribune' wrote in glowing terms on the whole vessel, commenting on all of it, but particularly on the orderly domesticity below decks. Virginia and her daughter

Jessie were sewing, with the baby fast asleep in his Chinese cradle, and young Victor busily sketching whilst Ben tidied his room. Surprise was evident in the young reporter's article. He evidently expected to find everyone asleep in hammocks or knocking the weevils out of hard tack biscuits.

All hands on *Northern Light* saw Krakatoa during its monumental eruption and her decks were awash for days with pumice thrown up by the fearful explosions, which killed thirty-six thousand islanders and threw a Dutch gunboat a mile and a half into the jungle.

At this time Virginia's health was failing and in consideration of this and a change in ownership of the vessel Joshua sold out his shares and bought outright the *Aquidneck*. A three hundred and sixty-five ton Baltimore clipper, "a little barque which, of all man's handiwork, seemed the nearest to perfection of beauty."

Slocum's joy in his fine new ship which, 'asked no favour of steamers when the wind blew' was shortly to be cast in shadow. Virginia, his treasured companion of countless adventures, died at sea after a short illness and was buried under the Southern Cross in the English cemetery at Buenos Aires.

The *Aquideck* was wrecked on a sand bar several voyages later as an indirect consequence of some skirmishes with Brazilian officialdom. Slocum, in the meantime having married again, his new bride Henrietta was with him along with his two elder sons Victor and Garfield. The two youngest children, Ben and Jessie, staying with Joshua's sisters in Boston. Weeping over spilt milk, though nearly destitute, was not one of the Bluenose traditions.

Undeterred, the family set about building a boat in which to sail back to Boston. The tools with which to build this thirty-five foot ocean crosser consisted of two handsaws, an axe, an adze, a jackplane and some augers and bits. Her sides were lapstrake built of cedar planks all hand sawn and jackplaned to size over a heavy ironwood bottom, which greatly improved the stability. All yards and bracing timbers were bamboo as were the multipole sponsons lashed along her gunwale giving great reserve buoyancy where needed. All fastenings were home made; mostly from scrap fittings re-cast into nails. The new Mrs Slocum sewed the junk rig sails

A QUIET DAWDLE THROUGH LIFE

and even young Garfield was found a job holding the dump hammer to clench the nails.

At first, the Brazilians politely (for 'Brazilians were always polite') refused to grant a passport for so dangerous a voyage in so small a boat. Knowing more ways than one of skinning a cat, Slocum rigged his vessel out with fishing gear then applied for a fishing licence, which was granted with a nod and a wink by the port official. "How far outside the bar would the licence apply?" asked Slocum. "Quien sabe!" shrugged the Brazilian, "Adios Senor, we will meet in heaven."

The *Liberdade,* launched on the day the Brazilian slaves were set free and named in their honour, was built with simple hand tools and successfully sailed home.

"When things for freighters got bad, as at last they did" says Slocum, "I tried to quit the sea, what was there for an old sailor to do? I was born in the breezes and studied the sea as perhaps few men have, neglecting all else."

His dilemma was resolved when he was given an antiquated sloop by an old whaling Captain. The sloop was thought to have been built about 1800 and descended from a North Sea fishing boat. Even then she was considered quaint. Slocum set about rebuilding her, replacing every timber but retaining her shape. "My axe felled a stout oak tree for a keel," he reports laconically. "It was my purpose to make my vessel stout and strong." This he most certainly did. The deck beams were 6"x6" section and the hull planking was $1^{1}/_{2}$" thick except at the turn of the bilge where it was no less that 3" of best pitch pine. "It was the charming tales about arctic whaling that inspired me to put double breast hooks in the *Spray* that she might shunt ice." Neither did he believe in fooling around with ground tackle. His main bower anchor was a monstrous one hundred and eighty pounds. "With that down," said Slocum, 'A man could sleep easy." I should think a man would need to in order to gain enough strength to get the damn thing back up in the morning! Everything about the vessel was rugged.

During the thirteen months of construction, he chatted to old whaling Captains from nearby New Bedford who continually 'worked up alongside for a gam.' They also proffered much advice and at last pronounced *Spray* 'fit to shunt ice.' She cost him $553.62.

Slocum, The First To Sail Alone Around The World

On July 2 1895, a small sailing vessel put out from Yarmouth, Massachusetts. On board as Skipper and crew was a fifty-one year old Nova Scotian, Captain Joshua Slocum. He had recently been made redundant, by the advent of steam, from his hard won position as Master of one of the finest ships afloat with her billowing clouds of canvas and lofty spars.

Now in the tiny *Spray* he was attempting to do what no man had done before, and many said was impossible. To circumnavigate the globe single-handed. Even now, a century later, this is still considered something of a feat, despite the help of self-steering systems, electronic navigation and radio contact.

The *Spray* had been given to Slocum in jest by an old whaling Captain, Eben Pierce. The joke was that she was a wreck. Slocum rebuilt her plank by plank while she was propped up in an orchard. "The seasons came and went while I worked," he wrote, in his book Sailing Alone Around The World. "Hardly were the ribs of the sloop up before the apple trees were in bloom. Then the daisies and cherries came."

After a short spell for sea trials, the Captain loaded such stores as he could afford, including dried cod, butter and a barrel of potatoes. His only chronometer was a one-dollar alarm clock, which he later said worked quite well after being boiled.

Within two days of losing sight of America, a gale overtook the *Spray* bringing heavy seas and dense fog. Slocum admitted to a feeling of awe and desolation. "An insect on a straw in the midst of the elements," he said. With cocked head he listened anxiously to the scream of the wind in the rigging and the crash of the seas on deck as the vessel plunged eastward towards the Azores. The paraffin stove gave out a warm glow and pungent smoke as he boiled an onion for supper.

Hospitable Azoreans loaded the *Spray* with white cheese and ripe plums on which Joshua dined well but not too wisely on

A QUIET DAWDLE THROUGH LIFE

leaving the islands. He became seriously ill with stomach problems and fell into a delirious sleep. On awakening he found a strange figure at the helm, in the garb of a foreign sailor of centuries ago. He announced himself. "I am one of Columbus's crew, the pilot of the *Pinta*. Lie quiet Senor Captain and I will guide your ship tonight." When Slocum recovered, he said the vessel was dead on course, the decks as white as a shark's tooth and swept of everything moveable.

At Gibraltar the *Spray* was treated royally by the admirals of the British man o'war fleet, re-fitted, re-provisioned along with the battleships *Collingwood, Barfleur* and *Cormorant,* and then eventually towed out by Her Majesty's tug. Slocum left with a profound respect for British hospitality.

Off the North African coast he was chased by pirates and escaped only when their vessel was dramatically dismasted in a sudden squall. The *Spray* now crossed the Atlantic again, heading for Brazil.

He visited old friends in Rio de Janeiro, Montevideo and Buenos Aires where he met an entrepreneur who sold whisky and made coffins. The more barrels he emptied, the more coffins he filled. Here Slocum changed the rig to a yawl before facing 'rude Cape Horn.' He reduced the vast mainsail, fitted a mizzenmast and shortened the bowsprit, though he declared he still felt far enough from home when on the end of it reefing the jib.

Later in the roaring forties, she was engulfed by a mast-high wave, but after being submarine for some time emerged to ride grandly over the rollers that followed. Then came desolate Tierra del Fuego where the Captain spread carpet tacks on deck at night as a sort of burglar alarm against barefoot natives intent on pillage and possibly murder.

Surviving the terrors and gales of the Cape Horn region the *Spray* slipped into the Pacific, visiting Juan Fernandez, Robinson Crusoe Island, before meandering on through this vast ocean. At one island the enterprising Slocum taught the natives how to fry doughnuts in tallow, a large quantity of which he had salved from a wreck in Tierra del Fuego. The islanders were so impressed with doughnuts; he ended up by selling them the entire cargo of tallow in return for gold coins, which they had salvaged from another wreck.

After many adventures in Australia and Tasmania, the *Spray* sailed up the east coast of Australia heading for Keeling Cocos Islands, a Trade wind run of twenty-seven hundred miles taking twenty-three days. Here the *Spray* displayed her legendary self-steering qualities without which the voyage could not have been accomplished. Slocum reckoned that, on this leg, no more than three hours were spent at the wheel.

At Cape Town Slocum was cordially received by President Kruger who still believed that the world was flat and that the *Spray* had sailed over it but not around.

After many more adventures the little ship cast anchor in home waters having sailed forty-six thousand miles in just over three years. As for me, I was so impressed by Slocum's zestful account of the trip in his book that I built myself a copy of the *Spray* and recently sailed her on a year long, ten thousand mile voyage. But that, as they say, is another story.

Chapter 10

The *Spray* Lives Again In Steel

In the unlikely setting of a large barn in the Midlands looms the shape of a large black boat. She has a clipper bow and her wide stern may have given rise to the expression 'avast behind.' Her outlines are unmistakeable though her origins are shrouded in the mists of time. She is the *Ospray*, a reincarnation of Captain Joshua Slocum's famous vessel, the *Spray*, in which he achieved a place in the Guinness Book of Records as the first solo circumnavigation of this globe of ours, completing his voyage in 1896, after a complete rebuild of a derelict hull given to him, probably in jest, by an old whaling skipper named Eben Pierce.

The building of the *Ospray*, my steel hulled version of the *Spray*, began with the arrival of a set of plans by Bruce Roberts, and from which the vessel may be constructed in steel, G.R.P. or strip planking. My reasons for choosing steel were connected with the fact that my eldest son is a welder. I now feel my choice was a wise one. Steel is incredibly strong, fun to work with and is ideally suited to rugged vessels modelled on working craft such as the *Spray*, descended, it is thought, from 18th century North Sea fishing craft, later modified to reap the harvests of the oyster beds on the eastern seaboard of America. My decision was clinched after reading 'Sailing Alone Round the World' by the good Captain Slocum, in which he describes his wanderings on the deep with such zestful pungency. One cannot fail to be impressed by his affection for a beloved vessel. This Master Mariner, after a lifetime at sea having command of such prestigious ships as *The Northern Light*, 'she was the finest American vessel afloat', was captivated by the sea-keeping performance of a stumpy masted little tub like the *Spray*. This old girl must, it would seem, have some magical quality to enchant such as he. Slocum wrote, "I judged her by a blow of the eye and was not deceived." However, even he was amazed by her extra-ordinary self-steering qualities. He sailed from 'Thursday Island to the Keeling Cocos Islands, twenty-seven hundred miles in twenty-three days, with no one at the helm in that time, save for about one hour, from land to land.'

Captain R D Culler, who built the first copy of the Spray in Chesapeake Bay, had a lifelong love affair with this little ship and earned a living chartering and carrying the odd cargo. In his book 'The Spray,' one can almost sense the tear in his eye as he writes wistfully, "As to the vessel herself, she was just plain majestic."

My decision to build a boat based on fishing boat lines was influenced partly by my own passion for fishing and, if I must be ruthlessly honest, by the view that in such a vessel rugged construction is not only acceptable but paramount and many hefty fittings can be home-made, saving cash for other essentials.

When the plans arrived from Bruce Roberts, I confess to being daunted. The mass of detail deemed overwhelming. However my eldest son Rob and I soon learned to take one step at a time and confidence grew rapidly. Let me say at the outset, "pour encourager les autres," that at the beginning of the job, I had no constructional skills whatsoever. A coffee table with a wonky leg, and a stone fireplace, which has been likened to the north face of the Eiger, being my principal achievements. In other words, if I can do it anyone can. Mind you, I have spent countless hours with my nose buried in such excellent reference books as John Leather's 'Gaff Rig,' 'Own a Steel Boat' by Mike Pratt and Ian Nicholson's 'Small Steel Craft,' and many more. In fact, I could not have managed without their advice.

In 1980, New Year's Day, I started building my copy of the *Spray*. This galvanized me into wanting to voyage and as I did not have the wherewithal to buy a boat I must build my own!

I was still working full time at Severn Trent and had been given the use of a barn large enough to build a boat. So this I did, with my son Rob, boat building in my spare hours. Rob and I worked out how many days we would work per week so that there was no conflict. In other spare time I spent reading and researching. I must have been a p... in the a... I liked to go to a pub to write where I didn't know anybody so was undisturbed while writing. These articles helped to pay my way to buy materials such as welding rods, gas, the steel etc. I also catered for weddings, funerals and other joyous occasions e.g. medieval banquets at Shrewsbury Castle. I would go to boat jumbles to sell and buy surplus boating gear. I found the most amazing equipment available at literally chuck away prices upon which I would pounce unerringly!

Rob taught me the art of welding with great patience. He is a thinking welder, a much rarer beast, who was not only prepared to study the craft but was willing and desirous of doing so.

Normally the first metal working job in building a steel boat is the construction of the frames. Bruce Roberts provides full size paper patterns, to save lofting out, and these shapes have to be transferred to a hard floor which, in our case, was four sheets of second-hand ¾" ply painted white. The plans were taped to this surface and panel pins tapped in at each angle. The plans were then lifted off the floor and frame shapes drawn in with felt-tipped pen by 'joining up the dots.' After wasting much time laboriously measuring all lengths and angles with rule and protractor, we hit upon the idea of using cardboard strips the same width as the frame bars, in our case 2½", to make templates of each section of frame by laying the strips on the drawn out patterns and cutting across at each inter-section. Using the templates to mark off, frame sections are then cut from the 2⅓" x ⅜" bar with an acetylene torch using a fine nozzle. Using this method our final frames were made several times faster than our first ones, which were painstakingly measured and cut with a disc cutter.

As the ends of the cut section have to be bevelled for welding, so the slightly cleaner cut of the disc cutter is no advantage. Distortion was negligible. Initially we made the mistake of making up each frame in two halves and then welding together. This can, and did, result in large errors of up to 1½" in width. Frames should be made full size by drawing full size patterns on the timber floor by flipping the plans over and creating a mirror image, and holding each frame section in place on the pattern with nails whilst being welded.

THE *SPRAY* LIVES AGAIN IN STEEL

We had a visit from a local vicar one day. He roared up on a powerful motorbike, earning himself the nickname of the 'biking vicar'. He commented musingly on the aptness of the name *Os-spray* relating to the bones of the *Spray*. He was looking at the skeletal form of the boat.

We elected to build our hull upside down so that gravity would assist us to shape the heavy steel plates over the frame. Our building jig which had to support the full weight of the hull was fashioned from scrap angle bar and channels of very heavy section 4" x 3" etc. Cross braces on which the frames were bolted were 2" x 2" x ¼" angle bar with slotted holes at each end for lateral adjustment. A 3" steel tube was rigged over the jig and from this the frames were suspended at 18" intervals by threaded rods that provided vertical adjustment. The frames were faired up using a fairing batten and tapping the frames in or out a little before finally tightening up the adjusting bolts in the slots. The frames were notched with the torch at each chine to receive the stringers which were ¾" round bar. This was draped round the hull and we welded into each notch. The plates of 5mm steel were cut to size using an acetylene torch after making hardboard templates.

The templates are made by holding the hardboard sheets against the inside before carefully cutting out the shape with a jigsaw. Time spent on accuracy at this stage is well repaid as hardboard, we discovered, cuts easier that steel. The hardboard template was then laid on the steel and, after much tedious trial and error, we discovered to our astonishment that the hardboard template may be used as a profile to cut around, becoming only a little charred round the edge in the process. The edges of the plate are bevelled to a 60-degree angle to give a full penetration.

After much trial and error and many heaves and strains and minor injuries, we found that it was quicker in the long run to weld on strong lifting lugs to each plate before offering it up to the hull with a small block and tackle, then tack welding to the stringers. Persuasion to its final curve was by levers, again welding on lugs where required, usually after, rather than before, the loss of a fingernail. A large steel plate suddenly released from constraint with a deafening clang will frighten the living daylights out of a corpse!

The welding on of the plates is an exciting stage in steel boat building and the temptation is to blast away and cover a large area in a short time. Eagerness, however, should be tempered with caution. Plates should be made as snug a fit as possible. To equalise stresses in the structure a sequence must be followed when plating up a hull, usually starting amidships and tacking on alternate port and starboard plates. More satisfying work I have never known. The day the final plate goes on is a day for backward somersaults and a late night at the pub!

The final welding of the plates, involving thousands of feet of weld, is in my view undoubtedly a job for the M.I.G. welder. This device feeds a continuous wire electrode through a stream of inert gas, usually an argon/CO_2 mixture that replaces the flux on a welding rod. Consequently the weld is free from slag. There is much less local heat input and no changing of rods. Continuous runs of weld can be made with less risk of distortion and no risk of slag traps, which can form hidden pits of rust. However lip service must still be paid to distortion, that old enemy of welders, by stitch welding runs of three or four inches with equal gaps to be filled when the first weld has cooled. M.I.G. welders are much better for gap filling and several times faster, besides making difficult positional welding somewhat easier. The plates should be welded to the chines and their butts to each other from both outside and inside the hull, welding alternate plates port and starboard to equalise the stresses.

The next job is vile, being dirty, noisy and endless. Grinding off the surplus weld to leave a smooth hull on a forty-foot boat is, I assure you, no joke. Neither is shelling out three quid a time for one hundred and nine grinding discs and I often kicked myself for scorning a bulk offer of a pack of one hundred for £98! Wise after the event, that's me. In addition to its other unpleasantness, an angle grinder is an arm-aching tool to heft for long periods. So Rob and I rigged up a devilishly cunning contrivance to ease the burden. This consisted of a rope thrown over a beam with the angle grinder suspended from one end by a piece of shock cord

THE *SPRAY* LIVES AGAIN IN STEEL

and a 15lb. lump of scrap on the other. Result? Half an hour's grinding without a pause, instead of five minutes. Progress!

Shot blasting the hull was the next stage. This is essential to remove millscale and rust and provide a proper key for painting. A forty foot steel hull will take between twenty and thirty hours inside and out and use up to fifty bags of grit. No great skill is required and if I were to do it again I would hire the equipment and do the job myself, recycling the grit several times. The hull must be prepared within hours of blasting as the super clean surface, resembling fine emery cloth, begins to rust immediately. I chose a zinc epoxy primer for *Ospray* and was staggered to discover that the primer alone cost £270. Nevertheless we felt a glow of pride to see our upside down little ship in her smart new coat.

The job of turning that huge hull over in the confines of the barn had occupied my thoughts for many sleepless hours. Crane drivers had taken one look and withdrawn with indecent haste, filling me with foreboding.

However, reverting to methods deployed by the ancients for knocking up the odd pyramid, Stonehenge, etc, the vessel was rolled to the edge of the barn on pine logs. A derrick was constructed from two telegraph poles from which was suspended a three and a half ton block and tackle. The derrick being substantially guyed in all directions, the side of the vessel was hoisted until she lay looking ponderous and unbelievably immense on her side. The lower side was then winched towards the side of the barn and the top lowered away gently until she came to rest on a mass of straw bales and old tyres placed beneath her as a safety net. Oh ye of little faith! The whole affair lasted four hours and went without a hitch. Another late night at the pub! New Year's Day 1981, a year to the day since the cutting of the first metal!

Bulkheads on a steel boat are complicated shapes but easy to install by welding to the frames. This job is infinitely easier if a full-length gantry is slung over the boat in the form of a 3" steel tube pipe from which all manner of heavy objects may be suspended in complete safety. Constant use of the spirit level is vital whilst installing bulkheads, which are clamped roughly in place by not too tight mole grips, then tapped into precise position before being welded.

Next on the shopping list was seven and a half ton of ballast. Now ballast can be mighty expensive stuff but a good fellow, chance met over a pint, just happened to know where there were several tons of used steel blasting shot awaiting disposal on the tip. Apparently this stuff is widely available at engineering works. Experiments with a sample demonstrated that this could be mixed with cement to give the required 320lb per cubic foot density required in the plans. Two weeks later, my stalwart sons and I accomplished another task, which I had contemplated with dread, with ease in one weekend at a cost of nine bags of cement and seven bottles of dandelion and burdock. The shot and cement were mixed in a borrowed cement mixer then poured into a dustbin, which was slung in a rope corset from a block and tackle. The bin was hoisted into the ship with the tackle, and then poured into the box section keel, a half bin at a time, weighing around 500lb.

The curved deck beams of $2\frac{1}{2}$" x $\frac{1}{4}$" bar were welded into place without problem. These had been rolled to shape by a local engineering firm after an unsuccessful attempt with the sledgehammer method, which left my hands tingling for days. A fairing batten was used to ensure a fair curve where the deck beams were cut off in way of the coach roof. The cut out sections were welded to uprights to form the roof beams of the coach roof.

The installation of the decks in 3mm steel was a major event in the building of the *Ospray* and when no one was about I used to stroll round 'on deck' and imagine her lifting purposefully to the ocean swell.

By now the confidence of two such tyros as Rob and I had grown to the extent where many of our ideas were being incorporated and the coach roofs presented no great problems. For the cockpit seats some 3" diameter steel pipe was cut into four lengthways to give rounded edges to the seats. The cockpit itself was made in the form of a lift-out tray to facilitate future engine removal and installation.

THE *SPRAY* LIVES AGAIN IN STEEL

Corrosion is the main enemy of steel hulls and apparently that which takes place insidiously inside, behind linings, being more sinister than the outside, which is easily seen and dealt with. Accordingly, to prevent condensation and also insulate the boat against extremes of temperature I arranged for her to be sprayed internally with a one-inch layer of polyurethane foam. The job was completed in one day, but due to me being lazy about masking off areas not to be sprayed, scraping off the drift took many hours. The effect was dramatic. A cold ringing hull being transformed into a cosy cave.

Joshua Slocum was not a man to molly-coddle himself. It was wooden ships and iron men in those days, whereas mine was an iron ship and.... Well, anyway, Bruce Roberts, with my full support, caters a little more for creature comforts so we set about filling this great cavern of a hull with all the comfort we could devise. Ian Nicholson's 'Boat Data Book' is a mine of information on measurements for all manner of internal fittings from berths to lockers for gas bottles.

As marine electrics are a specialised job, I handed this task over to Paul Curley, one of Rob's friends. The engine was a Ford tractor engine, which I arranged to be marinised and installed through the cockpit.

Steel boats are relatively easy to fit out and rapid progress can be made. Angle bar framing is welded to the main frames of the ship in a way that confers immense strength to the structure, then clad with timber bolted to the angle bar. A mixture of teak-faced ply and English hardwoods was used for the furniture. Masses of beautifully grained chunky elm giving a very solid effect. The coach roof sides were lined with strips of Douglas fir and varnished to a rich golden brown. All these timbers were locally grown and sawn, some of them felled by myself. This can represent a huge saving and a pleasant change from the ubiquitous teak and modern preservatives will guarantee considerable durability. Rob made a very good job of the companionway ladder out of the elm, fashioning useful lockers on each step, for such apparel as binoculars and other handy tools.

The masts and spars were felled from a stand of Sitka spruce high up on a Welsh mountainside and whilst the distance between the growth rings indicates that the quality is inferior to best Canadian Sitka, it is much better than southern grown Sitka which is very spongy indeed. After seasoning for twelve months the pole masts were dressed in the round with power planes and belt sanders before being coated with epoxy resin.

The rig is to be gaff yawl with a standing lug for a mizzen. This is the adjusted rig Slocum chose to face 'rude Cape Horn' and the terrifying williwaws blasting down from the mountains of Patagonia.

Galvanised wire shrouds are to be tensioned with lignum vitae deadeyes bought from Beaulieu Boat Jumble that, along with the Solent area in general, is a happy hunting ground for traditional boat gear, which is extra-ordinarily difficult to find in the Midlands. A weekend's browsing amongst the delightful boaty junk shops in Burseldon, Southampton and Lymington usually yields a sack-full of treasure.

The sails for *Ospray* are in tan Duradon which looks and even smells like canvas. I bought them second-hand from a Harley Street dentist whose boat had come second in an argument with an Indonesian reef.

The next problem was to get her out of the barn and on to the lorry. The driver of the lorry was a grumpy soul before he even started to load *Ospray*. We had a struggle getting her out of the barn and the grumpiness of the driver did nothing to lighten the mood. Eventually, she navigated the narrow tree lined road from the barn through Shrewsbury and thence to the coast eighty miles away. There were several stops along the busy roads to allow traffic to pass doing nothing to lift the driver's mood! Then at long last she was safe at the harbour.

Ospray is now almost ready for launching after just over three years hard but joyful work. Any regrets? Yes, I wish I had done it years ago. Building *Ospray* has been one of my happiest times, busy but with a glorious end in sight, which pulled us along in a happy frame of mind.

On launching day my next memory is of my Mum with her fox stole, all dressed up for the occasion, bottle of champagne at the ready; Mum proudly anointing the bow of the vessel and

THE *SPRAY* LIVES AGAIN IN STEEL

naming her officially *Ospray of Boston*. Dad was silent but looked on with obvious pride amongst other family and friends.

Her home was to be a berth at Port Penrhyn harbour where the Harbour Master had his office and whose name was Captain Metcalfe. This was a well-run working harbour but very friendly and affordable.

After *Ospray's* shakedown cruise, I was introduced to a gentleman who hailed by the name of 'Cale the Sail' in true Welsh fashion. He did not quite care for the way that I had rigged the gaff saddle, re-furbishing it with obvious improvement.

Jim with pup Misty Blue

Medieval banquet at Shrewsbury castle to help finance boat building

Chapter 11

Personal Jottings

The following are some jottings from my diary on *Osprey's* build initially intended for my personal use, (forgotten about and just found)! It starts a year and a half into the build.

July 4th 1981 Beautiful hot day. Cut out both companionway hatches, the forward hatch and the scuppers! Made template for the cutting out of the scuppers after reading all I could find on the subject which wasn't much. Made scuppers slightly larger than on plan. If a large wave invites himself aboard, I don't want him hanging around trying to find his way off again.

Jonathan pestered me to show him the bees in the hives by the horse pasture. When about 50 yards away a cluster of a dozen or so made straight for us with hostile intent. Halfway across the field Jonathan's armful of firewood suddenly erupted as one stung him on the head. I could hardly run for laughing as Jonathan, arms going like windmills, cleared the field gate like an Olympic hurdler, with me only one stride behind.

In the evening Jason went sniffing around the hives hunting rabbits. Watching covertly from a safe distance, chortling and expecting Jase to come hurtling across the field at about twice the speed of light, but the bees ignored him completely.

July 5th Cooler today, looks like rain. Baling the second half of the hay but the crispness has gone from it. It is 'sad' as Albert would have said.

Finished cutting out the scuppers that look quite grand. Spent ages deciding how to fabricate the slides for the washboards. More time spent thinking than working. Must be strong and able to drain. Cut out the last plate for the foredeck, including arrangement for holding bowsprit.

The smell of the new hay was intoxicating and, as I bent to admire the bowplate, the sickle of the new moon was sharp and clear through the loading port on the barn. A good day's work.

Life seemed good. Then I remembered I had a bottle of Guinness to drink with my supper of home-made bread and it seemed even better. Mishka and Janie came trundling back soaking wet and deliriously happy after hunting rabbits all afternoon.

Mark went on holiday today with his friend Martin. Trying hard not to look pleased with himself as he spread his wings for the first time. Couldn't help wondering how far those wings will carry him. Canada maybe? Doesn't seem long since I carried his carrycot down the cliff path to the beach near Saundersfoot.

July 7th Mike Herod came to quote for foam spraying boat. £550 plus VAT Whew! Tandoori chicken for lunch and red wine. Excellent. Minor work fitting plate in coach roof etc.

July 11th Made hatch coamings for forward hatch using 4 inch tube 'quarter sawn' for radiused corners. The smell of the new hay in the barn was sweet and strong. What a setting in which to build a boat. Old Slocum would have been well pleased. Roy came today and brought me a spare starter motor and oil pump. Hope we shan't need them but they will be a comfort to have on board.

July 17th Went down to Croydon. Masses of nautical junk – many bargains. Bought tar epoxy paint intended for Polaris submarines for £9 per 5 litre pack plus epoxy adhesives and a magnificent compass with a lovely little oil-lit binnacle. We found some oil and turned all the lights out at home. How cosy it seems. The compass seemed completely disorientated in the steel boat. I hope we can find some way of compensating for error.

July 21st Arranged loan with Nat West. Very favourable terms. Interest paid only on amount outstanding at any time. Hence benefit from pay cheques etc. Estimate cost of completion about £3800.

Aug 1st Beautiful day but rather hot in the boat with the infrared lamp and the gas cutter etc. Good progress and very satisfying. Fitting the frames for the furniture in the after cabin. As usual spending ages thinking about each part. Everything must be just right. Wondering whether to have an enormous lazarette or more personal stowage at the foot of each bunk. My idea of being able to convert the settees and single bunks into two doubles is working out fine but requires much thought and measuring. Sat in the crook of the settee with backrest – just testing – felt grand. Could almost imagine the coal stove glowing warm with the wind moaning outside and everything snuggled down and cosy

Eyes bad at night. Mild arc eye. Must be more careful.

Aug 3rd Completed foaming in after cabin. Looks real cosy. Misty Blue came up ladder for inspection and pronounced the installation A1. A dog knows a cosy berth when it sees one.

Heard a muffled roar whilst working below. Came up on deck to investigate to find two huge balloons sailing past losing height rapidly and heading for the cables and pylons across the river. The roar was from the burners as they gouted a huge tongue of flame up into the canopy. Looking very Conan Doylish they cleared the wires with little to spare. The horses galloped round the field in a frenzy of excitement.

Went back below after taking hurried photographs and welded in a grab bar cum roof pillar by the galley area. Planned out refrigeration area for large quantities of fish!!!

Aug 8th Frustrating day. Little done. Went to Jan and Eric's Garden Party. Guests playing putting on the lawn. Jan 'put' one straight through the open door amongst the party! Good old Jan. Very tiddly. I ate a large number of Jan's curried eggs.

Aug 9th Fabricated the frame for the companionway into the main cabin. A bit on the hefty side but better that than the other way.

Winston loomed into sight and went on a tour of inspection chuckling with delight at every new aspect. He pronounced it a 'men only' job and stated emphatically that it was 'all there.' He forced me against my will to go out for a couple of pints.

Aug 10th Fitted the frame I made last night and fabricated the other one. Rob has been doing some work to complete the keel and stern area and general welding where required.

Aug 21st Heard of possible berth near Bangor from Dawson the Sail.

Aug 24th Went down to Port Penrhyn to explore possibilities. What a cosy little harbour! I have been past it scores of times and not known it was there. Port Penrhyn is an old trading port from which slate was exported. There are some sketches in the harbourmasters office showing schooners and barques tied up against the wall. There is also a fishery based here with deep-freezing capacity and an ice-making plant which discharges ice down a chute into the boats!! Nets, otter boards and other fishing gear lie around everywhere plus an enormous pile of scallop shells. Shades of Mull. The *Ospray* will be very pleased to take the room, thank you very much. I daresay old Josh Slocum would have nodded his approval.

It transpires that the Harbour master and family are, as Mrs Metcalfe put it, fanatics about traditional boats and their son is author of the sketches of old Penrhyn. They were as pleased to welcome the *Ospray*, as she was to find such a snug berth. What a find.

Aug 25th I find I have diabetes. Bit of a blow but I went around the shops and soon determined that there are plenty of diabetic foods available with which to furnish a ship's stores for a longish voyage. Might even write an article about the subject. That would be a poke in the eye for old Lady Fate. Ha!

Aug 31st Have fabricated the sliding hatch frames for forward and aft cabins. Drilled all the holes in the Mellor patent adjustable mast tabernacle. It will be a simple matter to move the mainmast forward a foot if circumstances dictate. Not many boats have this facility. Deslagged welds in forward cabin and primed the deck beams and intercostals again.

Sept 1st Applied a lavish coat of anti-corrosive to deck beams and intercostals. I now have the finest pair of bollards you ever did see. Bragging again! This pair would hold the *Queen Mary* in a hurricane; "It was my purpose to make my vessel stout and strong." I hope you don't mind a bit of competition Josh. You sure did start something with the old *Spray*. It's like a fever burning me constantly. Even after nearly two year's slog I think of little else. Every piece of metal I see, every commodity almost, I convert to and measure as possibilities for the boat and her voyages. What a privilege to be given the chance to do something like this with my life. Tobermory Bay will hear the rattle of my anchor chain yet. God willing.

Sept 4th and 5th Beautiful golden September days. Crispy tang in the air first thing laden with the scent of leaves on the turn. From our 'gallery' in the barn I could see Mishka hunting partridge in the inimitable spaniel fashion. Just like her granddad who is steadying up a little now. Yip, yip, and yip, away they go. Never win a field trial but they don't half have fun.

Welding in fuel and water tanks today and fashioning the bowsprit gammon iron. Made two more splendid bollards for after deck. Raked towards amidships they look mighty boaty. Could hear curlew flighting in just after dark and the mutterings of flighting mallard.

Sept 6th Took my bollards to be galvanised today. Whatever turns you on! They can't touch you for it.

Sept 9th Have been making parts for the rudder this week. As usual, much head scratching and reading. Claude Worth as usual has 'worthy' things to say on the subject – groan. Have also been giving much thought to the rig and the exact form it will take.

Must say I am somewhat influenced by Claude Worth's love affair with a 'snug cutter rig.' Still, I expect I could always chuck the mizzenmast over the side if it gets in the way. On the other hand if I rigged her as a cutter I could always lop a couple of feet off the boom and install a mizzenmast. Hmmm!

Watched a particularly good film on vampires last night starring James Mason. 'Salem's Lot.' Mark had left the farm gates open so I insisted he went down to close them. I turned off all the lights and laid in wait behind a buttress in the buildings so I could give him a scare.

Sept 10th Raining hard all night with the wind moaning through the eaves of the buildings and the rain battering on the roofs. The moon being almost full moves fitfully between the racing black clouds. "The moon was a ghostly galleon tossed on cloudy seas." I was beginning to wish I hadn't scared Mark last night or watched the vampire film. Vampires were everywhere while the tin sheets on the roofs banged in the gale. There was one (or two) in the building with the broken windows, which I gave a wide berth as I passed looking frequently over my shoulder. There was another one in the old swill-boiling tank. Lurking there ready to creak open the lid and fang hold of me as I went past. Yet another skulked in the lavatory waiting for nature to send me into his toothy embrace.

Whilst I was engrossed in the finer points of rudder construction, the wind still whining in the rafters I became aware of a sinister scratching from a gloomy corner of the room. The hairs on my neck prickled as I stared, seeing nothing to explain the noise. No paper moved in a vagrant draught whilst the sound from the corner became louder and more frantic. I was just about to fasten the top button on my shirt and turn up my collar in order to provide more difficult access to my jugular vein when, with staring eyes and flailing wings, a large Daddy Longlegs struggled from the centre of a roll of plans in the dark corner. Of course I knew all the time there must be some logical explanation.

Sept 15th Travelled to Harrogate on conference. Took a large bale of reading matter on boats and enjoyed several cosy evenings ensconced in the van. Curtains drawn, stove going gently and all snug. Great difficulty though in finding a 'diabetic supper.' Everything is pasta or pizza up here. Eventually settled for a chicken Tandoori then went back 'home' to read.

Sept 16th Went to Wetherby to large chandler and spent three hours looking round. Bought masses of solid teak trim and steering pedestal.

Aug 17th Found bookshop specialising in marine subjects. I find it difficult to stay in such a shop for very long. I get fed up after about eighteen months. Bought fabulous collection of old nautical books. Thousands of hours of utter boredom reading yarns and sea lore!

Sept 19th Journeyed down to Southampton to Boat Show with Jonathan and Jase the Base. Arrived in Southampton at 10.30pm on Friday and went in search of fish and chips shop. After a long search we found one which sold fish bearing a distinct resemblance to old magazines soaked in bilge water only not quite so tasty.

We made up for it the next day after a great day at the show and a good night's sleep in the snug van and a splendid ghost story for Jonathan. Found a Greek café. The haddock were out of this world. I went stark raving mad and had two, each about a foot long. Jonathan had a huge haddock, mushy peas, a mountain of chips and bread and butter and we both had three cups of rosy lee. Beautiful it was, Boyo!

Sept 20th Another full day at the show. Not a boat built like *Ospray*. Bought a copy of PBO from their stand with our first article in it! Jonathan got two autographs. Des Sleightholme and son Aled Rose who was very genial to a young admirer. Bought a very 'Breton' fisherman's smock for working in. Found many people on the Stands very off-hand to a small potential customer like myself. Very sad. Offset by some extra nice folk like Chris and Polly from 'Boaty Bits' from whom we bought a somewhat Victorian loo for £35 plus some anchor chain and a few odds and ends.

Oct 4th Finishing off odds and ends of welding now and priming all bare metal ready for foaming in. All bilges and hull up to above water line inside is being lavishly painted with pitch epoxy. Belt and two pairs of braces. Nowt like it lad.

Oct 11th Welded in an extra mast support, a great lump of 4x2 box so that a bridge could be formed by my patent tabernacle and the position of the main mast adjusted. Trying to think of everything before it is too late, i.e. when the foam is in.

Oct 18th Welded tabernacle in place and trimmed corners. Looks very smart and ship-like. Should prove useful for bolting on winches for halyards etc.

Oct 23rd Tony and Steeve from CAS brought gear to spray foam in hull. What a job. Foam spray seems to get everywhere and smells quite strong. Tony emerged after several hours resembling a ferret after a night on the tiles. The foam has a beauty of its own, rising like space age bread and resembling drifted snow. The inside of the cabins are transformed. Cosy and warm. I wish though that I had done a better job of masking off. Many hours of scraping are the penalty for my laziness.

Oct 29th The cooker arrived today. A Taylor's No 040 against Jonathan's wishes. He had fallen in love with the 030 paraffin stove. I must admit, so had I. The muffled roar of the burners was comforting on the demo model at Southampton. The gas stove on arrival failed to live up to my expectation. Nice looking certainly but not over substantial and poorly designed.

Nov 6th The bowsprit went on today and the whole aspect of the vessel is altered, looks fantastic. The angle is jaunty but not 'snotty' as Don Street puts it. Mary came round as usual and seemed thrilled with the new look.

Have spent two weeks planning and making the fittings – outer and inner forestays plus cunningly incorporating bow rollers. Have had them galvanised at Corbett's and they look superb. I quite enjoy the delicious feeling of accomplishment that it gives one to acquire competence in these different skills and blacksmithing is especially satisfying. Cost of galvanising for all bowsprit fittings from 3/8 plate and together weighing about 30lb is £350.

April 1982 Painting ship! Whole boat rubbed down with sanding discs, then primed with light orange primer. *Ospray* looks somewhat embarrassed by her bright raiment and is only mollified when after a few days we covered up her clown's outfit with her black dress of No 9 gloss. What a black! A black, with the lustre of a raven's wing.

After a long day's work with Rob I scaled the hay at the other end of the barn for a distant survey. Pete Culler chose his words well when he said she was "just plain majestic."

Next came Chris with roll of wallpaper on which to map out the name on her stern. There was, he said, no substitute for genuine gold leaf for a classy job. It didn't seem fitting to cheapen *Ospray's* new black dress with a tawdry imitation so I dug my hand deep into my shrunken pocket and bought 20 quids' worth of bullion. The effect was worth every penny. Gold on black, a Rolls Royce job. Gives the boat a look of Edwardian elegance.

Installed the bog, mounted on a mahogany plinth. Varnished and raised to a comfortable height by much experiment standing, sitting, kneeling, bending etc. Got to cater for all functions by all sizes of both sexes and the permutations are endless. More to this design lark than meets the eye. Well not so much the eye really.

Rob built other half of cockpit. If nothing else this will prevent people asking if the rain won't drive in just a little. Slightly embarrassed as though they half suspected that something was intended to fill the six-foot by five-foot gaping hole!

I keep sneaking round the stern to look up at this breathtaking feature of the *Spray* with the bold letters proudly proclaiming her name and origin. Sometimes I can almost feel the strong hand of old Josh on my shoulder and his silent approval. The vessel, even to one who has loved every waking moment and many sleeping ones – in the spirit if not in the flesh – for over two years is still vastly impressive. I look at her and am breathless with wonder and excitement. Slocum said "I judged her by a blow of the eye and was not deceived." She is cloaked in the aura of power and purpose and the ponderous grace of the whale we saw in the sea of the Hebrides.

May Went down to Southampton with Jonny, Jase and Misty Blue. On a two day shopping trip. Slept the night in the van and woke up on Lymington Yacht Club surrounded by a forest of masts. Made some brecky and a good strong brew whilst Jason and Misty Blue sloped off in order to get as dirty as possible in a nearby marsh.

Lymington is boats. The whole place revolves round them. Went 'boat watching' round the marina. Very few character boats and even fewer with decent ground tackle. Small anchors and thin chain was the norm. Nearly all electric windlasses were cocooned in plastic sheet!! Why? Decided to look for a good big hand windlass. Found one – in Harry Haze's emporium. A hefty brute of a thing with two speeds, two handles and a merry clank to the pawls.

Spent all Friday and Saturday dashing between Lymington, Burseldon, Southampton and Portsmouth (Harry Pound's yard where you can get shackles weighing over a ton each). Spent hours in Gerry Foulkes place at Burseldon and came away mighty pleased with two big bronze winches for £10 each, seized up solid but only requiring a strip down and clean. Adjustable pitch prop came from Yot Grot in exchange for some money, six life jackets and a hydraulic steering pump. Found a beautiful bronze winch by Merriman £9 and a bronze steering gypsy. Marvellous weekend. Jonny is coming along fine in knowing a good bit of gear or fancy rubbish. Slept three nights in New Forest. This is an enchanted atmosphere of 'olde' England.

Rob made the cockpit sole from Dougie Fir and copper nails. I made the floor in the heads from same. Both look mighty smart. Rob putting in ceilings assisted by George and Mick and hindered by Barney who is allergic to work. The wiring of the lights is run through battens of Dougie Fir, which are rebated with devilish cunning and a portable router. The ceilings are painted white with George's meticulous brush and the battens are varnished. The whole boat is now transformed and looks cosy with the glow from the varnished wood and very, very shippy. Have just realised how many times I have written that the boat has been 'transformed' but this is true. You can slog away for weeks with little to show but from time to time certain jobs have an almost magical effect and are a real shot in the arm.

June They are clear felling a large area of wood at Attingham in order to return the park into a semblance of its character of last century. Another lucky find. Bill Onslow, the chief woodsman allowed me to choose all the timber for my remaining spars from among the Norway and Sitka felled last November and now seasoned, having had last winters heavy snows to 'work the sap out' as Pete Culler says of Chesapeake Bay practice.

Fancy rigging my little ship with spars under which Jase the Base and Janie have hunted rabbits and retrieved in fine style with swagger and swank the fallen pigeons. Perhaps the mizzenmast was the tree that Mike blew a branch off with a blast from the old Beckwirth intended for a pigeon flicking over the ride. Maybe there's a couple of No 6 shot embedded deep beneath the protecting varnish as a momento carried forever of a former life when the man who now carves her into immortality once hunted and laughed and lived with jolly dogs and good companions beneath her branches. Seeing her in all seasons and times of day. Drooping and heavy with the hush of the first deep snow, suddenly powdered by the crashing of a cock pheasant springing from the yip, yip of ecstatic spaniels beneath or whispering fury tip brushing the disc of the moon on a velvet June night, witness to the crooning owls and the furtive fallow melting into the moon cast shadows of her branches on the forest floor. And now to gyrate beneath the pole star. The rearguard of the ship, watching the surging wake. The companions of your second life being those of your first.

Romantic flights of fancy guaranteed to bring them crashing down to earth are fibre glassing. Oh my eyes and my liver. How I do hate it. Smelly, sticky, stodgy and spiky – fibreglass gets right up my nose and everywhere else. It is, however, good for encasing rudders made of other materials in order that water should be kept out. So my steel rudder covered in polyurethane foam was encased in GRP.

July Working frantically hard getting ready for sea. A million things to think about so it seems. Working every night till eleven or twelve o'clock. Making the spars now. Lovely work. Using an electric planer to rough them out constantly eyeing up to detect lumps and bumps, then the bell sander in an up and over movement. Sculpting out the shape. Everywhere covered in shavings and sawdust. The old barn really does look like an old time boat yard such as Pete Culler built his *Spray* in, smelling of pine shavings. Fitted all the cracks with epoxy filler made up from resin and micro balloons. First lot went off too quickly and had to throw it away.

Coated the mast with resin. They have turned an exquisite golden colour like a conker when you first prize open the shell. A hive of activity, Chris drilling and generally lending a hand. Mary and Ruth varnishing spars. Rob making fancy wooden fitments for everywhere and everything. Paul Curley with bedewed brow attacking the electrical system with characteristic vigour and enthusiasm. His Mum would be very proud of him if she could see him now. The wiring of a ship is vastly more complicated than I should have imagined and is riddled with pitfalls for the unwary. I should have been hard put to manage without someone willing to read up on all aspects and design a proper system. Have asked Paul and his lady friend for a week on the boat by way of a small thank you.

I feel that the pace is beginning to tell on me. I often work 17 or 18 hours a day but I think it is more the anxiety surrounding the final push. Shall we be ready? I should have been wiser to finish first then arrange the transport.

Shipped the rudder. Completes the profile. Technical forum. Dave asked me to speak on the building of *Ospray* and to visit her.

Up at 4.30, yes am. The last small flight of curlew were flitting through the early morning mist as I walked down to the barn which smelt strong and heady with the new season's crop, which was heating up having been harvested between showers. The steam from the stack rose in tendrils, which became entwined and lost in the mist.

Rob made splendid box for engine instruments in mahogany lined with leather over from our upholstery.

Decided to postpone launch. Feel ill and disillusioned. There are too many things not done that should have been. I have enjoyed building the boat and have often been touched by the interest and help of friends, some of whom put themselves to some trouble. I have also realised how few there are one can really depend on when things get tight. It all makes for self-sufficiency, which perhaps is a good thing even though it is impossible not to feel frustration and anger. The prospect of dropping anchor in Tobermory Bay has been the carrot in front of my nose. These many long months and I see the possibility shrinking with each delay. The stern gear is now installed after many hiccups and promises of being ready. People like that are a pain in the bum.

Should have launched today. No use dwelling on failure. Must make positive use of the time gained. Make sure the ship is better for it. It would have been a shame to send her not quite up to scratch after all the slog and sweat. A bit like sending a girl to her debut ball in a rumpled dress.

Paul Curley has been installing more lights and we now have lights for every purpose. Every time I come home from work there is a new light. If all were connected to the National Grid another coal mine would need to be opened to keep up with demand. Nevertheless I am glad that I have been able to leave all this aspect in capable hands.

Rob and I spent all day forging the mast fittings. Picked the wrong day for this work, as it is hot outside but unbearable in the forge. The work itself is most satisfying. Rob and I were soaked in sweat. The lurid glare from the forge and the merry clang of the beaten metal being hammered into its final shape to snugly fit the masts and spars is probably seldom experienced by the amateur boat builder. How lucky I am. The mast fittings have all been designed by us and I have as usual spent hundreds of hours reading what everyone also has to say about them, especially Claude Worth. How many hours' pleasure I have had from his jottings and infectious enthusiasm. Whether I have designed enough strength into the fittings and whether all moving parts of gear will clear each other, only time will tell, but if it doesn't it won't be for lack of scheming.

The pressure to get finished is very great. Things haven't gone as well as I'd hoped. I feel I can't keep this pace up much longer.

August Started engine yesterday to see how she ran. Wouldn't tick over. Vibration horrendous at about 1/3rd revs, spanners jumping around on floor. Roy came today and eventually got engine running sweet and regular. The exhaust panting out of the side with misty spurts of spray. Stood on deck and felt the throb beneath my feet. She was coming alive! The engine beat like a great heart deep within her. My joy was, however, short-lived. Later after Roy had departed, I couldn't resist trying the engine again. She started without hesitation but refused to run evenly. Instead, surging badly and creating terrific vibration in the shaft, which obviously requires another bearing. This seemed to me to push the possibility of a launch on the 5th beyond the bounds of hope and I decided with heavy heart to postpone yet again. After two big build ups and two big let downs the sparkle of the launch is beginning to dim a little. Paul said the other day, "Nothing great comes easy!"

I feel like a bowstring and have arranged to spend a few days away. Eric and Frank have spent two days trying to locate a caravan at short notice and Frank has offered me his tourer. Have decided to take up the offer. May go to Borth. Slight change from what I had planned for this week.

Went to Machynlleth and bought three old books. The Adventures of Captain Voss, who sailed round the world in a dugout canoe. Boleh, the voyage in a junk rigged boat by a certain Mr Kilroy, and the Last Voyage by Ann Davison. Have just finished reading the latter almost without pause. It is enough to put anyone off boating. Almost but not quite. A heart-rending tale of delay, disaster and death by people much like me.

Must ring Nick Cole about the sails. Nick has a suite of Duradon sails in tan from a cutter he owned in Indonesia but which was wrecked on a reef after only 500 miles. Nick says the sails are 'bloody heavy' but soft like canvas. Hand finished and roped. The mainsail is around 780 square feet. Wonder if I could get a mizzen out of it as well as the main. The sail is horizontal cut, which means it should keep shape better than the usual material. Have offered £500 but this is not enough. The man wants more. Nick is a dentist in Harley Street and seems a good sort. He says some very complimentary things about my articles so he can't be too bad.

Feel much better after a few days' break and have eaten like a horse. Les, as usual having baked enough for an arctic expedition, and I have freely indulged myself. We had curry Monday night made from the second of the two chickens Lesley brought, having had the first on Sunday night with potatoes, carrots and peas with blackcurrant pie and cream, followed by biscuits and a mellow piece of Stilton accompanied by a little Soave. The curry was a little fiery and I required two more lagers afterwards.

The chronological order of this passage is chaotic. I keep remembering things I have forgotten as the Irishman said. Sunday dinner was at 10pm all snug and cosy in the caravan with rain drumming on the roof. We had been to Llanach market where in a moment of delirium I had bought two continental quilts and I returned from a walk to the beach with Jase the Base to find my bed made up and ready by Les. Sat up in bed feeling ecstatically snug in our quilts reading the last voyage of Captain Cook and reflecting on the day. Having been to Aberystwyth looking at boats and buying five fresh crabs for £1.50 with which we made a great pile of butties for Sunday tea. Kept awake by Jonny thrusting about most of the night.

I have now read three books this week. Each one goes into detail about the hassle and delays and disappointments in getting a ship ready for sea. So it seems we are not alone, which is some consolation.

Went to Aberystwyth, had a browse round a bookshop and bought a few more boaty books including What Happened On The Bounty, Arctic Rescue, Worsley's account of Shackelton's voyage and a splendid book of knots which I presented to Jonathan as he is showing much interest in sailorly things and I regret to say – or do I – that he can tie a Mathew Walker knot neater and quicker than his father. What a start for a lad to have, seen the building of a little ship like the *Spray* and only thirteen. He has been on all my gear buying trips some of which have entailed a day off school. Education however, can take many forms. Found a real chandler, a nice old chap having shortly to sell up because of near blindness but knowing about ship's gear and the old way of doing things, (I wish we had him in Shrewsbury) and bought many galvanised fittings. Three solid copper nav. Lights and some tarred marlin twine which smells very shippy. Mike would have loved it here. Some of the old boats here seem to be rigged with whatever comes to hand, polyprop. rope for halliards, everything down to binder twine.

Back home now feeling much refreshed. Been a bit near the edge I think. Finding it hard to pick up the threads. Just picking quietly away doing a little when I feel like it. Going to bed early in my new continental quilt (which is the bees knees for comfort) and reading until sleep claims me. Great pile of delightful books by my bed from holiday.

Rang Nick Cole and struck a bargain for his sails – £600. Went to collect sails with Jonny and Jase but not Misty Blue, much to Johnny's disgust. Nick and Sally most pleasant. Talked boats until 10.30 then drove down to Southampton, went for a stroll along dockland until 2.30am then turned in. Tall Ships tomorrow.

Woke up early in the car park, couldn't resist getting the big mainsail out on the car park. Big? The thing is stupendous and weighs about one and a half cwt. I don't wonder Nick calls it the Mother-in-Law. Or rather, the London cabbie that loaded it in his cab, asked Nick, returning from Indonesia, "Got the bleeding Muvver in Law in there Guv?" Passers by on the car park boggled in amazement and I couldn't stifle a slight smugness at the thought of being considered to be part of the Tall Ships scene. Wish I were. One day perhaps. Went to waterfront café for the full cooked brekkie, egg, bacon, tomatoes and beans. Not 5 star. Not even 1 star. Queued for nearly an hour to get into the dock, then a forest of masts. A spider's web of rigging, bowsprits bigger than *Ospray's* mainmast but blocks and sheaves smaller than I would have imagined. Great yards, again bigger than *Ospray's* mainmast and 150 feet up! These beautiful things made from man's dreams for men's dreams. Sails to billow, bows to plunge and keels to tread the oceans. Masts to sway among the stars and timbers to creak with the rhythm of the deeps. Beauty built to exult in the power of the timeless trade winds.

September After failing to get to grips with anything all day, at last after tea I spent five hours in the forge making mast fittings. The heat and the glare are intense. The metal cherry red becomes submissive under the hammer and forms the shapes I want. How wonderful to beat out of the earth born minerals the strength to harness the gales. Earth, fire, air and water are surely never more in harmony than a forged fitting to hold sail to mast against the blows of the wind high above the plunging water.

October A month of pottering. Find it hard to get stuck into anything. Lesley tells me she has taken up an old association with Keith. I just wish them well. She has been a good friend to me. Always the same and always reliable. Given a lot and asked for little. Good old Les. I hope she's happy.

January 1983 Dawn of another year. Let's hope it's a good one. Let the New Year in as usual with a couple of barrels up the old conker tree. It's a wonder the branches don't fall down with the weight of lead in them. Enclosing the engine room with a solid elm bulkhead. Great improvement. Built in a chart table cum vanity unit in after cabin with bookshelf over. Makes the whole place look snugger and should keep out the noise and smell of the engine quite a lot.

March Decided I must make room for a large ice box/fridge. Reluctantly took out my lovely shippy engine room desk that I spent so long on. Built instead a new chart table with icebox under, the whole thing out of an old wardrobe. Looks less shippy but more yachty. Shame really. Still you don't have to squeeze sideways past it to get to the bog. Hope I am seldom in such a hurry.

Decided to render my two built in tanks water-tight – or fuel-tight as the case may be. All seams inside are welded but on top of this I put a filet of epoxy putty. Climbed inside to get at an awkward corner and got stuck inside the tank with my head at about 90 degrees to my neck. Frightened the living daylights out of myself. I had visions of being found a week later stark raving mad permanently fixed in the form of letter Z. After that I got Jonny to do it. It will be all right lad, I said, if you get stuck you'll only take up enough room for eight and three quarter gallons.

May Decided to fit rail round bulwarks. The one on the *Hans Christian* looked so grand. Ordered 120 foot of 6x1 Iroko – £73! £12.50 per cu ft. Planing would be £2.50 per cu ft extra so decided to do it myself. First big mistake. Planing 16-foot lengths of timber is mighty difficult. Hired belt sander instead. Long, long job. Wish I'd paid the extra. Live and learn. Jonny and I rigged up steamer from a 20-foot length of 7-inch pipe and a 10-gallon oil drum resting on half of a 45-gallon drum filled with sticks and oil etc. Wrapped the pipe in sacks and soon had a good head of steam up. Steamed the wood for about 3 hours then frantic rush across the yard up the ladder and on with the warps whilst still hot. After cooling, the lengths were uncramped, scarfed and glued and screwed into position. Five twelve-hour days. Unbelievable. Looks fantastic. The sheer of the boat is shown to great effect. A great powerful sweep from stem to stern. Carving the tailboard. Worked out great design and started to carve it in Iroko.

Went to Tywyn and slept by the river. Fishing at 6.15. Very cold and squally, river high, torrential showers, river very grim and dour. Caught two small trout.

Went to Aberystwyth to get another mast fitting. Met an old boy that was looking after the shop whilst the boss was away. He was over 80 and had been on the square-riggers on the Australia run round the horn. Bought some tarred marlin twine from him. "Good for piles is this," he said. "Beg pardon," sez I. "Haemorrhoids," he said enthusiastically. I glanced around shiftily to see whether anyone else in the shop had heard. A youth was sniggering hysterically and a lady, probably his mother, was making a close inspection of a coil of rope. "Better than any of your modern remedies," said the old salt warming to his subject. He leaned over conspirationally, "Not a lot of people know that." I said the world was full of ignorance. Thinking, I suppose, of ligatures or something, I said didn't they run into problems getting someone to put a finger on the knot? He stared blankly at me for a moment, then as one explaining the obvious, "You don't tie it, you use it in a ball," I glanced down in disbelief at the ball of twine, which was the size of a small grapefruit. "No," he snorted beginning to lose patience. "You tease the fibres out, roll 'em up in a ball and shove it up yer back passage." The youth exploded and the lady coughed and choked. I remarked that one learned something every day and that I should one day, no doubt, be grateful for this sovereign remedy for one of life's nastier afflictions. The old guy had been on the three master barque – Mountebank – and had once jumped ship in Australia to set up with a colony from Mevagissey, which he left after a row because he wouldn't join the choir, it being assumed that all Welshmen were natural songsters. There were, he said, only two medicines aboard ship for all ills including broken legs. Caster oil and black cat or black strap. I asked him, which he preferred, the sailing ships or the steamers? "It was grand under sail. All you could hear was the wind and the creak of the timbers but you were never really off duty, you could be called at any time to shorten sail. On the steamers you were sure of your 4 hours." The old man took me to see a mast he had just made from a Norway pole. I was pleased to note that my own compared very well indeed.

The Dovey valley was exquisite. A tapestry of colour. I could live in this place. The glistening expanses of mud in the estuary, curlews calling with the cuckoo. There were four young squirrels playing in the tree above my head while I was fishing. Alas, no fish, but lovely warm day and a promise in every cast. Saw a pair of divers. Misty Blue and Jase the Base gave usual rapturous welcome on return to van.

Worked all day 'till 9.45 sanding and oiling rail. Looks quite superb. Made a start attaching fittings to masts. Discovered robin's nest with four eggs in it in the concrete block supporting the mizzen and the boom. My old jacket was draped over it concealing the entrance. There are three nests within 15 feet of my boat. A turtledove's beneath the eaves of the barn. A starling's with young in it on top of one of the central pillars and of course the robins. Its almost as though they are there because of the boat rather than despite it. Nevertheless I bet it's the first time a robin, a dove and a starling have shared the same house with an *Ospray!*

Found two more blackbirds' nests in the barn. The robin is still sitting tight on her eggs and looks at me defiantly when I peep in through her curtain – a piece of blue rag I hung in front of her front door to give her a bit of privacy. Mary came down and helped me with a mass clear up. Boosts my morale no end. Looks much nearer the launch when she's neat and tidy. The bee man came today. Beautiful, mild and sunny. He says he has seen some bees working the holly blossom. I thought he was pulling my leg but he says it produces almost black honey.

Fixed both trailboards on today. Looks real shippy. Finished boom gallows in Iroko. Very pleased.

Worked 9am – 11pm cleaning decks for painting and putting undercoat on.

Painted decks with non-slip. Exquisite day. From my vantage point on the deck I can see the fields and hedgerows dripping with blossoms and fringed with frills of wild parsley. A field of rape is a bright slash of yellow just below the ruined abbey at Haughmond. Our bees have found it and are working it steadily. Must be about two miles as the bee flies. A vixen has cubs down the field and most nights at dusk is seen carrying a rat to them.

June Marked out waterline with Mark using the U-tube method. Hard to see the water level in the tube so we coloured it with juice from a jar of red cabbage. Can't help feeling that beetroot juice would have been better. Probably all the finest vessels had their waterline marked using beetroot juice.

Money getting desperate. Just can't see my way clear at the moment. Every day brings fresh bills or reminders of old ones.

Brought the boat out of the barn today! Rob, Paul, Chris and Derek. She started to move slowly and ponderously on our homemade bogie, waddling like some vast prehistoric creature from the swamps. The day was hot and fine, the air was heady with the scent of elderflower. Just as *Ospray* emerged from the barn a skein of 25 Canada geese flew low directly overhead and yelped in greeting. "We're heading north, care to follow?" They seemed to say. Oddly this was the first time in 14 years at the farm that I have seen geese fly directly over the barn. Seems very strange but exciting. Manoeuvred the boat into position jacking the wheels of the bogie every few feet to bar the wheels round. Arranged transport and launch for 28th!

Last few days of frantic haste to get all those little jobs done. Working about fifteen hours a day and more.

Chapter 12

Ospray Flies North – Her First Shakedown Cruise

The tide was just short of the full. At Penrhyn Dock in the wee small hours of July 19th, there was a muffled hustle. Six shadowy figures bustled up and down boarding ladders. Last minute loading of dogs, fuel, water and the pungent ingredients of Mac's fearsome curries were taken aboard. Then a huge basket of fruit given by a friend, 'to ward off the scurvy.' At last all was ready. The big diesel throbbed into life, lines were cast off and *Ospray* thrust her bowsprit into the velvety blackness of the summer night.

Where was she bound, this relic of the past? Not the Polar Regions or the three great capes as the mass of stores may have suggested but Scotland, the land of the mists and heather, only a few hundred miles distant. Yet, for us, there was all the excitement of the unknown, for this was *Ospray's* maiden voyage. How would the result of four years joyful toil cope with the mischievous Irish Sea? Would she display the legendary self-steering qualities of the old *Spray*? How would she perform under our interpretation of the gaff yawl rig favoured by Slocum with its standing lug mizzen? Many ideas were to be tested and many questions answered before she returned in early autumn.

The black whaleback shape of Puffin Island was passed to starboard just as the first glimmer from the east silhouetted the jagged peaks of Snowdonia. The oil lamp in the binnacle showed the needle pointing due North. This, however, was an approximation for the compass had yet to be swung and this was the reason for our first port of call, Ramsey, Isle of Man.

At 7am by the ship's clock the sea was glassy calm in a developing haze. No land was in sight when the skipper, who is a fair to middling cook, served the pampered crew with the full English plus. Eggs, bacon, beans, mushrooms and black pudding with a strong brew of fragrant Assam tea. Hardly had the spaniels snapped up the scraps when there was a dull roar, the origin of which was obscure. Curious eyes searched the skies for an aircraft. Frowning faces peered down into the engine room. Even my black pudding came under suspicion. The noise died away after a minute or so and the flat sea developed a popple that lasted nearly an hour. Later we learned that we had been near the epicentre of an earthquake registering 5.6 on the Richter scale.

Log entry shows that we sighted the Isle of Man coast in poor visibility at 12.20. For nearly two hours we crept up the coast with the big Ford engine idling along until we rounded Queen's pier, Ramsey with visibility less than one hundred yards. Taking a bearing from the chart we ran more in hope than expectation in the general direction of the harbour entrance half a mile away using our unswung compass. With every diminishing half fathom in depth the voice of the man on the echo sounder increased in pitch by half an octave and no one complained when the twin pillars of the harbour entrance loomed through the murk.

Welcoming us as we tied up on the North Wall was the broad smile of Mr William Barr, the veteran compass adjuster. His father and elder brother had pursued the same profession, being known in maritime circles as the Father, Son and Holy Ghost. The young Mr Barr, a mere lad of some seventy odd summers skipped nimbly down the ladder with his bag of tricks required to correct the special problems when a compass is surrounded by sixteen tons of steel.

Under Bill's genial direction *Ospray* was headed out to sea for about a mile. The visibility was still far too poor for landmarks to be used but the surface haze allowed a good look at the sun. Obviously a man of foresight, Bill had worked out all the azimuths the previous day and lost no time in setting up his pelorus which indicates the direction of the sun with great precision. The boat was headed on different points of the compass whilst Bill positioned and re-positioned magnets until the errors were reduced to acceptable limits that ranged from zero to four degrees.

The errors were recorded on a deviation card for future reference. Before Bill departed he introduced *Ospray's* crew to Jock and Arthur Middlemas who are nearing completion of a steel *Spray* in Ramsey and had followed our tales of the building of *Ospray* in Practical Boat Owner. After an eager inspection of *Ospray* we were shown proudly over their magnificent vessel *The Pinta's Pilot*, soon to be in the water after less than two years of full time work. Wow! The crews of both *Sprays* gravitated to the nearest pub to swap ideas, mostly on the Practical Boat Owner's favourite topic. Where to get the finest materials at the lowest price. Ian Simpson, a *Spray* builder from Edinburgh comes pretty high on the list. A lorry load of mahogany for £10 from a demolished bank. Just don't get caught with the gelignite!

Another nightcap, then we to our bunks after a stroll round the old harbour, watching the lights winking off one by one on the many character boats of which Ramsey has more than its share. *Ospray* was snuggled against the wall, high and dry with three ten gallon water drums ballasting her port side and, for belt and braces security, a line from a shore bollard led to a shackle running on a shroud.

Next day dawned bright and clear. *Ospray* was ready to depart when the tide lifted her gently off the nest her keel had dug in the mud. Harbour cleared, up went the jib and staysail, then the mother-in-law, (the mainsail so christened by a previous owner following a remark concerning her vast and ponderous bulk). Soon we were romping along in a brisk breeze. Cascades of spray were flung into the sunshine, as Slocum put it "like diamond necklaces."

The Isle of Man steam packet swept past close by on our port side heading towards Ramsey. Her passengers lined the rails and waved to us. *Ospray* rolled heavily as she entered the packet's wash and there was a terrifying crash from aloft. The massive mainmast of ten-inch diameter spruce began lurching from side to side with sickening violence. The cause was immediately apparent. The upper mast band carrying all six shrouds and the inner forestay had slipped six feet down the mast and brought up hard against the lower mast band. This put five feet of slack in all shrouds allowing the mast to whip round the sky in an arc of perhaps twenty feet, being brought up by the shrouds on alternative sides as she rolled, with a jar which shook the boat from stem to stern, to say nothing of the skipper's nerves.

Without warning a six-ton breaking strain forward shroud parted, the broken end hissed viciously past my face. The steel deck distorted visibly as the tabernacle was wrenched. Ominous creaks and groans announcing the imminence of a total dismasting.

The crew sprang into action with alarming disregard for personal safety, the sails were rushed down, then sheets, warps, in fact any spare rope, was used to form a cat's cradle either side the ship to take up the slack in the shrouds. Every time the vessel rolled, a little was gained until the mast came under control sufficiently for us to creep back to Ramsey under engine for repairs.

Our friends from *Pintas's Pilot* came to join our struggles. A crane was secured for early next morning, which hoisted the mast band back into position, whereupon Bernard spent three hours swinging at the masthead. Snatches of bawdy ballads alternating with puffs at his fag whilst he laboured with mallet and chisel letting hardwood whelps into the mast below the band. These were doubly secured with epoxy and coach screws to prevent any repetition of the incident, which I regret to admit was caused by a design fault of yours truly.

Problems traditionally associated with mast bands are; crushing of timber caused by mast band being too tight or weak spots created by a shoulder in the mast, or a through bolt which can also provide a site for hidden rot. In an attempt to overcome these snags crafty old me had devised a cunning scheme which, (so we now know) met with resounding failure. I had inserted a packing of ¼ inch conveyor belting under the band before tightening up the bolts until the assembly seemed rock solid when tested with a sledgehammer. However the forces involved were enough to pull the band off its 'packing' leaving it slack on the mast. A warning to the wise!

We cleared Ramsey for the second time at 16.25 on Friday, again in brilliant sunshine. We made good time on the ebb tide and by 19.35 the Mull of Galloway was on the beam. With a force

A QUIET DAWDLE THROUGH LIFE

5 or so breeze coming over the tide the well-known rip off the Mull was having a frolic. My son Mark was sitting astride the bowsprit watching *Ospray's* black bow plunging ponderously. The exultation on his face changed suddenly to horror as his eyes widened with the shock of armpit deep cold water and, shortly afterwards, he vacated his perch.

Bernard, being a man of remarkable foresight, interrupted the self same sea on its way from the bow to the scuppers. Whistling jauntily through his teeth he hoisted his dripping trews (for we were not in Caledonia) to the masthead causing our speed to drop by nearly a quarter of a knot. Then he hunkered down in the cockpit sucking hungrily on a damp fag and defiling the beauty of Galloway with the spectacle of his hairy, goose pimpled legs.

After a wet and windy passage through lumpy seas, which tested Bernard's masthead carpentry, we arrived off Port Patrick just before midnight. The leading lights were carefully aligned, then under plenty of power to combat the strong cross current, *Ospray* surged into the sudden calm of the harbour, being wary of the rock lurking just under water on the port side.

By the glow and crackle of the wood-burning stove, amber liquid tinkled into glasses as a beef curry was got under way, into which Mac shovelled garlic like a demented stoker. The fumes were frightful. It was alleged that a yacht tied up nearly developed osmosis overnight!

During the next few glorious weeks *Ospray* wandered the highlands and islands of the Clyde. A cruising ground to cater for all tastes. From the awesome grandeur of the rearing peaks of Arran we sailed in company with Henry the flute maker from Glossop on *Kaltar* into the breathtaking tranquillity of the Kyles of Bute to anchor off the pier at Tighnabruach, whose tongue in cheek brochure proclaims that 'sometimes as many as several people may be seen walking in the street!' Be not deceived. Beneath the surface in Tighnabruach is more life than a tramp's vest. Off the beaten track and reminiscent of scenes from Doctor Finlay's Casebook this is a place to unwind. A stroll for buttered scones and tea, a glance at the morning newspapers, perhaps a gentle cruise up beautiful Loch Riddon to look for a seal on One

Tree Island, or trail a lazy line for mackerel, then a warm welcome in the pub at night.

From here *Ospray* ventured again upon her first circumnavigation. Non-stop round Inchnarnock Island in a single afternoon! The desolate 'lost soul' cries of the grey seals are not to be forgotten and must have given many a lonely sailor an attack of the 'willies' in the dark of the night.

Thus acquiring a taste for reckless adventure, *Ospray* began tilting at windmills and set forth on yet another circumnavigation, of the Isle of Arran. Although being twenty miles long this required three overnight anchorages. Well there's no sense in wearing yourself out! Cruising back to Arran we saw a basking shark before anchoring by the ruined castle in Loch Ranza. Magic was in the air next morning with the skirl of pipes drifting from the kirk where a wedding was taking place with all guests in full highland dress. Misty Blue, our spaniel, marred the hallowed atmosphere by provoking a bout of aggro. with a passing swan.

Carradale on the Mull of Kintyre was our next anchorage, sheltered from all but southerly gales when you must slip round the corner into the tiny harbour or run the fifteen miles to Loch Ranza. Carradale Bay has a great sweep of white sands where Roger Bannister trained for his epic four-minute mile beneath a turreted castle, set like a gem amongst pine-forested mountains. Next day we up-anchored and sailed with many a backward glance, round Pladda Lighthouse and up the east coast of Arran to Lamlash crouched behind the mass of Holy Island affording shelter, if sometimes a rolling berth, from almost any quarter.

Ospray was welcomed and recognised everywhere by P.B.O. readers with interest and affection. She handled well and self-steered under many conditions but with a tendency to gripe in a stiff breeze from ahead. I have made provision for moving the mainmast position forwards if need be but after reading Denny Dessoutter's dissertations on balance I shall try trimming her by the stern and observe the effect. Apart from slight adjustments required to the gaff saddle, which needed strengthening, everything else worked well. *Ospray* lived up to her name and fish came aboard in goodly quantity by line, pot and barter from trawlers to whom we often tied up for the night.

It was indeed a log worthy occasion when the crew of *Ospray* were warmly entertained aboard Her Majesty's minesweeper H.M.S. *Dulverton*. Six hundred tons of G.R.P. and high technology. Two things struck me, as we were shown round. Firstly, it was nice to know she was on our side and, secondly, I was thankful not to have to mix the resin! *Ospray* acknowledged a friendly wave from the bridge as she passed us on her way south.

After leaving gannets and guillemots, fulmars and shearwaters for our daily companions it was with some regret that we too headed south. She is now back in her berth at friendly Port Penrhyn. Plans for next season are already being hatched.

Getting the feel of Ospray *with Misty Blue*

Misty at Port Penrhyn, down the ladder

.....and back up the ladder

.......and surveying the harbour

Chapter 13

Odds And Sods

1984 – 1985, Yacht masters Certificate.
1984 – 1988, Voyages to Ireland, Scotland and Hebrides.

Whilst still working, I took a leading part in the design, construction and running of a lagoon, created on the site of an old rubbish tip and used for the polishing of sewage effluents before entry to the river Severn. Making a silk purse from a sow's ear? The lagoon and surrounding area was planted with carefully selected species and has now become a natural and attractive haven for a great diversity of birdlife much valued by the local ornithological society. I helped to introduce a few different species of duck e.g. teal, widgeon, pintail, and mallard, also encouraging more grebes to nest on the river. Unfortunately, the grebes did not always have success breeding because of the numbers of mink in the locality.

1987, Took early retirement to do other things but mostly to enable me to write full time.
1987 – 1989, Converted large range of farm buildings attached to my home, into workshops which are rented out providing me with an income which allows me to research my writing properly.

The buildings were made secure so that there was available a variety of workshops, all white washed, with an electricity supply, a stout door and a good padlock. There were some small units suitable for say a carpenter to store his tools and some stock, larger units for at one time an antique dealer, a black smith, car mechanics and a barn suitable for storing larger quantities of merchandise, machinery and road maintenance etc. Upstairs, in the Granary, I partly soundproofed smaller units suitable for band practise. One of the rents that came in was from the Bee Man who kept hives along the hedges of the fields. Twenty-four bottles of prime Shropshire honey were very much appreciated. These units kept me well occupied, maintaining the grounds as a whole, advertising as needed and interviewing of potential clients of which there were many. I had researched the other sites where industrial units were let to give me an idea of rents and rules and regulations. The one problem I did have looking back, was the fly tipping both on site and further down the lane belonging to the Council past the units on my property and adjacent land. On the whole, our tenants paid up and a friendly atmosphere prevailed. Although threats were made of small claims court action, none was taken. Living on site, I was able to keep everything reasonably in order and my next-door good friend and neighbour, Alister, a farmer, walked around the site every night checking his animals and keeping an eye on the units. Thank you Alister.

My eldest son, Robert, has just returned from an extensive European tour with T'PAU, the leading pop group. He plans to write of his experiences and the fascinating interplay of personalities in a tightly knit community living under great pressure. He has helped with the building of *Ospray*, an enjoyable experience especially being able to do such things with my son. Unfortunately Rob did not sail on her much because of mal-de-mere, but was able to enjoy her with his family, while alongside the harbour at weekends.

My second son, Andrew, sailed to Australia as chef on the topsail schooner, *Tradewinds*, on the first fleet re-enactment expedition. He has a large fund of stories and photographs of the voyage, which I propose to use in one form or another.

My third son Mark, when he was doing his 'A' levels, became ill with a myeloma and needed urgent surgery and treatment in London. This entailed travelling up to London for Ruth and myself. Luckily Andrew was working and living in the city so lived reasonably near to Mark. This was a tough time for Mark and the family. I remember one day, Mark throwing a chair and saying "Why me?" How do you answer a question like that from your son? Thank goodness, he has made a full recovery, despite several operations, and although he has lost his quadriceps on one leg, he is a very able young man. He travelled widely to see the world, as I suppose he knew not what lay ahead of him in life. Money was not the main goal in life, working for Greenpeace and similar activities seemed more important. Mark joined us for four months of our voyage, across Biscay, down to the Cape Verdes and across the Atlantic to Trinidad before flying back to the UK.

My forth son Jonathan also helped with the boat though still quite young. I have a wonderful memory of him selling a multitude of life jackets at Beaulie Boat Jumble and having his pockets stuffed with £5 notes! He also has a love of wood and has worked for many years with Rob as a carpenter. They were well known for their work in oak renovating barns and old buildings.

In 1989, I started going out with Else, whom I had known for many years and we started to plan a voyage in *Ospray*. I wanted to head north to Greenland to fish for cod but Else wanted to head south to the West Indies. Else won. We'll see what happens at the next throw of the dice. And so the idea took hold and plans were made over the following three years. What spare parts and equipment would we need? What crew would we invite and how many should we be for the longer crossings? Where would we plan to go? And what victuals would we need? There were lists upon lists of the must haves and would haves and could haves!

We drove up to Mull for our first Christmas together via Poynton to introduce Else to my parents. Unfortunately, that was the only time Else was to meet Mum as she died while we were away. I am sorry that Else did not get to know my Mum better because they would have got on like a house on fire with their many common interests e.g. in sewing and needlework, shopping for bargains and gardening. Else now treasures her pin box.

Over the next few years we holidayed in Scotland, one Christmas and New Year with Halldis, Else's Mum, when we rented a house on Mull. It was a cold and wet year and Halldis did not feel well with the 'flu. When Jim said that he might plan to move to Scotland sometime, she told Jim vehemently "Over my dead body will you take my daughter to live in Scotland."

And where do we live now? And she had been born and lived in Norway!

Else applied for a sabbatical from her work as a physiotherapist and was given a year off without pay. She made arrangements to rent her house while I arranged for Rob and Kerry to live at Monkmoor Farm, my home, to live in the house rent-free and run the business for me and look after the two dogs, Misty and Mishka. Else had the paperwork finalised for her divorce.

Chapter 14

Ospray – Trans-Atlantic Voyage 1991-1992

Schedule – All dates approximate and subject to weather conditions etc.

August 1	Depart Bangor for Kinsale, Southern Ireland to await suitable weather for crossing Bay of Biscay. 550 miles. Crossing time 5-6 days to Cape Finisterre. First port of call Vigo, Northern Spain.
August 20	Depart Vigo for Funchal, Madeira. 800 miles. Crossing time 8-10 days.
September 10	Depart Madeira for Canary Isles. 250 miles. Crossing time 3 days. Cruise Canary Isles visiting Lanzarote, Fuertoventura, Gran Canaria, Tenerife and Gomera.
October 20	Depart Canary Isles for Cape Verde Isles. 800 miles. Crossing time 8-9 days.
November 5	Depart Cape Verde Isles for West Indies. 2100 miles. Crossing time 15-21 days. First port of call, Port of Spain, Trinidad.
January 3	Depart Trinidad for extended cruise through eastern Caribbean. Visiting Grenadines, Windward Islands, Leeward Islands, and British Virgin Islands until end of March. Aprox. distance 600 miles.
June 1	Depart Virgin Islands for Bermuda. 700 miles. Crossing time 12 days
June 10	Depart Bermuda for Azores Islands. 1820 miles. Crossing time 18-20 days.
July 15	Depart Azores for U.K. 1300 miles. Crossing time 12-15 days

Crew   1st leg, Jim Mellor, Else Goss, Mark Mellor, Vanessa Jones.
Joined by Sean Vicary in Spain. Vanessa left in the Canaries.
Bangor to Trinidad.
2nd leg, Jim Mellor, Else Goss, Paul and Lill, Emily and Nick Quesnel.
Trinidad to St Vincent.
3rd leg. Jim and Else, Andy Mellor and girlfriend Tracey.
St Vincent to Antigua.
4th leg. Jim and Else.
Antigua to Bermuda.
5th leg. Jim and Else and Sam Richmond.
Bermuda to Faial, Azores.
6th leg. Jim and Else and Geoff Knibb.
Faial to Graciosa, Azores to Ireland and then Bangor, North Wales.

Getting Prepared For Our Trans-Atlantic Voyage – Spare Legs For Sailors

Sailors throughout history, in life and in legend, have been prone to shedding bits of anatomy with almost nonchalant stoicism.

Nelson managed to lose both an arm and an eye. Captain Hook found a passable substitute for a missing hand in his fearsome steel hook, which must have often caused him to think twice before scratching his more tender parts. The bold Captain Ahab ended up short of a leg after a tiff with Moby Dick and henceforth kept the watch below awake by stomping around the deck, in an understandably foul mood, on his ivory leg which he had carved from the jawbone of a sperm whale.

It seems that sailing has always been a hazardous business though with any luck at all and a modicum of common sense, most of us will escape being crunched by a crocodile or snapped up by a sperm whale. We may even go the whole of our lives without once being raked by grape shot. But, for those of us who derive pleasure from wandering the seas on pitching decks surrounded by whirling ropes and flailing blocks there will be hazard and injury enough. It will behove us to know how to cope.

Now it seems that Captains Ahab and Hook were into orthotics! According to my first mate, bless her heart, who is a Chartered Physiotherapist, and from whom I milked most of this information, orthotics is the use and application of orthoses. "Well stone the crows," I can hear you say. Have patience dear reader and all will be revealed. An orthosis being a device which supports, corrects, or compensates for an anatomical deformity or weakness however caused, while a prosthesis, from the Greek 'in addition' is a replacement or substitute for a missing part i.e. an ivory leg of a steel hook for a hand.

Now if the two worthy Captains had tangled with their sperm whales and crocodiles in this day and age then Ahab's crew may not have been raving insomniacs and Captain Hook himself may have slept the sounder without the morbid dread of impaling himself during an absent minded nocturnal scratch.

Orthotics has come on in leaps and bounds since steel hooks and ivory legs. Even the Navy, not noted for softness, have abandoned the ritual of laughingly dipping the gory stump into molten pitch before strapping on a wooden leg. Unless, for the sake of tradition, which dies hard in the Navy, the patient insists.

Sorry to disappoint you but I am not about to tell you how to amputate a limb, fascinating though it may be. However, for more repairable damage there is a recently developed range of materials, which may well find a place in the substantial First Aid inventory of a well-found ocean voyager. These materials are a new range of thermoplastics. Plastics, which can be cut to size from a flat sheet, softened by the application of only moderate heat, then moulded to shape round an injured limb.

They are successfully used for the treatment of fractures, soft tissue injuries such as muscle, tendon and ligament tears and also in the protection of serious burns. Any of the above can have serious consequences if occurring on a short-handed vessel possibly weeks away from medical assistance. In many cases sufficient support may be obtained from a well-fitted orthosis for the limb to be used within limitations. Indeed there may be no option for a single hander. Also of importance is the alleviation of mental stress given by protection to a damaged limb, especially on a moving vessel where one may get flung about sustaining further pain and injury.

Advantages over traditional materials for supporting or immobilising limbs such as plaster of paris, bandages etc, are many. Extreme lightness, water resistance, greater comfort and easier to apply and remove for inspection of wound, cleaning or just for a good scratch. Oh heaven! Soggy bandages or plaster of paris would lead to extreme discomfort and possibly salt-water sores.

Even in the absence of a crisis or after it when snug harbour is reached, thermoplastics are far more suited to recovery and rehabilitation in a marine environment where ladders, hatches and companionway steps are a part of everyday life.

Another useful attribute of thermoplastics is to fashion a purpose made splint to hold an injured hand in a position of function such as grasping the spokes of a wheel or a winch handle, or a pencil for plotting the course. The mind boggles at the possibilities! In fact the material can be moulded round anything as a handle or holder and be used to fabricate or repair many items of boat gear. Even a temporary repair to a broken boom!

The basic principle of using thermoplastics is fairly simple. The material is softened in hot water (usually about seventy degrees) or by hot air, then moulded round the limb to be supported and allowed to cool after trimming off any surplus. A lining of stockinette or foam may be used and the device is held in position with Velcro tape if required.

Obviously the complete technology and full range of applications is beyond the scope of an article so a few examples are shown. The potential for ingenuity in orthotics is huge. The Duke of Wellington managed to contrive an ear trumpet that also served as a walking stick. Or perhaps it was the other way round!

Supply of material. Now although life is full of surprises, it would be folly to bank on finding much in the way of thermoplastics on a coral atoll so anyone interested should make enquiries in the U.K. I have found the following firms particularly helpful. Each one manufactures a small range of products differing slightly in application and are able to supply further information and instruction in the use of their material.

> Orthopaedic Systems, Unit G.22,
> St Michael's Industrial Estate,
> Widnes, Cheshire WA8 8TL
> Product – Hexalite

This is a mesh material that can be used single thickness or several, laminated together with hot water to give the rigidity required. The open structure allows quick drying and can be worn in the bath or shower and also, I assume, in the monsoon. Some applications would require a layer of stockinette or waterproof foam for comfort.

Orthopaedic Systems will supply a basic kit for splint making at a cost of £40.

This comprises; One Pack of Hexalite Sheets

> One Roll of Stockinette
> One Roll of Padding
> One Rolling Pin
> One Water Ladle

A water heater can also be supplied but it is assumed that a boat would have a baking tray and thermometer on board.

This firm also produce an innovatory method of managing injuries to the lower leg and ankle. These are pneumatic braces and are very successful in treating simple fractures and severe sprains. Enthusiastic reviews have appeared in the medical press and it is claimed that not only do most patients remain mobile but the limited movement allowed by the brace promotes quicker and better quality of healing whilst the massaging effect of the inflated compartments during exercise is believed to reduce swelling. A big advantage is that almost full up and down movement of the foot is retained allowing such activities as driving. Perhaps most useful is the ankle brace which will fit most adults from 5' 2" and cost £28 each. Unfortunately, due to the way the Good Lord made us, you will either have to decide which ankle to break or buy a right and a left. However, the walking brace which will cope with lower leg of ankle injuries costs £116 but will fit either leg.

Another supplier is Smith and Nephew Limited

> P. O. Box 81
> Hessle Road,
> Hull HU3 2BN

Shopping list of equipment needed for the voyage: –

Rented a life raft for the year – 6 man – and never used, thank goodness!

SSB radio – Single Side Band – able to keep in touch with family in the UK via Portishead Radio in England, which provided worldwide maritime communications from 1928 until 2000, and to contact other ports of call and nets that were formed to keep us safe. I said, "Herb's little ducklings sailing across the pond."

VHF Radio.

EPIRB – Emergency Position Indicating Radio Beacon

GPS – Global Positioning System – 'is a space-based satellite navigation system that provides location and time information in all weather conditions where there is an unobstructed line of sight to four or more GPS satellites.' – (Wikipedia.) The Americans took out the satellites for several days while we were en route to Trinidad causing us much consternation at the time.

Cetrek – autopilot or autohelm.

Depth Finder – to avoid some of those nasty reefs and pinnacles!

Sextant

Extra rope and chain and sails

Medical stores

We already had life jackets, life ring with its rope, harness for working on deck, thick rope to trail overboard. A sea anchor or drogue was given to us by Dr John of Selattyn in Shropshire, who also instructed Else in the use of injecting relating to diabetic problems, as I was a type 11 diabetic, and wrote out a list of medicines to procure for the voyage. These were supplied on prescription from the dispensary at the hospital where she worked.

We wished to be self-sufficient for 12 months at sea!

Chapter 15

A Taste Of The West Indies

Trinidad and Tobago – The Best of both Worlds
(Written in 1993)

In the rich and colourful crown of the Caribbean, Tobago is surely the jewel. On its deserted beaches one expects to find Long John stumping along or, maybe a chap in a goatskin cap. In fact legend has it that the discovery of a castaway on Tobago inspired Defoe to write 'Robinson Crusoe.'

In every turquoise bay you expect a vessel like the *Hispaniola* to be swinging to her anchor, creaking gently on the swell. And indeed, sometimes there is!

Tobago and her sister island of Trinidad are usually missed out by sailors heading west across the Atlantic. I think this is a great mistake. Although Barbados or Antigua are slightly closer, especially if leaving from the Canaries, one often has to swing so far south to find the best of the north east trades, that a call in the Cape Verde Islands becomes logical and, in my view, highly recommended. From the Cape Verdes the difference is trivial.

However, we on *Ospray*, our home built copy of Slocum's famous *Spray*, had a special reason to visit Trinidad. Our first mate Else, was a Trinidadian and the entire crew of myself, son Mark and his friend Sean, had been invited to spend Christmas with her family.

We left Mindelo in the Cape Verdes to a rapturous send off from the locals and a brisk force seven Harmatten laden with Saharan dust. For twenty-one days, seeing not a ship or a plane, we rode the majestic but benign trade wind rollers with only the wheeling shearwaters and flying fish for company. Occasionally a roving band of dolphins seeking, like Mister and Missus

Ramsbottom, for further amusement, came for a romp on our bow wave before dashing off leaving us infected with their sparkling joie de vivre.

We entered Galleon passage, between Trinidad and Tobago, in the dark of night, as did Slocum when returning from his epic circumnavigation nearly a century before. He spent a wretched night tossing as he thought, amongst frightful breakers and cursing the goat that had eaten his charts, before collapsing with relief on a pile of rope when he realised that "It was the great revolving light on the island of Trinidad, throwing flashes over the waves that had deceived me."

Normally coming from the east, Tobago should be visited first owing to the wind and current systems, which do not favour a voyage from Trinidad to Tobago. However, eagerness overcame prudence and we headed straight for Trinidad. Soon after dawn on December 4, accompanied by frigate birds, pelicans and ospreys, we came into the Gulf of Paria through the Dragon's Mouth and tied up to the little dock at Power Boats in Chaguarmas Bay. Else's family, some with tear stained cheeks, were there to greet us. Soon we were sitting in the shade of a palm tree sipping an ice-cold beer, and this at seven o'clock am! Half a mile away in the forest, a howler monkey screamed.

Christmas was a blur of rum punches and other drinks based on rum, which is amazingly cheap, about three quid a bottle, and Creole dishes with huge quantities of meat, which is also amazingly cheap. Between the social rounds, swimming and sight seeing, we had *Ospray* hauled out, shot blasted, primed, painted, anti-fouled and dropped back in for less that £1000, in under a week over the Christmas holiday! A smiling team led by Jerry Ferreira of Industrial Marine Services Ltd accomplished this.

Trinidad is by far the more commercial island of the two, with lots of facilities for the repair and maintenance of yachts, good supplies of local teak and skilled labour to work it at excellent prices. There are plenty of dining out facilities representing Trinidad's mixed ethnic origins of Europe, Asia and Africa and the most friendly and efficient banks I have seen anywhere in the world. With its well stocked, air conditioned supermarkets and

A QUIET DAWDLE THROUGH LIFE

good prices, Trinidad is ideal for re-stocking a vessel before moving on up the islands. Lying in eleven degrees latitude, only seven miles from the coast of Venezuela, Trinidad offers a perfect refuge during the hurricane season from July to October. Medical care is excellent but expensive so make sure you have adequate insurance. Ours cost £400 each for twelve months.

I lost a front tooth whilst surfing. Arrangements were quickly made and I found myself being treated by a delectable lady dentist who murmured soft and comforting words while cradling my head on her soft and comforting bosom. The resulting replacement is superb and the memory lingers on. How often is one sorry to leave a dentist's chair?

During the year's cruise, we had four medical problems requiring professional help, two dental emergencies (six visits), despite checks in the U.K. just before departure, one severe eye infection and one nasty ulceration of the leg due to a coral scratch.

Moorings and sometimes pontoon berths are available at three main centres all snuggled in the crook of the arm of Chaguaramas Peninsula just to the west of Port of Spain, Trinidad's capital of some two hundred thousand souls. Trinity Yacht Facilities (also known as Power Boats) has a fifty-ton lift and a waterfront café and bar in a delightful setting overlooking the islands. Customs can be cleared from here; the building is close by and has its own pontoon berth. Yachting Association has showers, snackette and temporary membership is available.

We also went to Trinidad Yacht Club, which has moorings, pontoon berths, showers, bar and café. All these offer fairly good security. If you intend to stay for Carnival, you should definitely make reservations. Carnival in 1994 is February 14 and 15. This is spectacular! One of the largest in the world, it is a pulsating extravaganza of colour and rhythm. The streets become rivers of gaudy humanity in bizarre costumes; iced coconuts and tropical fruits are on sale, literally by the truckload, and the whole affair is gleeful and good humoured. If you can keep your feet still at this event you surely must be dead!

'If my friends could see me now,' I thought, chippen' down Tranquillity Street with the best of them, skinny legs sticking out of my old colonial shorts. They would probably have died laughing!

There are lots of wonderful places to visit in Trinidad. Asa Wright's Nature Centre is a paradise for naturalists. In this part of the Northern Range (rising to three thousand feet) many of Trinidad's six hundred species of bird can be seen. Trails through primeval rain forest echo with the strident call of the toucans, and humming birds can be photographed within feet of the lens. For the patient and sharp sighted, there are ocelots, armadillos, wild pigs and monkeys. In the Caroni Reserve, which is a huge area of mangrove swamps, you can go on a guided boat tour through these 'everglades' and see flocks of scarlet ibis and white egrets coming to roost at dusk. If you peer into the tunnels between dense jungles of mangroves, you may see a cayman or a turtle rippling these death still waters. Giant leatherbacks nest on the eastern beaches of the island.

Noel Coward described Trinidad's natural Pitch Lake as "Twenty two tennis courts badly in need of repair." It is ironic that with this unending supply of asphalt, Trinidad's roads should be so badly in need of repair, seeming to prove the old adage that, 'A cobbler's wife is poorly shod.'

Tobago, as I hinted earlier, is a yachtsman's paradise albeit with fewer facilities than Trinidad. If you have hastened to Trinidad first and do not fancy the hard slog against wind and current, you can fly there for about twelve pounds and hire a car. However, you would be missing the chance to anchor in some of the most exquisite bays on earth. Tobago is as yet unspoilt, the people are exceptionally friendly and the whole island seems to have been designed by the Almighty on Capability Brown's principle of 'a surprise round every corner.' This may explain why the island changed hands eighteen times in the course of history. Some of the forts of these occupations can be visited and provide an interesting insight to the colourful and turbulent history of the island. Sometimes neighbouring forts were occupied simultaneously by English and French garrisons. Apparently they would lob shells at each other to while away a quiet Sunday afternoon. Place names are a quaint mixture of Anglo Franco origin. Charlotteville sits happily in Man-O-War Bay and Scarborough terminates in Bacolet Point. Scarborough is the port of entry and provides fuel and water and basic facilities with some moorings available.

According to the time of year, the wind is likely to be fairly consistent from one direction or another. This will help you decide which bays afford the most comfortable anchorages. A dive to ensure your anchor is well dug in and not likely to foul a coral head is reassuring. It is no hardship to dive into these crystal turquoise waters with temperatures well into the eighties and visibility as much as one hundred and fifty feet. The greatest danger is being killed in the rush. Quite often, throughout the Caribbean, you will find it possible, and sometimes necessary, to tie up to a palm tree with a stern line after backing in from a bow anchor. From King's Bay, a secure anchorage in all but a strong southerly, you can walk along a woodland path like a botanical gardens to a waterfall tumbling several hundred feet down precipitous rocks to a pool below. It was quite something to cool off under this hammering cascade in mid January, thinking of the folks back home trudging to work in drizzle and fog.

The quality of the diving and snorkelling off Tobago is superb and has been compared with Australia's Great Barrier Reef. Equipment can be hired from half a dozen centres and expert dive masters will guide you on anything from a novice dive to a challenging deep-water dive. Even snorkelling you will see a stunning variety of fish and coral in gorgeous colours, the fish so tame you can feed them by hand or photograph them with ease. We often swam and snorkelled for six hours a day. One day we took a trip in a glass-bottomed boat over the Buccoo Reef with its fantastic corals including huge brain corals before anchoring in five feet of water for an hour's snorkelling. There were fish everywhere. Black and yellow striped sergeant majors, stoplight parrotfish, predictably red, orange and green, eight or ten pounds in weight cruising round at arm's length. On another occasion, in less than twenty feet of water, we saw a manta ray, barracuda and turtles plus a host of brilliant small fry.

It goes without saying that seafood features largely in the local Creole cuisine, which is wholesome, spicy and delectable.

Crab and dumplin', flying fish, shark and bake, callaloo soup, doubles and Trinidad's claim to fame, the Roti. A meal in itself, the roti is the Caribbean's answer to the Cornish pasty. A multi-layered envelope of fine bread/pastry is stuffed with a generous filling of spiced meat, or seafood, and vegetables. Takeaway or eat in, you can often choose from a dozen fillings or more.

The sailor visiting Tobago will be greeted by smiles and waves everywhere. If the Caribbean is laid back then Tobago is horizontal! The islanders are remarkable for their flair for doing absolutely nothing with panache. In the face of such an example we changed down a couple of gears, putting us in the correct frame of mind for a leisurely dawdle up the islands. Grenadines next stop.

Further information and a booklet – Discover Trinidad and Tobago can be obtained from: Trinidad and Tobago Tourist Development Authority,

8 Hammersmith Broadway,
London W6 7AL

Chapter 16

The Following Notes Are From Else's Diary Describing Day-To-Day Life Of The Crossing From Bermuda To The Azores

Sat 6 June

Up at dawn. There is a small boat warning 'till 9am. Quite a few yachts are leaving. I spoke to Bermuda radio, told them we were going and found that the channel was clear. So anchor up and stowed below decks and we were off, 9am.

We motored for the first few hours but soon were on main (one reef) and two jibs going at a good speed. By now we were on to the large chart, small scale, and the Azores look far away when you see the small distance already covered. Sam is feeling ill and looking like a ghost. Both Jim and he are wearing travel bands. So far, I feel O.K.

Oh, Jim rang son Rob to say we were off and later, before supper, I managed to get Lill and said 'goodbye' to everybody with good wishes for the voyage.

Sam stayed below and tried to sleep, Jim and I taking the watches and self-steering because the autohelm appears not to be managing. Don't know why. So a long night, rain, Jim feels tired, but going at a rate, once I noted we were doing 7.6 knots. Jim managed some baked beans; I had a cup of soup only. Sam had nothing. Just as well we all had some toast for breakfast.

THE FOLLOWING NOTES ARE FROM ELSE'S DIARY

Sun 7 June

10 days off Jim's birthday, I hope the weather is better then, it's raining and overcast and we're manually steering and still going at a rate. One of the sheets broke on my watch during the early hours, getting frayed on the rail. So woke Jim to drop the sail and put on another.

Our first day's run was 124 miles by GPS. Keep this up and we'll soon be there, but everyone's feeling ugh! We can't have it all ways.

We've even had gale force rains gusting well up to force 6 perhaps 7 but *Osprey* is riding the waves beautifully, the rigging is the thing that we are the most worried about. The sheets getting a good battering.

By noon, the weather was clearing from the south and by sunset we had a lovely evening, you could see the stars and the first quarter moon (today), perhaps it will clear. Listening to the radio, *Taura* is turning back with some mechanical problems. As yet, we can hear the chat on 6A and 12A but even though I have programmed the radio, we are unable to contact Herb on *Southbound II*. At least we know what the weather is doing from him. Jim's just sent his apple overboard; perhaps it will be my turn next! While trying to sort some warm clothes out for the bunk, I had to lie down once and then tried to go to sleep after.

The two men had hot chocolate and I had a cup of soup. Sam is now helping with the watches and we've decided to do 2 on and 4 off, especially as it's manual steering at the moment. We think it may be damp in the compass. Sam has almost beaten being sick; the main thing is keeping dry when off watch.

Mon 8 June

It was soon overcast and squalling and raining and the wind being fluky during the night. But what a surprise when I woke to a beautiful morning. Herb said that the front should start breaking up today.

A QUIET DAWDLE THROUGH LIFE

There was a change in the wind SW instead of SE, so we played with a change of sails and let out the second reef (we'd reefed down during the night). With the sun out everybody felt much better and we all ate scrambled eggs with one slice of toast. Some Gatorcade to follow to top up our fluids and electrolytes.

I rinsed out the salt-water clothes and soon had two lines up, trying to get everything dry. Carpets up and drying outside, floors mopped with Ajax so not greasy anymore, the table fixed which had fallen over and the glass picked up that broke falling out of the cupboard when Jim was getting out his pills. Then a little relaxation.

Sam has his shirt off, I changed into a swimsuit, Jim came up after his sleep and he soon had the Cetrek working again. We think it was damp in the compass. Fingers crossed it will keep doing its job well now.

A lazy afternoon. I decided to make a chicken soup, which is now on the go. Unfortunately, it looks like the clouds are building up so we may have another rainy night in store. Oh well, we should be accustomed to it. Also the roar of a wave coming to get us and then silently slipping under the hull. It's the quiet one sneaking up that gets us down the back of the neck and even up the arms of your waterproofs!

Everyone enjoyed the 'stew chicken' and kept it! It ended up being a lovely night, the moon hiding behind some dark clouds before going to sleep. So I steered by the stars until they too disappeared. Sam had self-steered so I continued on manual to let Jim sleep better. Towards the end, the Cetrek (autohelm) wouldn't take being on, calling out 'Batt. Ala.' (Battery Alarm). Just as well Jim checked the batteries as he also found water in the oil, salt water. Probably back tracked from one of the drainage tubes. I suppose water in the bilges is far better than water in the sump! With the extra weight, the drains are below water level now. The day's run was 94 miles.

Tue 9 June

Jim managed to 'fix' things once again although the Cetrek kept alarming on him, a nuisance! I thought Sam was letting me have

THE FOLLOWING NOTES ARE FROM ELSE'S DIARY

a sleep in this morning. An hour later I got up and he was sleeping peacefully propped between the compass table and the hatch. After waking him to go to bed, I next found him asleep on the seat. He was knackered!

Still overcast but a nice morning, I've started reading the Indian book, Lame Deer, and had my first cup of coffee. It didn't taste very good.

The day didn't brighten but neither did it rain, so most of us took turns to sleep. At one time the main jib gybed and started pulling the rail up, we were trying to get the genoa and mainsail on opposite sides. It worked well for almost two minutes.

We're gradually starting to eat and drink a bit more, Sam still limiting himself, only supper tonight, cauliflower cheese and sausage.

It has now begun to rain, 6'ish so all hiding below decks. I threatened to have a shower but it is a bit cold. Jim and I had a nice shampoo though; Sam wasn't up to going below. Today's run was 82 miles but only 59 miles in the Azores direction. Now at 18.30, we have 1503 nautical miles (nm) to go to Faial as the osprey flies!

A good night, no rain, but fluky winds often so ended up motoring quite a lot, when the engine is off though we end up going further north. Soon we will need to be catching up on the easting.

Wed 10 June

I woke with the daylight just before 6am and the start of my watch. Sam was reading up on the Azores in the Atlantic Islands guidebook. The seas are steely grey, spread with flecks of white foam once they have passed under the boat. On the other side, they approach with white horses, no pretty blue to be seen today, directing themselves at the port side. Some making the boat lurch to starboard, playing with her like a small cork in a huge wilderness of water. The ride is still reasonably comfortable despite all I've said. All objects appear to stay below in their ordained places even though they may object at times making crashing noises.

It will soon be 09.00, Jim now at the helm, so I will do a plot and see how our last day's run compares.

Oh, a small swallow had a ride with us for a short time while I was on the radio listening in for the weather. Jim thought that he was hungry; there are still breadcrumbs on the stern coach roof. He asked me to get some mince out but I didn't hear him while concentrating on the radio.

Not a pleasant day, the weather worsened to gale force winds, keeping one watch at a time in the cockpit, safety line hooked on.

Then it started to clear, how beautiful. We winged out the genoa and jib, racing off in the right direction for the Azores, but a dicey rig to keep going at night. So far, the Cetrek is working; Jim just found some condensation in the face of the compass. It stayed fair to have supper in the cockpit. None of us have been able to face a full meal below decks yet. 'Stew chicken' (as the West Indians say) with dumplings this time.

During the night figures were flying across the moon changing in shape and size every few minutes, from lovable to sinister. I think Jim also drew them in his diary. I drew a picture of a large black bear which soon changed into something else and ended up as a blob with a 'cake slice' out of it and yellow from the moon emitting from its mouth (so to say) and a hole that looked just like an eye, glaringly yellow. They told me to "Be strong in the bad weather!"

Thu 11 June

A very rainy night, the Cetrek complaining again, so has been covered in a plastic bag. Being covered, you can't get at the controls when he shouts 'bleep.' The weather man, Herb, advised those yachts north to go south of east because of the bad weather, gusting up to 30 knots plus. Just why we have been having foul weather!

When the wind backed to NW from SW, it also dropped but now the seas still remain quite confused so we are rolling and the water tank is leaking slopping pints of water into the bilges. Oh, for a sunny, decently calm and windy day, to clean up and dry the

THE FOLLOWING NOTES ARE FROM ELSE'S DIARY

leaks. Jim has been round with the tape trying to plug holes; I do appreciate dry feet in bed!

About suppertime, we crossed the '1/4 of the way there' mark which was also 500 miles out of Bermuda. Listening to *Magic Carpet* on the radio, she is 950 miles from Bermuda, averaging 130 miles a day and hopes to do the trip in less than 14 days. I don't think we will be that lucky. However, yesterday, she had waves fill her jib and cockpit so is heading fast for Flores to hide!

Tonight's supper was sausage soup/stew. I am just about to warm the rest up for Jim coming on at 2am. We now have the engine on but still making very little way, 2.4 knots, and the GPS says 1294 miles to go to Faial. Flores is about 100 miles closer if that is our first port of call. Off to bed now.

Fri 12 June

Up at 06.10 with the sunrise, lovely golden colours below floating white clouds. There's blue sky, about 40% cloud cover, the weather to the south still looks very grey. It's noticeable immediately how much colder it is, checking the temperature, it was 73 degrees during the night, and it has now fallen to 67 degrees. I can smell the fresh coldness. I wonder if there are any icebergs around? At the moment we see shearwaters and Portuguese 'man-o-war.'

We sailed all day, the Cetrek coming back to life which made things easier, we are now running with the set of 'Lucas' sails and the mainsail with one reef. The speed is not fantastic and we are making more south now.

I'm finding it difficult to get NMN's (Coast Guard long range communications station from Chesapeake) other forecasts. The one clashes with Herb's roll call. The chart at the moment has cold and warm fronts drawn across it as well as a high-pressure ridge. There are all sorts of weather about! And we are getting a lot of it!

I eventually managed to get through to Portishead radio and booked a link call for Jim. He spoke to Kerry and described some of the large waves. She asked, "Were they very frightening?" Jim replied, "Yes, but *Ospray* and her crew were well in control!"

The genoa taken down this morning has a huge tear along the bottom, which will keep me busy for a while, hopefully on a more settled day. Jim managed to bake bread and scones.

Tonight's meal was shepherd's pie with red beans and whole mushrooms in it. Not surprisingly, there are some leftovers. 1276 miles to go to Faial at 9am, with a 74 miles day's run.

Sat 13 June

At 9am, we've been at sea for one week. We've done over a 1/3 of the way, so it looks like the trip may take 21 days, even though the first 1/3 zigzagged quite a bit. It's now 1210 miles to go, yesterday's run being 85 miles.

I've decided that some of the waves like to show off. They come tumbling and growling up to the side of the boat and then dissolve in a cascade of crystal droplets quite silently. I can watch these waves forever, each one being quite different.

On my shift from 6-8am, I thought we might be in for some more bad weather. The clouds to the north were lined up like trains while those ahead, in the north east, were racing towards us across the sun, there seemed a never ending supply of them. Eventually, it did clear into quite a nice day, the wind 15-20 knots gusting to 25 but the seas gaining in height. So we are having a bouncy ride at the moment. Poor Sam's bed is getting wet, through the cowl and a little from the front hatch.

At 13.45 Jim sighted a red tanker, which I called up on VHF16. "How can I help you?" I asked for a weather forecast to which he said, "Wait a few seconds," but then I never heard any more.

While I slept late morning, Jim managed to fix the autohelm, there was a corroded fuse, and thank goodness it was something that he could do, the Gods are watching over us.

By evening, Sam was looking very pale and kept to his bunk, being showered every so often with seawater. Jim has tried to make all the leaks waterproof, but not very successfully. Water appears to get in when it wants to. I'm sure that's the problem with our electrics.

THE FOLLOWING NOTES ARE FROM ELSE'S DIARY

So Jim and I had leftovers of the pie, Sam said he would have a slice of bread when he went up on watch. I hope the weather improves, for everyone's morale and good health. I've been sneezing, Jim felt a bit achy yesterday, and so has been taking aspirin. At least the water tank isn't overflowing as much now that the waves seem to be settling.

Going to the heads is becoming quite an art. First wipe the seat; otherwise you get a wet bum from the sea water, which has come in, through the vent. My legs are too short to touch the floor, so one stays on the raised platform by the sink, the other leg dangles, too short also to be wedged against the door. So, instead I need to hold on. I gather the men need to be careful that the seat does not come banging down at an inappropriate time!

Sun 14 June

Another grey day when you can't see the sunrise. There is a lot of low cloud and limited visibility. There is rain not far away surrounding the boat. I stood in the hatchway peering through the gloom hoping that a ship would not suddenly appear. There was one on the horizon when Jim was taking over from me at 2am. It now looks as if it might clear a bit but with the wind direction from the NNE we are sailing ESE and heading for a low. Hopefully it will be moving away as well with all of its bad weather. Wouldn't it be nice to have a few sunny days around Jim's birthday on Wednesday?

I've just finished reading the Indian book about 'Lame Deer, Seeker of Visions.' It certainly makes me think of nature, back to basics, and perhaps able to enjoy this bad patch of weather, appreciating what the elements can do. The clean sea smell, the colours, the everlasting movements and patterns in the sea and sky.

I didn't start on the sail, not a very nice day though the afternoon did clear up a bit. We enjoyed supper, beef burger (home made), mashed pumpkin and potato with salad, then a fruit salad for dessert. It was Sunday, so we had a dessert!

Mon 15 June

Quite a pleasant night though there was no wind at all. I called Jim half an hour early to drop the mainsail but he decided to leave it. I'd tightened the ropes so at least it didn't bang on the gallows.

So we continue with the calms, (before the storm perhaps) and motoring. I listened to the group of yachts nearby on 6A, Wendy on *Faydra* being the net controller. I must try and get in touch with her about my transmitting frequency. Perhaps on VHF.

Then it was a really beautiful morning, so after breakfast Jim and I had a lovely bucket shower and shampoo on deck. The water was reasonable, not too freezing! The sun was lovely and warm to dry our bodies. Sam then woke and had his shower while we politely sunbathed or read! So enjoying the sunshine, taking sun sights (for an hour), mending the sail and trying to find the leaks before it all gets wet again.

I had a lovely sleep and was up at 7pm. Couldn't believe I'd slept so long. Just in time to listen to Herb and his gale warning for Wednesday, not far from us. Luckily we are now further south so hopefully will be out of the worst winds. Hence the calm that a lot of the boats are having! NMN didn't mention a gale but did predict the low areas, they are all around.

Tonight's sky was really quite awesome. About every type of cloud present with huge swirls behind us, I should have taken some photographs. None of us ate much for dinner, bread and soup even though the sea is calm. We did have a good salad for lunch though and a fresh bread roll at teatime. I suppose we weren't sure how quickly the sea might start getting rough again!

I was dreaming that I'd been working at a hospital, something to do with a building, and was trying to find where I'd parked my car. Other cars kept coming past and then one set of lights was blinding me. It was Sam waking me up for my watch just after midnight!

Tue 16 June

A lovely moonlit night with faint stars because of the light and I could still appreciate the weird clouds all above in the heavens.

THE FOLLOWING NOTES ARE FROM ELSE'S DIARY

Full moon was last night. No nasty clouds across the moon like the other night, quite often it shone out alone.

Towards the end of my watch, the autohelm came apart below the quadrant but Jim soon had that fixed. I thought that the noise must have belonged to a strange fish. Then later, when I went to wake Jim up, he was lying facing the fishing rod. He was all neatly covered with the duvet and with a squid looking at him in the eye. What a laugh we had!

The day has been so-so; overcast most of the time but no terrible clouds building up that we could see. *Faydra's* morning net all reported in well, suffering the same calms as us. NMN was a real man today having difficulty keeping his tongue up with his words. The two lows that may affect us are still about with winds of 20-30 knots and seas 10-16 feet and the other with winds at 25 knots and seas 8-12 feet. We'll wait to see what Herb also has to say tonight. We've been going south very slightly as 35 degrees N seems to be a dividing line for good or bad weather.

It's now nearly 7.30pm., squally outside and we will shortly take a reef in on the mainsail. It was just quite gusty but seems to be settling again. We are almost half way and are at 35 degrees 33 minutes N, 48 degrees 25 minutes W, C.O.G. 087 degrees, S.O.G. 3.9 knots.

Because it was getting quite lumpy, supper was curried sausage stew, quite hot!

Wed 17 June

Happy Birthday Jim, my love, and the sun is trying very hard to come out. It however remains a grey morning with drizzle, building grey cloudy horizons and not much wind but a confused sea. So, we are not getting anywhere very fast hence have put the engine on.

Listening in to the 9.30 net, some of the other boats had bad weather like we did last night, are climbing or walking on walls and looking for a ticket home. Neither Jim nor I slept much last night. One yacht, we think called Grand Pesto, has lost her rudder and has been out of contact for a few days. No VHF contact has been made with her either.

Jim liked his cards and presents; he now has more reading to do when he wishes. He doesn't know that he still has one more surprise to come. Wait 'til later.

The day cleared, a blue patch and some sunshine over the boat but clouds still on the perimeter of the horizon. Sam put the fishing line out. Jim was and looked very tired so went for a ziz while I finished making the trifle, out of the left overs of a pound cake. The ingredients I managed to hide in the food cupboard.

We motored most of the day as there was no wind but from NMN at 15.25, there is a developing gale in our area, so we should be getting some wind.

At teatime, Jim blew out the candles on his cake while Sam and I attempted to sing Happy Birthday. I put them in the shape of 55. He never asked why the cake was so small!

Still no fish and we tried a variety of sails but ended up settling on the genoa for the night. Another two hanks had gone on the larger jib, these we replaced.

Supper was steak and kidney pie, boiled carrots, onion and potatoes with spinach, and a bottle of just chilled bubbly. The ice has certainly kept extremely well, the best ever, 12 days. Half an hour later, I brought out the trifle, the rest of the cake, well imbibed with the rum given to us from Uncle Chic, which we all ate with relish.

The wind picked up nicely during the night, about 5.6 knots, when I was looking. We steered by hand to save current. Although it was still very overcast, the moon behind the clouds still gave enough light to read the compass, instead of using a torch.

Oh, *Grand Pesto* had her rudder fixed by a passing merchant vessel but there is still a look out for *Ripple*, who left the Virgins seven weeks ago and has not been heard of since. I think we saw a notice in the Harbour Master's Office in St Georges about her.

Thu 18 June

The sky is clearing, huge rollers are coming from the north to northeast and we are coasting all the way down them heading east. There's a good breeze, averaging for us 4-5 knots.

THE FOLLOWING NOTES ARE FROM ELSE'S DIARY

There was nothing special on *Faydra's* link up except that we were doing better, speed wise, than a few other boats. I went for a sleep and didn't wake until 3'ish. I feel much more rested. Poor Jim looks like he could do with a week's sleep. He hasn't shaved for ages and that also makes his face look quite different. So I then took the helm to let him and Sam sleep, except in ¾ hour, he was up again and going to put on the solenoid. I asked Sam if he would steer so that I could finish sewing the sail. The sun had been out warming my back beautifully.

Jim was having difficulty starting the engine. When it did start, he still wasn't sure why. We tried to get through to Portishead but left it, as there was so much static. Supper on tins of chicken, peas and mushrooms mixed on a bed or rice and the end of the trifle.

Fri 19 June

It's almost 01.30, the engine is still on as there is very little wind so the Cetrek is also on. Hence I'm writing to keep awake. The sky is lovely and clear, moon, stars, and the few large clouds moving ahead of us from north to south. Herb didn't mention anything too terrible so we are slowly making our way north again. Oh, the lads saw a shark pass the boat yesterday while I was sleeping. Sam said it had white spots on it.

We have now passed the 45-degree longitude mark so will probably change the clocks again today. We did this, the other way, as long ago as November, a whole seven months ago, which seems an age away.

A lovely warm day so I did some washing and sunbathed. Soon it was too hot and Jim and I had a cold shower on the deck, Sam politely refused. Jim's been working on the engine and replaced the solenoid. It started using the key for the first time in a while. We replaced a hank in the genoa, which with the mainsail is pulling us along quite well in the very light winds.

Supper was a beef stew, still with fresh potatoes, onions and carrots. Rice pudding and apricots for desert and feeling very full.

Now that we've changed the clocks, it's much later by the time I've finished listening to the radio. So tonight, the watches have also been put on an hour. I could have slept on the spot, with the receiver to my ear, and trying to make out the words spoken by the various stations. If it's worse tomorrow, I may have to go onto 12A.

Sat 20 June

Today at 09.00, we will have been at sea for two weeks. Our daily runs have not been fantastic and we may have anything up to another week to go. At the moment there are 698 miles to go to Faial. If we do stop at Flores instead, it is 100 miles nearer.

It is now 02.30 and there is a lovely clear night outside, the moon has a small halo around it, so perhaps some rain somewhere. The wind is changing to a southerly direction blowing the diesel fumes straight onto me sitting in the cockpit. So I've come below for a short while to catch up on my writing. Doing a reasonable speed, up to 5.3 knots.

A lovely day, calm waters and while I was chatting to Jim over coffee, I saw a fin, not five foot from the boat, a shark's fin I think. But that was all we saw of it, my exclamation was enough to startle Jim. I put the fishing line out early but unfortunately no bites.

We had some spotted dolphins come to visit and they stayed alongside for quite a while coming and going. Sam took the line in. They were up to six foot long, looking beautifully sleek, blowing at us.

I'm trying to do a bit of sewing again and also enjoying my book, 'The Wayward Tide,' and I also want to have a midday sleep.

Surprise, surprise. After listening in to *Faydra* this morning, I changed the frequencies back to the original ones and someone spoke to me, it was *Moonshine* and then *Kirituck*. I told a little lie about how fast we were going! So perhaps we will join *Faydra's* roll call tomorrow morning. Jim was extremely pleased about sorting out our transmitting.

NMN did not transmit in the afternoon, we don't know why and in the evening I was not able to hear much from Herb on *Southbound II* . It didn't sound as if there was anything terrible

THE FOLLOWING NOTES ARE FROM ELSE'S DIARY

about, perhaps I can catch up tomorrow. 12A started about 22.45 by which time I was also very tired.

Jim made supper tonight, corned beef hash, went down very nicely with a G&T. We expect to arrive in about a week from today.

Sun 21 June

Another lovely day and we have passed the 40degree W longitude mark. At 9am it was about 480 miles to go in a straight line to Flores, but I don't suppose we'll end up sailing a straight line!

Listening in to the chat with *Faydra* this morning, three yachts have seen whales, so they are about. One also saw a huge drift net just waiting to tangle an unsuspecting propeller or two no doubt! Three other yachts are staying with *Nana* who is still taking on water but coping. Someone is trying to fix her rigging and another helping with the engine. He is worried about running the engine and opening up the hole now filled with epoxy cement. He is a single hander.

I had a lovely long sleep at lunchtime, waking up just in time for NMN, who never came on, again. It was so hot sewing up on deck earlier that Jim and I even had our hats on and were once more putting on suntan lotion, not to get too burned.

Sam cooked supper tonight; mince with loads of onion and garlic, red beans and rice. I got the last sponge pudding out for desert. We didn't bother with custard, as we were already quite full.

Then for my stint at the radio. It was much better listening to 12A so would probably start at 22.30 instead tomorrow night. Looks like there may be some nasty weather ahead again. One boat called *Straight Up* asked about a VHF message that he'd heard. That *Spirit of Iowa*, a square rigger we saw in St Georges, has met with some accident perhaps and that all of their crew were OK and picked up by a freighter? Herb knew nothing of this and would check when he last had contact with them.

Mon 22 June

It's now 04.10, the moon shining through the porthole and the first night for a while that we are sailing along, well at 4-5 knots.

Recently, the wind has dropped at nights causing us to motor for approximately twelve hours. There is a small halo around the moon and the clouds are rushing past heading in a north-easterly direction. I wonder what's going on up there? I know there is a low-pressure system about 47 degrees N 45 degrees W moving east and south by Tuesday. Also a squall line covering a large area moving towards us from the Azores stretching from 30-40 degrees N and will soon be at 37 degrees W. It's interesting to plot the weather and to see how quickly the systems change. We are very lucky to have contact with someone doing the weather like Herb on *Southbound II* out of Bermuda.

Looking over my shoulder Jim saw a whale, it turned over twenty feet away from the starboard side of the boat. After a while of looking, we could see it blowing behind us, a massive spout. A sperm whale thinks Jim.

We could tell that the weather was getting blowy again, see what Herb says tonight. The mainsail had one reef, the genoa was up and we were going like the devil. Quite often 6 or 7 knots.

We managed to eat a good supper; Jim made curried eggs, as the sea was still reasonably calm. However during the night it sure rained and blew! Herb said to expect it to get worse during the night and tomorrow. Be prepared! However we did leave the genoa up, as we seemed to be doing so well.

Tue 23 June

Half way through my watch, 4am I think, a big wave suddenly stopped us and I couldn't work out why we didn't pick up speed again. Both Jim and Sam awoke feeling the change in momentum. Then I noticed the foot of the genoa had torn. So all on deck to put the stay sail up instead. Then at 7am, Jim had us up again to lower the mainsail. So we motor sailed until 3pm, by which time the genoa had been sewn and could go back up. Talking on *Faydra's* net, a few other people were having squally weather and *Arcadia*, further north was in 40-45 knot winds. *Destiny* was hove to off Flores because of SE 25-knot winds gusting up to 40-knot winds. There's a low just north of the islands. *Geneve* is

THE FOLLOWING NOTES ARE FROM ELSE'S DIARY

about 60 miles away from Horta, so everybody is gradually getting there. *Pall* contacted me for a chat about going to Ireland when we got to the marina in Horta, perhaps on Sunday or Monday.

Otherwise, today cleared up more than we expected, even though there is quite a lumpy sea. We are rolling a bit now doing 3 knots. Jim's worked the diesel out and we have about three days of motoring left, I suppose the weather will decide whether landfall is Flores or Faial.

NMN gave warnings of two gales north of us so there's still a lot of weather about. Herb tonight told us not to go further north until Thursday unless we wanted much stronger winds, up to 35 knots. Also that a boat called *Casandra* hadn't clocked in for two days and there was possibly a tanker called *Pacific Dawn* drifting about 3000 miles away east of Bermuda. *Geneve* has reached Horta. Supper was simple, bread and soup for Sam, beans on toast for Jim and I. We expect a bit of a lumpy night.

Wed 24 June

It's almost time for me to go off watch, 04.45, there's a wind springing up from the south west again so perhaps Jim will switch off the engine. We'd taken the genoa and main down and put the staysail up from midnight, especially as Herb said we might have quite a lot of weather tonight.

On the net *Grand Pesto* was having rudder problems and heading for the rocks off Horta. One of the other yachts was helping her, *Tandojam*. *Destiny* was still hove to off Horta, *Kirituck* was 37 miles from Flores, *Missy* was adrift with sail problems, *Moonshine* was bare pole in big seas not enjoying life, *Sea Bass* was 55 miles from Horta, *Sunrise* was 6 miles off Flores. So everybody was busy one way or another. Yachts are now rafted five deep and the local time is one hour on from that we have now. The net will start at 7.30am tomorrow; I shall have to get up early.

When I listened to the radio, *Destiny* was now also having rudder problems, a sea anchor out but still broadside to the wind. Both *Moonshine* and *Osprey* offered help although we are both behind her. *Moonshine* is behind us and is having howling winds 30-40 knots and horrendous seas. *Kirituck* contacted me to say that they passed about 15 miles south of Lajes so couldn't report on that anchorage but that the weather further north was moderating, that would certainly be better for *Destiny*.

I treated myself to a hair wash and then cooked super, tuna pie and asparagus. Sam is still feeling queasy so only had some bread and water earlier and then a cup of soup going on to his watch at midnight.

Herb gave us some good news for the next two day's sailing. The winds are moderating as the system moves NNE. We would have W, NW 15-20 knot winds tomorrow during the day and the night.

Thu 25 June

It is nearly 04.30. The clouds are setting up again hiding the stars but the moon is just managing to shine through a bit leaving a gold carpet thrown out to *Ospray*. We were sailing well on genoa alone but Henry, (the Navigator), started blinking, so the engine is now on. I'm sure my headache is due to the continuous noise of the autohelm and engine or the radio, the static; Morse etc. can be very piercing! Jim and Sam also have headaches, it may also be tension with the effects of the weather and being at sea with a lumpy movement, the boat rolling and lurching a lot at the moment. Yesterday's run was 101 miles, so we are ticking them off very nicely. At this very moment, there are 178 miles to go and the ETA in Horta is Fri 26 June at 18.21. As long as it will be daylight, I don't mind!

We are heading for Horta because of the weather further north and it is a much better anchorage than Santa Cruz on Flores.

Well, I was up again for 7.30 but *Faydra's* net didn't happen. A few of us did talk, *Destiny* is about to put up sail and take in her sea anchor having solved her problems. We think Wendy must have slept in, as I'm sure we will do with our first whole night's sleep.

THE FOLLOWING NOTES ARE FROM ELSE'S DIARY

Oh, Jim rang Geoff, a few nights ago and he has made provisional arrangements to come. That has pleased Jim no end to know that we have a third person to crew on the next leg, and such a good friend. We ring him again on Sunday.

About 4pm the wind died so on went the motor. It looks like we may not get into Horta in the daylight now, but the other yachts have said the anchorage is well lit, although we would prefer not to be next to fibreglass yachts, we might just have to raft up along side them. I must also find Herb's address to send him a thank you note/postcard. Perhaps find out a bit more about him. He is most helpful when he comes on at night, well worth waiting up for his comments and good wishes on our watches.

Supper tonight was leftover pie from last night, again Sam did not eat. We had ours with a glass of wine and then pineapple with evaporated milk. Sam had plain pineapple.

Fri 26 June

Will we make it today? It's 81.7 miles to go plus another few to get into harbour; the co-ordinates I used for Henry (the Navigator, our GPS) were about the centre of the island. It is now 04.10. We are motor sailing at 4 knots with very little wind from the southwest.

We have had the motor on all day going full speed ahead to get into the marina in daylight. There has been another yacht to the north of us with main up but we haven't been able to hail her. *Osprey* has had a tidy above deck, rust removed, ropes and anchor at the ready if needed, fenders inflated, and Sam caught a mess of net full of crabs and barnacles on the fishing line. I've been catching crabs and putting them overboard for the last couple of hours. We also had a visit from some dolphins, leaping in the air and cris-crossing on our bow wave, the common dolphin, with white around their eyes and white bellies.

Moonshine, behind us, is very happy to be so much closer, at roll call this morning they had 160 miles to go. You could hear the smile all over her face on the SSB! *Destiny* is making her way around the north of the island.

We decided to cook a meal, as it might be late by the time we docked, so ham and turkey pie, with the last of the cabbage, potatoes, carrots and onion. Jim made a delicious apple pie; we had some of that at teatime.

Land has been in sight since 3pm. I was asleep at the time but you can now see most things as we are about a mile away making our way along the south coast. I've tried calling *Faydra* on VHF but no answer.

It was soon all happening, rounding the breakwater, looking for a berth, the light fading and then some folk came to help us come alongside *Palmares*, an English, very white, fibreglass yacht!

As soon as we were safe and spruced up we went to find Café Sport, a beer and our post. *Faydra* had been on the VHF to welcome us.

Sat 27 June

We found the authorities all in one building and all of the paper work was soon done. The only drawback was they kept my passport, as I don't have a visa. But I can get it out again to go to the bank.

Then a stroll up to the marina, a drink and a sandwich at the cafe, looking at the hundreds of boat logos on the walls. Some very clever and extremely artistic. We met a single hander called John, Jim and he got together for a long conflab, and was soon joined by Angus and Maria, their two dogs and a Swiss friend. Beautiful hot showers and clean white towels were next on the agenda. I couldn't get through on the telephone via the operator. A walk into town to find the various supermarkets, open markets, post office, hardware/chandlery stores etc., stopping for a drink and then a shop to buy bread and one cake with the last of our escudos. Jim then found more in a pocket, so we returned for another two cakes. Only to find we had left the bread, the locals had a good laugh! Sam in the meantime had found a travel agent but everything was shut, so will make plans on Monday.

In the evening we went to a restaurant with no name, just a sign for eating outside, where they cook on hot stones (slabs

THE FOLLOWING NOTES ARE FROM ELSE'S DIARY

of marble) or, we cook on hot stones, I should say. A lovely evening, each of us trying something different, T-bone steak, chicken and pigfish washed down with 3 bottles of Portuguese red wine. Then we went downstairs to listen to music and chatted to the folk from *Geneve*. They are heading for Tangiers. They previously lived on Gran Canaria where he had a job with the ferries – hydrofoils. The meal was on Sam – thank you Sam.

Sun 28 June

A lovely lazy morning. I've sorted out clothes and linen for the laundry tomorrow. Done a tidy in our cabin. Shaved my legs and am actually wearing a skirt today! I must have lost a bit of weight because it fits. Jim has just made two fruit pies to take with us for the luncheon today and I'll take some channa (salted chickpeas) as well as we've still got plenty.

Sam was going to go for a motorbike ride today but didn't find anywhere open. So we are now off to Café Sport to ring homes and perhaps get some postcards and stamps. Then to our party at the Club for 3.30-4.00pm to meet the folk and discuss plans for a net to Ireland and the U.K.

Telephoning from Café Sport I could not hear Lill, so Jim and I spoke and then put the phone down. We bought a phone card and rang again from the marina restaurant where we could hear. Jim also rang Geoff who was unable to get a flight as yet, so we ring again on Wednesday.

We had a lovely luncheon at Club Naval de Horta where we met most of the other folk in the net. Wendy is lovely, Canadian, and we talked a lot to Peter and also Bill (the Russian) and his wife Kelly (Irish living in America). Laura from *Missy* stood up and told a poem about the trip mentioning all the yachts by name, very good, and of course Herb. The husband from *Sea Bass* ran the do giving stories and told about Hugh on *Arcadia* having an anchor and shroud ready for his friend who was going to die at sea. He had even written the service. The next crewmember, first on the helm, just kept turning the boat round in circles, I gather he was promptly put back on shore. The other crewmember broke his leg while still land based, so never left. There were many good stories and quite a few loosened tongues!

That evening we sat and chatted about the trip well into the night.

This is the poem from Laura.

> Twas in June of '92,
> We all sailed the ocean blue.
> We formed a net, some gales we met,
> And a sunny day or two.
>
> *Faydra* led the way by voice,
> The time for which was Wendy's choice,
> On Bermuda time or UCT,
> She greeted us most cheerfully.
>
> With Herb's advice to go here and there,
> North and South and who knows where.
> With all this effort to avoid the blow,
> I thought we'd be out till it started to snow!
>
> Last *Unicorn* at the head of the pack.
> *Janev* close behind on a fast port tack.
> *Tandojam* thought it a nasty sail.
> *Ospray* so excited to see a sperm whale.
>
> *Missy* flew along at 38 North,
> With water bad they continued forth.
> *Sea Bass* kept the fleet intact,
> So Herb could be more matter of fact.
>
> *Arcadia* and *Destiny* were side by side,
> Which made for a less lonesome ride.
> With the glow of *Moonshine* and the hope of *Sunrise*,
> A day with the sun was a welcome surprise.

THE FOLLOWING NOTES ARE FROM ELSE'S DIARY

Because *Currituck* had done this trip before,
We knew we'd find the Azores for sure.
Mambo-Hambo, Herb never got it right,
As we listened for weather during the night.

Blue Moves, *Nightwinds* and *Sea Bass*,
All should receive an honour.
For without their timely assistance,
Nania would be a goner.

We picked up a *Peryton*,
And we lost a *Free Flight*,
The *Blue Hen* was silent,
And *Safar* was out of sight.

With names like *Charity* and *Dreams Come True*,
Our net had a most romantic hue.
And as we socialise here at Club Naval,
We hope you've enjoyed this poem from *Pal*.

With thanks to Laura from *Pal*.

The above poem gives the impression of a jolly laughing crowd in constant contact. However it should be remembered that this crowd of ships were probably one hundred miles across. For instance, we never saw another vessel over the three-week voyage even though we were in constant radio contact with them and Herb in Bermuda. There was much good-natured banter despite some of the awful weather and the problems some of the other ships encountered. We thought there was only one good day's weather in the three-week period and luckily *Ospray* was one of the few vessels without a serious problem. We are now masters at one-pot meals!

From the Azores, five of us headed back to Ireland and England and formed a net of our own; again out of sight but feeling the security of radio contact. Three boats meeting up in Kinsale.

Arriving safely back in Wales, family and friends waiting on the harbour wall to greet us, certainly made me flush with pride at what we had achieved and how well *Ospray* had looked after us.

We really did not want to go back to landlocked Shrewsbury and our jobs. Both Else and I could have quite easily re-vittled and headed north.

Several months later, while spending the weekend on *Ospray*, as we regularly did, enjoying the evening light and the sounds of the curlew, I asked, "Where do you propose we go from here?" Else said, "I would like to get married." But she didn't say to whom, so I had to make an assumption. Fortunately my supposition was correct and we got engaged on her birthday, March 1993. Yet another cliff-hanger ensued, as my first wife's decree nisi did not come through until the day before the wedding!

Family and friends stayed at nearby hotels, B&B's, in the house and campervans. As we partied through the night, a police helicopter hovered overhead close above us, looking for an escaped convict, scary to say the least, flooding us with light. Next day many folk turned up at the house for breakfast and lunch. That evening we headed for the airport and flew to Trinidad to celebrate with Else's family and to spend some days in Tobago, one of our favourite islands.

Else, Jim and Geoff in Kinsale, Ireland

At Monkmoor Farm with friends – Geoff, Jim, Joyce, John, Else, Pat and Margaret

In Derbyshire with friends – Jim, Pat, Joyce, Else and Geoff, again taken by Colin

Chapter 17

Stags In The Clouds – Published In Stalking Magazine

It was a January day. I was basking on the deck of our home built little ship; we had just sailed across the boisterous Atlantic. Now safely in the West Indies, euphoria had given way to contentment. *Ospray* was tied up to a coconut tree and the startlingly turquoise waters of the Caribbean lapped lazily against the hull. The trade wind soughed through the palms fringing the beach. A stalk of bananas, about four feet long, hung from the mast and an iced rum with freshly squeezed limes was by my hand. Contentment? Well almost. My mind was far away. Five thousand miles and over a year back in time.

I was two thousand feet up on a bleak Hebridean mountain. Rob Cameron, the stalker/lessee of majestic Glen Forsa, and I lay soaked to the skin in a peat hag. We had been there an hour. A chill rain drove into our faces as we waited in vain for a bunch of stags and hinds to emerge from a shallow corrie. A lone, sentinel hind guarded the entrance, preventing our closer approach.

I, at least, was frozen stiff and the light was beginning to go. In desperation Rob gave a muted whistle into the teeth of the gale. The hind leapt to her feet, bristling with suspicion. Another wait – another whistle, the hind departed at speed for points west and the other beasts came out – at full gallop. We trudged empty handed down the hill.

Believe it or not, from the tropical paradise of the Windward Islands, I was longing to return to those windswept hills.

After a year of adventures, and seeing seventy ton whales only feet from the boat, our voyaging brought us back to our home port in North Wales. Scarcely had the vessel been snuggled down and all sails stowed, I was on the telephone to Scotland.

I soon made arrangements to share a fortnight with others of my persuasion. Stalking some days, fishing others, perfect!

The intervening weeks were spent in a tingle of anticipation, sighting in the old .308, tying flies, digging worms and a little training on those bumps near Shrewsbury that we call hills.

Before I knew it, I was on Caledonian MacBrayne's ferry, steaming out of Oban harbour towards Mull, shrouded in mist and enchantment.

Tir-nan-og – Land of the ever young – is the ancient Gaelic name for the Hebrides and it certainly takes years off me whenever I visit.

An hour later, in the cosy cottage hidden deep in the woods by beautiful Loch Baa, a malty, pre-dinner dram glowed amber with the light from a roaring log stove and I thought how good it was to be back.

The grunt of rutting fallow bucks and the smell of bacon only gradually lifted the velvety veil of a malt-induced sleep. Then it was away to the hill via the ferry terminal from where we collected Ivan, resplendent in plus-fours, on a sort of busman's holiday from feeding pheasants, vermin control and his novel way of deterring poachers, also John, an ex-patriot New Zealander and fellow fisherman whose knapsack clinked merrily as he walked.

Pausing briefly for a shot at the 'iron stag' to make sure man and rifle were up to the job, we jolted, amidst a certain amount of hilarity, up the five mile track by the tumbling waters of the Forsa to the head of this magnificent glen.

This being the last few days of the stag season, the plan of campaign was to fulfil the annual quota by cleaning up any poor beasts and bad heads, following Rob's policy of stock improvement.

There were also several good beasts that he thought to be on the verge of going back and therefore legitimate targets.

Parking the Land Rover by the headwaters of the Forsa where the silver salmon spawn, the party disembarked for a spy. After a few moments, the distant bellow of a stag guaranteed that we swivelled our binoculars to a ridge high up on the shoulder of

Sgurr Dearg which rises from the glen floor to a height of 2,429 feet in a series of steep and sometimes precipitous slopes bestrewn with crags and rocky ledges. Tiny specks, just discernable, were identified by one pair of experienced eyes as a decent stag with nine hinds. Another speck, some distance from the others, was declared to be a poorish beast and likely a switch. My query as to whether he had any teeth missing was ignored.

I surveyed the rearing hill with only a little foreboding. Had I not spent these last three weeks prancing round the Shropshire hills leaping blithely over ditch and brook? Lead on MacCameron! After half an hour I felt fine; after an hour I removed my hat to allow the escape of steam; half an hour later my heart was attempting to escape from my ribs. The lads halted every now and then, tactfully pretending to spy, allowing me to catch up with a shred of dignity. Obviously more training was required. At my own pace I can go for long enough but keeping up with these younger and fitter men was another matter altogether.

Robert nipped off for a quick spy from a hump. He returned to say that a ten-minute stalk should bring a Rifle within shot of the switch – for such it was. In a whispered discussion we agreed that John and Ivan would stalk the switch whilst Rob and I made a detour round a large shoulder in an attempt to come up to the beast with the hinds. The wind decreed that I should shoot first. At the sound of the shot, hopefully diminished by the wind, John would take out the switch.

The last hundred yards of our approach were in full view of the herd – a long, slow belly wriggle – until at last we were behind a rock ledge over which we peered between tufts of heather for a closer inspection. The stag, a fine beast, was chivvying his hinds in a boulder-strewn hollow a longish shot away below us. Rob decided he would be past his prime by next season and that I should try for him.

For fifteen minutes he trotted hither and thither, sometimes disappearing behind boulders or in a hollow. My cross-hairs followed his every move whilst my clothes soaked up the contents of a small but frigid lake on the rock where I lay. At length he came out of the hollow and stood broadside on its rim. At the kick of the rifle, the old fellow staggered, valiantly attempting to pursue his departing hinds, then collapsed into the hollow. He was dead when we came up to him and carried a nice well-balanced head of eight points.

During the gralloch John and Ivan scrambled down to us. The switch had been suspicious before my shot, whereupon he departed in top gear for healthier climes. We hastily agreed to intercept him by a quick trek over the top of the mountain.

"You'll travel faster without me," I volunteered, Titus Oates himself could have done no better! No one argued. Although I may have given the impression of wrenching self-sacrifice, secretly I wished to be alone to contemplate this splendid beast and the awesome grandeur that surrounded me.

Far below was spread a tapestry of greens, golds and purples through which ran a single silver thread. A hen harrier hunted, quartering the ground like a spaniel. Kneeling on a rock, I slaked my thirst from a dark pool by a waterfall, then lay back in the heather and munched on an apple. There are some moments in life....

Two hours later, three figures emerged from the thick cloud that, by now, engulfed the hill – weary, cold and eager for a hot flask of tea. When the first patches of cloud came swirling down they had crouched under a crag for an hour while a stone's throw away, a stag bellowed lustily. Then the clouds rolled asunder; hardly daring to blink, three pairs of eyes peered over the rock. No stag.

Next day was a fishing day for John and I. The weather was atrocious. Fierce squalls roared down the loch every half hour, between the squalls it merely rained. More in hope than expectation, we pushed the boat out from the jetty. Barely had we rowed a hundred yards when John's rod sprang into a tight arc and ten minutes later a nine-pound, late run fish flapped in the bilges. Salmon were rising all around us and after two or three heart stopping plucks I hooked and landed a beautiful grilse of four and a half pounds with the sea lice still on him. By this time large waves were building up on the loch so we headed for home, a warm fire and a dram. On the way back we spotted a dead stag on the shore so we beached the dinghy to investigate. A dripping figure emerged from the trees; a stalking party had shot the beast on a high ridge above the loch and it seemed the easiest route back was by water, so his majesty was heaved into the boat and off we set, the plimsoll line and occasionally the bows being well submerged. I pondered on the irony of drowning in six feet of water having just circumnavigated the Atlantic. However, it is a sound maxim that 'When it comes to water removal, few pumps will beat a frightened man with a bucket,' so we eventually tied up and squelched through the darkening woods to the cottage. Wet to the skin, gibbering with cold and deliriously happy. It's a funny old life isn't it? An employer insisting we do this as the requirements of a job might well be invited to leave the vicinity.

The stove was roaring heartily when Rob and Ivan appeared, having come to a successful conclusion with the switch after a hard stalk.

After John and Ivan had departed to resume earning a crust, the rest of the week brought three more stags to my rifle. Two cull beasts, one of which had brittle, chalky antlers and another old gent on the verge of decline.

The following week I was to share with, and by kind agreement of, Roy Nixon, another Mull regular. Roy rounded off the last day of the stag season with a very fine beast while I fished the river Aros with no success but much enjoyment.

Next day, the visibility being too bad for the hill, we had some woodland stalking in pursuit of melanistic fallow does, which the estate wished to be culled in favour of the true dappled type. The day's bag consisted of three does, and a fence post, shot by myself, unnoticed in long grass in front of a doe! Robert offered to have the stump removed and mounted and included in the record under 'various.'

The next day was a fishing day for me but so foul that I sat in the car for ages watching the curtains of rain drive past. At length, on the principle that 'Faint heart ne'er won fair lady,' I sallied forth; head bent against the deluge, and flicked a worm into the peaty torrent. To my astonishment, the first cast produced a tap-tap then a surge; I struck, and a bar of silver erupted from the burn, fighting like a demon all the way to the net. A fine sea trout of two and a half pounds. Four more were to follow, all from the same pool. I cursed myself for wasting half the day – you can never tell with fishing.

Meanwhile, Rob and Roy, out at the break of day before the rains came, had brought to book three hinds in prime condition.

The last day on the hill was a day of indifferent visibility and a cold, northerly wind, which indicated Beinn Duatharach, a desolate area of wild beauty and peat hags, as being most likely to produce success. After spooking three hinds at the last moment, the court adjourned for half an hour for a flask and a bite. On resuming the march, the hill seemed to be empty and after a longish ramble we were just about to turn for home when Rob went off for a spy. He returned to report a small group of hinds sheltering under a bank. An ultra careful crawl this time and, eventually, we made out the beasts lying down and very difficult to see amongst the tussocks. Roy and I chose our beasts and fired almost simultaneously, downing one each. As we came away after the gralloch, three eagles circled overhead and we could see ravens homing in. News of a feast travels fast in these parts.

Two weeks after I returned, a telephone call offered me the chance of a couple more days in the pre-Christmas week hind cull. Still smiling from some very satisfactory shots in October I needed little persuasion. What is it that comes before a fall? But that's another story.

I have rented the fishing rights on the River Aros on many occasions, while on Mull, which yielded many a fine sea trout and quite a few salmon. The White House on Aros is a large Victorian stately home with walled in garden, its own pier and ruined castle, on a point of land, which I always had a fancy for. Imagine my excitement when, after several years, I had a phone call from Bob and Sally Davies on Mull, Bob being my one time next door neighbour, to tell me the sparkling news that the White House was going up for sale. Else and I drove up in our campervan over an Easter weekend to view the property. I was filled with excitement at the prospect of possibly owning this superb estate. It consisted of a length of the fishing rights on the river Aros, a magnificent house, albeit in need of some modernisation, (you could take a bath in the huge Victorian sinks), several smaller houses, the pier, the ruined castle and many acres of wooded land. All for an affordable sum, but we would have had no money left over for the work needed to be done, which was immense. After a great deal of thought and much deliberation, it was regretfully decided to drop this delightful idea.

Richard Smart is a friend who now lives on the Borders but we first met when he was a chef in Banbury and have shared many a good day fishing and stalking. One very memorable occasion, we were stalking at Longleat near to the Safari Park. We were walking quietly through bushes when there came the most blood-curdling snarl, which almost caused an instant evacuation of my bowels, my heart to stop and the hair on the back of my neck to stay erect loosing any curl they had. Who was stalking whom? What I did not know about was the fence just behind the bushes where a pride of lions dwelt!

Richard has also shared stalking with me on Mull. I remember Rob driving the Land Rover, Richard shouting "Bingo," the vehicle coming to a lurching stop as he thought he had seen a deer. No deer. This happened several times more before one was sighted.

Hill Fitness – Published in Stalking Magazine

By local standards I am fairly fit! Trotting through the Shropshire woods I glide past old ladies walking fat Labradors with contemptuous ease. Bird watchers and courting couples fade rapidly astern as I don my most truculent sneer.

However, there is *fit* and there is *hill fit*, a phrase used in the Highlands implying a subtle distinction. The distinction is as subtle as an air raid, chalk and cheese.

I always arrive in the Highlands, on my increasingly frequent stalking trips, feeling in sharpish condition. Yet I never fail to return home vowing to be fitter next time.

STAGS IN THE CLOUDS – PUBLISHED IN STALKING MAGAZINE

The sheer scale of the hills, the peat hags with their hay-bale sized tussocks, the sucking bogs and leg-jarring burns do tend to sort the men from the boys. Even old boys like me (born and bred among the sheep farms of the Derbyshire hills) have lapsed and find it a struggle.

Just before my last trip, seeking to test my nouveau fitness and desperate for something to climb, I bounded upstairs, two at a time, causing serious alarm to my wife who was at the top. Apparently she thought I had suddenly come into rut. Her deep sigh as I immediately bounded down again could have been disappointment, or relief – one can only speculate.

A fortnight later I was steaming up a mountainside, which was certainly less steep than the side of the house but not a lot! As usual I was stalking with Rob Cameron whose territory covers a substantial chunk of the magical island of Mull and also with a friend, Richard, who was enjoying his first taste of Mull. Our objective was a group of hinds high up on a ledge at Gruline, a formidable range of cliffs, which frown out over the sea to Fingal's Cave on the island of Staffa. Rob was hoping to take out several beasts to make a dent in the substantial hind cull.

As I laboured upwards I felt a twinge of disappointment at my apparent shortfall in fitness, although it was a steep hill by any standards. I sucked a glucose tablet that, as a diabetic, I always carry with me despite Rob's assurance that I would drag easier than a stag. Having seen some of Rob's dragging, I shall stick to my glucose.

I became aware of a certain conflict in responsibilities. As I see it, the duties of a Rifle (not necessarily in order of priority) are: –

(a) To the stalker. To make the best of the opportunities he works hard to provide, by keeping up a reasonable pace, stalking out of sight and sound with all the skill you can muster and by taking a shot in reasonable time.
(b) To the beast you are about to slay. In arriving at the point of aim able to hold a steady rifle and in not taking chancy shots.
(c) To yourself. To enjoy yourself and avoid becoming ill or dead. This brings the sport into serious disrepute with wives and loved ones.

Anyway, to resume my tale. In order to attempt (a), hopefully ensure (b) whilst paying regard to (c) I stumbled upward taking a couple of short breaks, i.e. collapsing in a heap, to recover my breath which, fortunately, I do quite quickly.

After a final pause just under the lip of the crag, beyond which lay the parcel of hinds, Rob whispered the order "Right lads, over the top!" We crawled over the rock and peered through the heather in time to see the hinds clattering away over a defile on the far side of the plateau. Obviously the beasts had winded us whilst we were resting. Resting, mainly, because maybe I was not as fit as I ought to be? I felt somewhat subdued. Should I content myself with tiptoeing after roe and fallow in the dappled woods? However, much as I love my woodland stalking, around the tumbling cascades of the gold-bearing streams at Dolgellau and within sound of the lion's roar at Longleat, there is an exhilaration in the awesome splendour of the high corries such as I have only otherwise experienced during a storm at sea, peering apprehensively across a mile wide valley of water at the colossal mass of the next wave rumbling towards our small vessel. Dwarfed by the forces of nature.

Carry on stalking lad, but how hard should one drive oneself bearing in mind that, presumably, we do this for enjoyment? Ernest Shackelton, the famous explorer, held the view that humans are almost always capable of enduring more than they would suppose. His epic voyage across the wild Antarctic wastes after the loss of the *Endurance* in the ice would seem to bear this out. So is it all in the mind?

An episode last season whereby I astonished myself might add fuel to this theory. It was the last week of the stags and Rob was having a tidy up, concentrating on poor heads and old beasts. My week had started well with a seven-pound grilse from a shrunken river. I was fishing while the brothers Thompson traipsed for miles into the back of beyond for the pure joy of dragging their beasts over ground where Argos fear to tread, and working up appetites for Cameron's famous dinners.

Then it was my turn for the hill. Two elderly stags in moderately accessible positions were stalked and shot in the first two days. On the third day, flurries of sleet were in the air as we tramped the peat hags to the west of Sgulan Mor. We saw nothing until we came to a huge corrie with escarpments and banks of scree, which plunged dizzyingly to the glen floor below. We could hear stags roaring, but in the swirling mists and sleet it was only after prolonged scrutiny that we could identify the beasts. Twice we picked our way down several hundred feet to inspect two small groups, but in each case decided that the beasts were too good for our purpose, so we climbed carefully out again leaving them in peace. Just as we were about to abandon the hill and turn for home, we spied a grand old beast lying half a mile away with some hinds in a most difficult spot.

Rob deliberated long and hard and I could see that, like Baldrick, he was hatching a cunning plan.

"How do you fancy a crazy chance? Stalking within a whisker of the wind. Very long odds." "Suits me." I replied, ready to agree to anything, or so I thought.

A considerable detour led us round the rim of the corrie, below which we entered the head of the gully that sometimes became almost a chimney as we descended in a buffeting wind. The idea was, that if successful, we should bring the Argo across the glen floor to bring the beast out in the morning. Fifteen minutes later, peering through a tuft of heather on the edge of the gulley, there was his lordship lying with eight or nine hinds, about a hundred yards below us at a steep angle from which the most plausible shot was to the base of the neck. At the bark of the .308 the old gent tumbled forward down the gulley eventually coming to rest in the stream. Although obviously going back, he had a beautiful, lyre-shaped, wild old head.

Now we were well down the hill it became apparent that what had, from a greater elevation, seemed suitable ground for an Argo was, in fact, riven with gullies.

"What now?" I queried. A moment's speculation, then a shrug. "We take him out the way we came in." I bent my neck upwards. "Thou jest." I said. Or words to that effect.

I could only mutter a prayer as Rob began to uncoil two nylon Turnbull harnesses from his pocket.

And take him out we did. To my total astonishment. The gralloched stag weighed a touch over two hundred pounds, not enormous but quite enough.

By myself I could hardly budge him an inch, but by gripping and clawing with fingers, elbows, knees and toes and co-ordinating our heaves like a pair of dray horses, in a shade over two hours we hauled that beast, inch by inch, up the gulley to Argo territory. Never in all my life have I been so glad to see a yard of level ground.

While we were recovering our breath, and from my surprise that my heart hadn't burst into a thousand fragments, we were treated to a spectacle. A mile down the glen, a yellowish stag was chivvying his hinds when a very dark beast with his own harem breasted a rise some five hundred yards away. Both stags immediately left their hinds and trotted towards each other to do battle, for all the world like two knights in a tournament. They met with a terrible crash on a steep bank where a fierce fight ensued, each struggling for mastery of the high ground. At first, the black knight seemed to be winning on points but suddenly the yellow knight deftly sprang above him and, lunging downwards, caught the black knight a wallop which knocked him head over heels down the bank. He scrambled to his feet and clattered away to rejoin his hinds, no doubt thinking up an excuse on the way. No losses or gains, save pride, in this contest. No hero's welcome for the victor either. On his belligerent "I showed him" return, the yellow knight's hinds regarded him with that faint disdain that wives reserve for husbands who honk and shout at other drivers for some real or imaginary transgression.

Meanwhile, back on the bank, I was doing as well as could be expected, probably better. Having retrieved the rifles, I sat huddled against the now driving sleet and pondered on the mysteries of life, while Rob disappeared to fetch the Argo.

Living in low country, how does one achieve the degree of fitness, which makes stalking these elusive 'children of the mists' more of a pleasure than an ordeal? My wife, who is a physiotherapist and knows a thing or two about bodies, tells me that stepping up and down off a stool is good for the quadriceps. The trouble is,

I find that after the first couple of hours, tedium begins to creep in. Of course you can make it more effective and more realistic if you don full kit, including rifle, and close your eyes; maybe getting your wife to pour a cup of cold water down your neck every now and then. The realism is further enhanced when you miss your footing and crack a couple of ribs on the stool. It also affords the neighbours a good laugh if you forget to draw the curtains.

Pace is the secret on the hill, and the formula is the same as the old adage for financial contentment where income is fitness or available energy. It follows that the higher your income the more you can spend.

We found that we were enjoying the lifestyle in Scotland and decided to look for a property to buy. Else did not want to live on Mull, which I loved, because of the inaccessibility should there be a medical emergency. I had diabetes and was shortly going to have heart surgery. If we wanted to have e.g. a shed put up, it would cost more because of the ferry transport and in general, items were more expensive in the islands. So we spent holidays travelling from Appin in the north to Tarbert in the south along the coastline looking at houses.

Then one rainy Easter weekend, in 1997, could it have been anything else in Argyll, we looked at a bungalow on Seil. I did not like it. Else did, as it would be much easier to maintain than an old farmhouse in Shropshire. On our third visit to the property, the sun was shining so we walked down the sloping garden to the beach covered with slate where the sound of Seil flowed in a north south direction. I could see the famous Bridge over the Atlantic. And I found scallop shells, mussels, crab claws and was told that there were otters about. That did it, the house would be ours! It didn't take long and we entered the house in May with Else's sister Lill who came to help us move in.

Plans were made to go on holiday to Norway in 1998, camping with Else's sister and her family. Four adults and two children in the Mitsubishi, two tents, ground mats and sleeping bags on the roof rack, a small bag, per two people, with clothes and a picnic hamper fully equipped plus victuals. Nicholas and Emily sat in the very back on the two extra seats as they were the smallest. It was my first visit to Bergen and the beautiful surrounding mountains and fjords. A glorious ten days finishing up in Bergen with Else's family. I think Paul, Lill's husband found it very cold, despite wearing all of his clothing at nights, and would probably decline to go camping in northern climes again! Else's aunt Odny thought it terrible that we had slept in tents on the hard ground and in unheated huts. But imagine the scenery waking up to magnificent mountains and waterfalls, tasting the famous fare of the land, salami (reindeer), sild (pickled herring), geitost (goat cheese), fresh fish, prawns, cherries at the market in Bergen and so many different types of bread. The only drawback for me was driving through all of the tunnels. I needed to change my spectacles, going from sunshine to the dark of the tunnels, when Else would need to hand me the required pair. This was rather unsatisfactory and caused some alarm amongst our passengers, so Else did most of the driving in the end.

Back in Scotland, a long drive from Newcastle to Oban, we overnighted at Innishail and then next morning headed south. We males to pick up Glen and Gypsy from the kennels and the girls headed for Birmingham airport to pick up Annette and Stephanie visiting from Denmark, Else's brother's girls. Their wish for the holiday was to visit Ruthin Castle and attend a medieval banquet, which we duly did. It had certainly been a real family get together for Else. She had also decided to give up work and help me recuperate following my surgery, which was booked for September. We could then spend more time in Scotland if that suited us.

One day when I was stalking on the hills with Rob I felt decidedly rough and very out of breath. We did finish the stalk and get the intended beast after I had rested awhile but at the end of the day Rob said, "I think you should go and see your Doctor when you get back to Shrewsbury." To cut a long story short, I did, and ended up having an angiogram. It was suggested that I needed heart surgery. I had never felt any chest pain and was told that I probably had 'silent angina.' The wait on the NHS could have been many months or even longer, so I elected to go privately. Fate was at hand, as I had recently bought a catamaran and decided to sell it for the price of a quadruple bypass! This was 1998 and one begins to wonder about one's mortality. I asked the consultant about his success rate and was told the odds. I wanted to know that he hadn't used up his successes! He had a 97% success rate, what happened to the other 3%?

I am happy to report that my surgery went according to plan. But I did have one unfortunate incident. The story went like this. I was asked what I would like for breakfast and I really, really, fancied a boiled egg, my first decent food! I put a goodly helping of salt and pepper on the side as one does. What I did not realise was the effect the pepper would have on me. I sneezed, a huge sneeze. My chest felt as if it was being torn apart. Remember that my surgery involved entry via my sternum to access my heart, which finally involved stitches and staples. Later Else told me to tightly hold a pillow across my chest if I ever felt a sneeze coming on. This story and advice, I have given to quite a few friends who have undergone similar surgery.

I had many friends and family visit, Geoff among them, who never went near a hospital! I was honoured. Brother Bob would come before his work in the mornings and finish my breakfast and Else would come in the afternoons and stay for her evening meal. When she got back to Bob and Mary's house at night, there was always a gin and tonic waiting for her. Thank you Bob and Mary. Bob had shown her the route to and from the hospital the day before I went in.

Else would bring the dogs in the car and I could look out of my window, several floors up, when they would look up at my whistle. They loved to chase the squirrels in the gardens. I was very apprehensive on my first foray down the stairs to the car to see the dogs. I need not have worried about them jumping up on my chest as they seemed to know to keep away.

My walking and general ability improving daily, I would see any visitors to the stairs and kick my heels in joy (I was really showing off)! Soon it was time to go home. The advice from the medics was to exercise moderately and try my best to control my diabetic condition, have a reasonably fat free diet, no pork pies, and try to avoid very strenuous exercise and not become overtired. Apart from all that I could get on with my life taking everything in moderation.

That Christmas we spent at Innishail where I continued to increase my walking distance and I found that I was able to walk up some of the smaller hills at Ardmaddy. What wonderful views, fresh air and just being able to walk and enjoy life with Else and the dogs.

Rob Cameron and Roy Nixon having a spy for stags

Jim on Mull with two cull stags

Jim with a stag and a salmon on Loch Baa, Mull

Jim and Rob hauling out the stag nearly vertically – this is not to be recommended

Chapter 18

The Pull Of The Highlands

We found that after every holiday in Argyll, we really did not want to return to the hectic life in Shropshire. So I arranged to rent the house and asked Alister Evans, our farming neighbour, to manage the business. He knew the tenants in the units and already would do a walk about each night. This worked very well. I was still on the end of a phone if there were any problems.

One night before we moved, there was a knock at the door about 10pm. It was Alister and there was a fire roaring in the barn with the possibility of it spreading to the units nearer the house and even to the farmhouse. Luckily we live near to the river and the fire brigade were able to access water from the river Severn. We left the front door open to the 'watches' that worked through the night so that they could have refreshments and biscuits. I was warned that we would have a very early phone call from assessors and insurers with regard to the fire damage. Very true, very confusing and upsetting, and in the end I am sure we did not get paid out as much as we should have. It took many skips full of twisted galvanise, burnt out cars and weeks to clear up the site. This all happened after my heart bypass surgery and Else worried that I was doing too much. I did not rebuild where the large barn had burned down but instead bought three containers and put them on the concrete pad. These would be a safe and suitable lockup for future tenants.

When Else and I moved up to the Inner Hebrides, Isle of Seil, we rented the house in Shrewsbury as we were unsure whether we would want to move back to the south or stay in Scotland. You will find out which one won as you read on. Many of our family and friends visited and because we are so far away, would stay for perhaps a week. We then got to know them so much better, quite different to an evening socialising over drinks and dinner.

There were mountain or forestry walks to explore, which the dogs thought were fantastic. We soon bought a small motorboat to go sea fishing for mackerel, cod and whatever else we found in the sound and around the islands of Shuna, Luing and towards Mull and Oban. At this time we had Glen and Gypsy, two black and white Springer spaniels bred in Shropshire. Luckily they enjoyed travelling anywhere with us either by car, camper or boat. I was introduced to Harry Fowler who showed me some of his fishing grounds e.g. Loch Etive, a sea loch stretching many miles inland catching sea trout, rivers e.g. Scammerdale, catching sea trout, brown trout and the odd salmon. I enquired about pheasant shooting and got in touch with John Reid at Largie, several miles south of Tarbert. I joined the shoot and Else worked the two dogs picking up and beating. We had about an acre of garden sloping from the house down to the sea, which we regard as the right way!

Colin and Pat are regular visitors and could relate many a fishing tale or fishy tale! I introduced Col to fishing the sea around Seil, the local river Euchar at Kilninver and up to Scammadale, headwater of the Euchar, where we have caught many a lusty sea trout. Also the Lochgilphead Fishing Club Water onto remote mountain or hill lochs. Colin has always loved Scotland and has fished many of its inland waters.

An Eskimo needs a whole lotta snow,
But an Englishman needs time!

One year we stayed on the Borders in Dumfriesshire at a friend's house, Andrew and Di at Ae, near Thornhill. I had some ground near Sanquhar, which I rented off the forestry with red and roe deer. Col, Pat and their son Mike were with us. There was heavy snow on the ground. Colin and I went stalking with Glen, our spaniel. Else had advised Colin to kneel stand when holding Glen, as on hearing the shot, he would be off with Colin close behind. We were quietly making our way up the ride in search of a beast.

I hand signalled Colin to stop walking whilst I disappeared through the trees over a ridge. I shot. Then there was Colin being towed through the deep snow by a dog wild with excitement wanting to see the outcome and to be first on the scene!

There are a lot of stories about Glen who was quite a character of a dog. He loved his Uncle George (Wallace) who would be greeted with a catchy-jump on arrival into the house. And if George and I were going stalking to Dolgellau, he definitely had to be included in the party. He had a very good nose and would always let me know that there was a deer ahead, even if it were quite a distance away. He did have one slight fault though; he wanted to see the deer first!

Travelling up to Sanquhar once in the campervan, I had a blow out on the motorway, quite a frightening experience for any mortal, far less a hound. Glen jumped on to Nick's lap, saying in his canine way, "Save me, save me!" That night, a chilly night, we slept in the van in our sleeping bags. Nick (Williamson) made the mistake to vacate his bag for a call of nature. It was not easy to evacuate Glen, who had snuggled down into his deliciously warm sleeping bag. If we were ever watching a spooky film on television at home and Glen thought that, perchance, Else might jump or shout, he would very soon retire to behind the sofa. Only to emerge when everything was safe again. At Monkmoor Farm, I would wonder that the post had not come. Oh no, Glen had got there first and hidden the letters under my desk in the study. It was not unusual to hand in a cheque at the bank decorated with tooth marks!

When we were at Innishail, the name of our house on Seil, on a hot day, he would trot down to the sea and lie relaxing in the shallow water with a smile on his face. Clever dog.

When I bought Gypsy, I had been to see dozens of advertised pups, before deciding she would be ours. I took her into the tackle shop in Shrewsbury, to show her to Allan and Liz Dignam. All Liz could say was "Look at its eyes!" She really was a most beautiful black and white spaniel. And Glen hated the intrusion of this new pup. He would lift his lips in a terrifying grimace, no growl, to frighten her. It didn't work very well. She loved to play, more than I've seen liver and white spaniels play, and could amuse herself for hours with a tennis ball, lying on her back, balancing the ball between her paws and occasionally mouthing it. Her other party trick was if I balanced a treat on her nose and said, "Wait," even several times, "Wait," then "Get it!" She would flick it high and catch it and devour it. Glen, not to be outdone, also learned the trick.

My brother Bob was visiting us and we decided to have a weekend at Largie, where I had joined a shoot run by John Reid in 1999. We would be partly stalking and partly rough shooting. Else cautioned Bob, when shooting a rabbit, to make sure that it was well ahead of Glen. I noticed Bob put an extra cartridge in his pocket. On questioning Bob, the extra cartridge was in case he shot Glen before or after the rabbit, the next shell would be for himself. Lastly, when on the shoot at Largie, if Glen was by my side picking up, and I had the misfortune to miss a few birds, Glen would treat me to one of his specialities, a withering look of utter scorn, which was not hard to read as, "You could at least hit one." I would retaliate, "Well, I can't hit them all!"

My best day fishing ever was on ground belonging to the McNicoll brothers Hamish, Ian and Alister who live at Turnallt just north of Ardfern. Rob Cameron introduced me to the family. There are very few people alive today who have had the privilege to fish several miles of absolutely virgin river water (well nearly virgin) as it had been hardly ever fished. I think it is the Barbreck River.

Else dropped me off at the top of the glen below Loch Avich where the forested hills are drained onto rough grassland and where the river starts. I walked several hundred yards before finding fishable water over and around heather, juniper and stunted trees e.g. birch, alder, willow and bog oak, the land being grazed by sheep and cattle. Because of the rugged ground the use of heavy machinery was unsuitable so the farming was done on foot and more recently with the use of quad bikes. The cattle tended to be found nearer to the houses on the lower more suitable ground. The one striking thing about the three brothers was that they were all tall and lanky, without an ounce of fat, men of the hill and would or could walk the hills for miles non-stop.

In a long time of fishing I would rate this as my best day's fishing using the worm. I had my flask and 'piece' and fished from early morning until late afternoon. My catch, consisting of brown trout, sea trout and salmon, I shared with the brothers who were reluctant to take any as I had caught them and I should have them.

I was enchanted by the greenery and wildlife, seeing deer, buzzards and a golden eagle. The going was not always easy underfoot, there being the occasional path to follow, some scrambling down to the enticing pools and some runs on the flat. I had some small trout nicked, by what I don't know, probably a bird. I had good weather all day, the river at its ideal level, some rain in the past week but not enough to spoil the fishing with too much.

My delight was to watch Glen's absolutely boundless delight being with his Dad on an exciting fishing trip, and 'saying' that he would help. Even though he was standing at the river's edge frightening the fish being carefully brought into the bank. Glen would sit looking for any motion. Then when I caught a fish, he would want to go into the water to help me bring it in. Or so he thought! I would have to say a few stern words to make him back off from the water's edge. I would strike into a fish and only when it was getting near to netting it, Glen's enthusiasm would get the better of him needing a few expletives!

I have fished this glen three times and have no hesitation in nominating my first days fishing on this wonderful river as my best ever anywhere. That includes the company and enjoyment of the dog Glen, with his limitless enthusiasm for the day's events, the land, the fishing and the fact that not many people get the chance to have such a day's fishing in such a magnificent setting.

In the Highlands, hill farmers can be men of few words. One day I was part of a fox drive and observed three farmers resting on their tall sticks. They were standing round a foxhole observing the ground which they pointed to while nodding their heads. The only words I heard were, "Aye," said with differing intonations. That told the whole story. The evidence was prodded and all men knew what the fox cubs had been eating.

Gypsy as a wee pup in Shrewsbury

*Feeding the pheasants on
Ardshellach Farm*

Picnic walk overlooking Loch Melfort, taken by Sue

Chapter 19

Antique Guns

I was lucky to be able to collect some lovely old antique guns, some quite special with a bit of history, and had them displayed in my study at Innishail. Alongside these were flasks for powder and shot, some made of leather, horn and various metals. There was a selection of flints of various sizes, brought up from an East Indiaman, Earl of Abergavenny, sunk in 1805. For the firearms, there were various sizes of felt wads, card wads, lead ball shot; assorted sized pincer type ball moulds and wad punches, multi sized nipple wrench, several bore measuring callipers, various sized percussion caps plus various tools and accoutrements. I was also invited, for several years, to display some of my long guns and pistols and to show this collection at Scone Game Fair in the BASC tent. Wonderful things to collect and display, to research and talk about with friends and acquaintances that appreciated such craftsmanship.

If you should happen to have any of the following, this is the loading and firing sequence.

Cannon
Load main charge down muzzle,
Followed by wadding, ram.
Followed by ball, ram.
Priming charge into touchhole.
Fire with prepared fuse.

Flintlock
Pour main charge down muzzle.
Followed by wadding, ram.
Followed by shot or ball, ram.
Priming charge into pan, close.
Bring to full cock, fire.

ANTIQUE GUNS

Percussion
Main charge down muzzle.
Followed by wadding, ram.
Followed by shot or ball, tap.
Percussion cap on nipple.
Bring to full cock, fire.

And here are some gun related sayings from the past.

Lock, stock and barrel.
The three main components of a gun.
Everything. The lot.

Just a flash in the pan.
When a spark from the flint ignited the priming powder in the frizzen pan but this did not fire the main charge in the barrel.
A brief and temporary show of brilliance.

A deadpan expression.
The look of blank shock on the face of a soldier or sportsman when, charged by a deadly enemy, his flint failed to even flash the powder in the pan.

To 'spike his guns'.
When soldiers captured an enemy position, a soft iron spike would be driven into the touchhole of the cannon to render them unusable in the event of the position being re-captured.
To create a huge disadvantage for the opposition.

A loose cannon.
If a heavy cannon, often weighing several tons, broke loose from its restraining ropes during a battle at sea or a storm, it would charge about the decks as the ship rolled, causing death and destruction.
A person is said to be a loose cannon if by careless words or deeds, he creates mayhem.

A shot in the dark.
A nervous soldier on sentry duty might fire at a suspicious noise, or the flash from a gun, or a cigarette being lit. Occasionally it comes off! Hence the advice to comrades in the trenches. Never take the third light. A crack sniper would take only seconds to get off a well-aimed shot at the illuminated face.
Nowadays, a shrewd guess that proves to be accurate.

To 'go off at half cock'.
The hammers on a gun have three positions. Down – at rest, half cock – supposedly safe, full cock – ready to fire. Sometimes because of a jolt or faulty mechanism, a gun would go off at half cock, which could be fatal.
To embark on a project before one is ready.

At one of the Ardmaddy fete days to raise money for building the Village Hall on Seil, Rob Cameron and I did a display while Patrick Cadzow did the commentary.
It went like this.

> Many of you will have seen the antique guns on display.
> Cannon were used to defend Seville as long ago as 1247 and certainly by the English at Crecy in 1346.
> By 1413 Mahomet II had a huge cannon at the siege of Constinople. It was said to be four feet in diameter and fired stone balls weighing over six hundred pounds. Such a thing could spoil a man's entire day.
> It was not long before cannon began to be used in naval warfare and by Nelson's time a British battleship was known as a 74 as she carried 74 guns. It was common for the gunners to be ordered to fire on the upward roll of the ship so that a ball which missed the hull of the enemy ship might go high and smash a mast or spar and carry away rigging. Flying splinters of oak from the vessel killed many sailors.
> Now before we light the blue touch paper, I would point out that for safety reasons, all the wadding used in this demonstration is super soft toilet paper. Lab tested. We all know how well Labradors test toilet paper!

Demo – 'Fire on the upward roll' (a cannon was fired)

Cannon were fine for battering down castle walls, pounding enemy ships, or flinging projectiles into massed infantry. They were not ideal for sniping at soldiers, and sportsmen found them totally useless for sniping at snipe.

And so the handgun was invented. First the matchlock. The gunner had to carry a lighted fuse that was stabbed into powder in a small pan on the side of the breech. The flash travelled through a tiny hole into the breech and away she went. Unfortunately the amount of fuse used could be a serious item and the garrison sentries at York were said to have used one and a half hundredweight per night. Also the glowing of a fuse gave away a man's position at night.

A better form of ignition was sought which resulted in the development of the flintlock. This is accomplished by a piece of flint held in the jaws of the cock striking a steel plate called the frizzen causing sparks which fall into the priming pan and firing the charge.

Demo –   Rob and Jim firing a flintlock each.
First the powder charge down the muzzle
Then the wadding
There is no shot as this is a demonstration
Finally priming powder in the frizzen pan.

It has to be said that this system was not brilliant in wet weather and after a mere two hundred years a Scottish parson named Alexander Forsyth invented a powder which detonated when struck and so came the percussion cap. This speeded up the ignition process and made shooting of flying game more of a possibility. Some of us need all of the help we can get.

Demo –   Rob and Jim shooting a percussion gun each.
First the powder charge, then the wadding,

Lastly a percussion cap on the nipple of each barrel.

Up until now most guns were loaded from the muzzle. This took time and had to be done standing up with the butt of the gun on the ground. If you were a soldier, the enemy, who often were lacking in a sense of fair play, would be shooting at you, which could be very distracting, often resulting in multiple charges being poured down the barrel with disastrous results. One soldier was found to have eleven full charges in his gun. In the din of battle he had failed to notice the lack of recoil.

Inevitably after many attempts, the breechloader was developed, soon followed by smokeless powder by which many shots may be fired in amazing rapidity with no puff of smoke to shroud your falling game or betray your presence to the enemy. Very effective but it isn't half as much fun!

Demo –   Rob and Jim firing two very quick right and lefts with breechloaders.

Unfortunately my eyesight was deteriorating causing me to cease stalking and so I sold my rifles and more recently my gun collection. Although they would have been nice to keep it was unfair to leave Else with these to sell at some later date. I have a few pieces still to sit and stare at and reminisce about.

Display of handguns in my collection

Display of long guns in my collection

Jonah firing a pistol at the target with Jim looking on

Jordan firing the cannon, 'Princess of Thule', with Jim and Jon looking on

George Wallace commentating while Jim fires a gun at the Game Fair

Chapter 20

What Shall We Do For The Millennium?

To celebrate the year 2000 we decided to do some travelling abroad, visit some of the countries still on our wish list. George Wallace asked us if we would like to go to South Africa with him and his wife Julia where he had some connections with a wild life ranger. We arranged for the dogs to go into kennels near to where George and Julia lived and had started our anti-malaria tablets as well as having the relevant inoculations. So we flew out at the beginning of May and were met by Martin Shoeman at Johannesburg airport. There was a long drive through Pretoria to Ellisras and then to Sangioma Safari Lodge where Lindy, Martin's wife awaited us.

We had a wonderfully exciting fortnight, the first week on a private game reserve where we ate such things as ostrich and boboti for the first time. We saw lovely yellow hornbills which Lindy called banana birds. We drove for a full day through dramatic scenery of cliffs, stony areas and forestry. The second week, we travelled through the Kruger National Park. Else commented that it reminded her very much of Trinidad in that the daylight hours were similar, dawn and dusk at 6 o'clock, the cicadas sounded the same and the magical nights were lit up with fireflies. The days were hot but the nights and early morning game drives much cooler. The rivers were all quite dramatic to see as it was the year after all the heavy rains in 1999 and there were still some bridges impassable and huge trees blocking the waterways.

How do you look for a giraffe? What may one see? If it is next to the vehicle, you see giraffe coloured tree trunks. If it is far away, you may see nothing because it is browsing until it lifts its head, and then you may see some neck and the head. There is always a surprise around every corner of the road. Impala or other antelope crossing at the run, wild pigs their tails held high bolting across the road, and elephants. Well, they could be on the road; they could suddenly appear from behind some small trees where they were totally hidden or there could be evidence of them having recently passed by. Uprooted trees, bushes strewn all about or huge fresh dung heaps often heralded flapping ears and trunks uplifted moving in our direction. Time to reverse! On another day's drive looking at elephants; we were very much aware of a large bull elephant telling off a young teenage bull elephant who was approaching our vehicle with a look of an intent to charge. The wise old bull was giving him a thraping with an uprooted tree and giving him a severe telling off. The old bull seeming to say, "Packet it up you silly bugger, you will get us all shot!" What magnificent animals deserving our full respect. Especially too, when the big bulls were in musth. We never saw any rhinos but were lucky to see the other big five, elephant, lion, buffalo and leopard. We were both fascinated by the hippos and their huge numbers in the rivers.

One amusing incident happened when there was a traffic jam. All the vehicles were at a standstill, and then as the cars started to move, we noticed a tiny chameleon crossing. It placed its feet one at a time, stop, move, stop, move, seemingly not at all worried by the huge tanker truck that had stopped to let it safely cross the road. The speed limit on these roads is 30mph in the Kruger.

We saw a gnu and her calf every day, which hung out by the gates to the game farm. She was always there, but we did not gnow why. Perhaps she gnew better and that it was safer.

Impalas, after their productive years in the herd, are driven out into bachelor groups for the rest of their lives. It was one of these that I chose to shoot with a gun that I brought out from the UK. I was successful and we had it for dinner one night, the remains being given to the natives on the game farm. When it was George's turn for his game, he was successful in getting a kudu, which gave us some lovely meat and steaks and the rest given to the families on the farm. I also tried to shoot some guinea fowl or francolin but they never played the game and kept ducking behind the undergrowth and, being an Englishman, it is not the done thing to shoot game birds on the ground. Just not done!

While we were in the Kruger, safely tucked up in our huts, the baleful roars of lions often wakened us. It was something that we never got accustomed to and I must say we did also look out for creepy crawlies especially at bedtime! On our way to the airport we stopped at 'God's Window' to look at and buy local handicrafts and to marvel at the panoramic view, miles of spectacular rainforest. A wonderful holiday, well worth the long flights, airport waiting times and expense. The dogs were fine and we were soon back home in Scotland having our Hep B booster and finishing our malaria tablets.

Betty was a very close friend of my Dad's whom he met sometime after Mum died. They met as they attended the same church. Dad was unable to attend our wedding but Betty came with friends and her toast to Else and I was, "Here's to us, and them that's like us, there's very, very few, and most of them's deed!" This was followed by Betty's famous hearty laugh that had the whole room laughing! Unfortunately she died and we went south to her funeral in December 2000.

In February 2001, we went to New Zealand. This is where my son Andrew was living and working as a chef, in North Island. We flew via Kuala Lumpur spending three days there on the way out. We took several sightseeing trips, saw a variety of temples and went to a bazaar where I bought a watch. Else told me off for not haggling over the price. The taxi drivers were excellent, telling us about the history of the country and people. We walked in town every day trying the local food sold by the vendors. It was lovely though to get back to the hotel, have a refreshing drink, served by beautiful girls bending down onto their knees, in an air-conditioned lobby and to get out of the searing heat. Breakfast in the hotel could be a curry, western style food, a wonderful array of fruit or a variety of local porridge. Knowing my love for oats, I had to try it. I did not try it again! I decided that I did not like rice porridge!

Then flying off to New Zealand where we hired a car for the fortnight. Over the first week we initially stayed in Auckland, walking down to see the boats in harbour and the Maritime museum. We crossed over to Devonport one evening to see the area; a restaurant that Andy had worked in and then for a meal. We then drove as far north as we could liking especially the Bay of Islands area. It was sunny so we were in shorts most of the time but we found the water amazingly cold, so only paddled. We stayed in motels, which we found very comfortable, eating out at nights and found the food excellent. I was very puzzled by something in the countryside. There were no barns. We saw cattle and sheep, but no stored fodder. Then I realised that they probably did not need barns, as the weather was so much milder than the UK. The animals would be able to feed out of doors year round.

We visited many museums and were amazed by the subtropical Kauri forests in North Island and the huge tree ferns everywhere. At one of the museums, we saw some of the bog kauri, which is said to be the oldest workable wood in the world. It is found in peat swamps, the wood now called Ancient Kauri and it has been carbon dated to forty-five thousand years old. We saw beautiful furniture, and a variety of small crafty wooden objects for sale. Eucalyptus trees were introduced in the early mid nineteenth century. In one of the many museums near to Wangerei, Else was watching a video relating to the immigrants from the UK who settled in New Zealand. She suddenly exclaimed because the ruined castle that she was viewing was exactly where she had visited a fortnight earlier in Sutherland, Scotland. Ardvreck Castle, on Loch Assynt, was in one of the many areas from Ullapool to Oban affected by the clearances on the west coast. The Scots left home for Nova Scotia, Cape Breton. When the potato famine then hit Canada in the 1850's they left for New Zealand.

Then for our second week we stayed with Andrew at his friend Alan's house in Whitianga (wh being pronounced as an f) on the Coromandel peninsula. We were shown the sights, were cooked glorious sea food such as green lipped mussels, collected our own cockles on the beach one day, walked to see Cook's beach, a hot water beach, some glorious coves, Cathedral Cove that we have since seen advertised on TV. We visited a kiwi fruit winery that produced mainly white wine, which we liked very much and bought some to take back for the house. Alan took us out fishing when we caught red snapper and something like sea salmon. The authorities are very keen that small fish are returned to the sea and if you are found with an undersized catch, the fines are heavy. That night we had a fish curry and tasted tea tree smoked fish.

Before returning to Auckland we showed videos to Andy and Chrissie of family back in the UK and our house, garden and dogs. It was, generally, thoroughly relaxing in the warm climate and catching up with Andrew and his life halfway across the world. The one worry that we did have was 'foot and mouth.' The kennels that housed our dogs also bred pigs that are cloven hoofed and who could have been affected. We phoned several times and were reassured that there were no problems.

On our way back we treated ourselves to one night in KL at a more expensive hotel, the Shangri-La, breakfasting in our bedroom. Delightful fruit and an English breakfast at our leisure, a display of orchids also on the tray. I don't remember having any jet lag so the time spent at KL certainly made the travelling more comfortable and enjoyable.

Andrew sent this picture to us of a 7 １/₂kg brown trout, caught at the 'Quiet Lake', New Zealand in 2003, with the rod we sent for his birthday

Chapter 21

Our Interests And Hobbies At Home

I decided that I would like to put some pheasants down on nearby ground so that I could use only my black powder guns when shooting the birds. I wrote to Jimmy Gilbert at Ardshellach Farm on the mainland across from us. I asked if I could put down one hundred birds specifying that they were only to be shot with black powder.

Andrew unfortunately met with an accident while in Denmark visiting his Danish girlfriend. He was mugged and ended up having surgery in France for a brain haemmhorage. This was a very worrying time for Ruth and myself. He was eventually escorted to Ruth's house, my ex wife, in Shrewsbury to rest and recuperate and then they came up to us for a while. Mark, Becky and their child Erin also visited, so it was a full house. While my boys were here we finished off the enclosure for the pheasants on Jimmies ground. It was in a sheltered area with a grassy bank behind and an open area across a field to the sea, Seil Sound. I had a Shogun Mitsubishi and would drive with the heavy bags of mixed corn etc to the bin by the pen a field away. The food would be liberally spread around the area to keep the birds at home. We would visit daily, sometimes twice a day, to top up food and water and check that all was secure from four-footed mammals and flying predators.

Charlie at Ardmaddy arranged for us to have one hundred birds, which arrived on the third week of July. Great excitement, seeing how they progressed and making them a small shelter that also collected water when it rained so we did not have to tote huge amounts of water as well as food.

When the birds attained a sufficient weight and were in season, October to the end of January, I organised a few shoots. These were using black powder guns only. Simply because using cartridges was too easy and using black powder gave the birds a better chance. Especially as it was only a tiny affair and no way intended to produce a lot of birds for the table. We sourced pheasant blocks, food in a tub that they are very partial to and hopefully encourages them to stay near to home. These empty tubs made very good feeders is due course and then later as plant pots for raspberries.

It was only ever intended to provide a very few chosen friends or family with the odd couple of hours back to basics walk about. Everyone wore a waistcoat and was kitted out with powder flask, shot flask, pockets for wads and cap dispenser. They were taught the safe use of these ancient but fascinating weapons as few have in these ultra modern times seen Black Powder guns. We think too much emphasis is often placed on the size of the bag.

They were shown how to, according to an old adage:

> Ram the powder,
> Tap the shot,
> And you'll kill them dead,
> Right on the spot.

Observing the obvious safety rules especially when using a gun with more that one barrel i.e. taking care not to load the same barrel twice. This paragraph should not be necessary to write but it has been known that a ramrod has been shot in excitement or haste, a barrel has had a double charge and was only noticed when the result was a humongous bang and a very sore shoulder. Also, I always kept my head down while reloading, thus keeping my composure, and when loaded then looked up for my next shot.

When moving from area to area, the caps should be removed from the nipples to prevent accidental discharge. The cap fits on the nipple, with the hammer at half cock whence it should not be able to be fired. Only on sighting the bird in a safe position for a shot, should the hammer be put on full cock and the shot taken or the hammer returned to half cock.

Else, meanwhile, would have Glen and Gypsy seeking out the birds to flush in front of the guns. As you can imagine it was not easy to rein them in when the nearby gun was reloading. Very slow birds or easy shots were scorned.

We would spend half a day walking through bracken, rushes, heather and grassy wet areas where we had pheasant feeders. If we took home two or three birds, we would be well satisfied, Jimmy and Doreen happy to have a bird themselves.

Unfortunately, Jimmy is no longer with us, may he rest in peace.

We decided to upgrade our boat and drove over to Ireland in April, as I had seen some interesting boats advertised over there. And we like Ireland, the people and the musical evenings at the pubs not to mention the Guinness! One problem we had, as 'foot and mouth' was still active, was at Customs. They were checking through items in the back of the car when they came across 'Markies.' There is supposedly marrowbone in them. But they let us keep them so the dogs still had their breakfast! We enjoyed our week travelling around the island. As one does when shopping for shoes, one goes back to the first shoe shop visited to buy, I find the same with boats! I had been looking at *Fiola* in Ardfern boat yard for many months and having not found what I wanted in Ireland, I was back at Ardfern. And so *Fiola* was motored up to Seil with our friends Tim and Maxine Hall with their baby Elijah, in May. Our previous boat *Colisa* went in turn to the Ardfern area.

In 2002, we went to Trinidad in February. My brother Bob came and stayed at the house to look after the dogs for a while and invited his daughter Nicola and her husband Simon. For the last week of our holiday, the dogs went to Jimmy and Doreen's farm. Not sure how much they enjoyed sleeping in the barn! While we were in Trinidad, carnival was in full swing. Imagine being on a street called Tranquillity, while trucks blaring out calypso music pass by and a throng of barely clad dancing or 'chipping' Trinies smile and wave while they stream past. The sight of a scantily clad bottom, just a few feet away, remains a lasting and very pleasant memory. The music stayed in my ears for days, the loudness of it and the catchy songs. "One cent, two cent, five cent, dollar!" Nicholas showing us how one danced or moved to the song.

We saw a donkey cart full of chilled coconuts and decided that was the way to quench our thirst. As we were waiting our turn, a coloured man said that he wanted to buy them for us, noticing my English accent, and asked where I was from. I happened to think that he wouldn't know where Shrewsbury was so I said, "Manchester." His reply was, "Well you must know Henry, he lives in Manchester."

As always, we also visited Tobago and our favourite places to swim and eat. Not to forget the shark and bake at Maracas beach in Trinidad, roti, stewed meat and potato or prawns in a wrap, whenever and wherever always a favourite, and for breakfast Paul would take us for doubles. This is a type of fried bread called bara on which channa or curried chickpeas are served. Not easy to eat but absolutely delicious.

At Easter our visitors from Welshpool and Knockin were Roy and Kim, Kev, Ness and their youngster Jodie. Despite the cold weather, Easter eggs were scattered around the garden for Jodie to find. Ness refused point blank to go in the dingy to see *Fiola* as she had sworn not to go to sea again after her trip with us on *Ospray*. But they had all come up to visit and see where we lived which was much appreciated.

We like to be reasonably self sufficient, growing vegetables and soft fruit in the garden, and getting a supply of pheasants and venison in season. Along with catching and smoking mackerel, we also took up sausage making. This can be great fun. We met Mike and Helen Stewart at Largie where they 'picked up' along with Else on the pheasant shoots. I invited them to a sausage making session and then for lunch to taste our produce. Have you ever made sausages? Helen had the first attempt at putting the skin on the nozzle of the machine. Else and I watched her face intently. As her little smile developed on her face, I asked her, "Does it remind you of something?"

We also helped out at Dunmor Farm with fleece wrapping, this was in June. You know when you have done a day's work with the sheep shearer's working at full speed, trying to keep up with them, keep the fleece intact and roll it properly. Whatever you wear is full of bits of wool and your hands feel wonderfully supple having had a lanolin treatment, feeling like a baby's bum! Fiona always put on a wonderful lunch with ham rolls and cake and the best brownies ever! Eddie tried to tell Else the names given to the different ages of sheep but I don't think any of them stuck. We tried to help out with varying activities in the community such as shearing days, sports days, fox drives, fete days and shooting days, both of us being interested in wild life, the countryside and those who work in and follow country pursuits.

When I moved up to Scotland, I needed a place in which to do wood work and odd jobs, so ordered a wooden shed. This came flat pack from Yorkshire and Else and I erected it over a weekend. I had previously made a base as strong as possible with well-seasoned and thoroughly treated posts. Herringbone drains had initially been dug to take the majority of water away. The shed was erected without mishap, looked absolutely superb and has been very productive over the years. One job that I was very pleased with was my smoker. I had been busy for many days when I asked Else to come into the 'workshop' as I had something to show her. When she did come, I was stood saluting her entry in my 'sentry box.' This we put next to the wood shed. Its source of fire is a West Indian cooking coal-pot, which we bought on our trip, as there was plenty of room on *Ospray*. A stainless steel chimney completed this splendidly. It has proved to be very useful in smoking mackerel, pheasants, cheese and a variety of other game including venison.

Christmas was spent at Caplic Estate in Sutherland on the Oykel this year with Allan and Bridget Wyatt, their Labradors and our spaniels being old friends. For whatever reason, I don't remember, Allan, Bridget and myself felt a bit under the weather. Else took all of the dogs for a walk up to what we called 'pimple hill' on Christmas day and reminded me that it was a very warm day, so she was wearing no jacket. 'Pimple hill' was the highest bit of ground nearest to the house, which was in various stages of being built. Sat at the top of the hill in the warm sunshine, Else looked through her binoculars for the red deer that are usually about. She also made sure to keep the dogs out of the way of the Gascoigne horned cattle that Allan and Bridget bred.

Christmas dinner was well up to Bridget's high standard of culinary prowess, the rooms being heated by a huge log burning stove and a bar-b-cue! Even though most of the fresh air had been boarded off, we still had most of our warm clothes on. We laughed at the simplicity of the occasion and that we could all still enjoy being a little bit touched, a bit like the 'Mad Hatter's Tea Party.'

In 2003, we stayed in Britain but certainly visited friends so were away from home. We were often invited to celebrate Burn's Night in Oswestry, Shropshire, at one of the pubs and when this stopped would arrange a get together with friends at home. In Shropshire, Dougie Kerr would be the one to address the haggis, he being a Scot and then the rest of the folk sat round the table would do other readings. When we moved up to Innishail, Jimmie Gilbert would then address the haggis. Our neighbours Stuart and Ann Reid would be asked to do the address to the lassies and the reply from the lassies as they write most wonderfully humorous anecdotes about us, all lies I'm sure!

Over the years our Scottish pronunciations have improved a wee bitty, I hope! Even so, we still tend to recite what we think may be the easier poems such as 'To a Mouse' and 'To a Louse.' Over the years we have started to make our own haggis, which we feel is well ahead of the game. But we would say that wouldn't we?

In March we went to Rhyl in Wales where Colin and Pat's granddaughter was to be christened which was on our way, more or less, down to Towcester where we were invited along with

OUR INTERESTS AND HOBBIES AT HOME

other friends Rob and Michelle, to where Lloyd and Susan Evans live, or as they say in our area of Scotland, stay. We had invited them for meals at our house and this was their thank you. We were treated royally and went to London one day. We went on the 'London Eye', visited the 'Tower', had a meal at the Tower Carvery and then went to see the show 'Mama Mia.' The next day we went clay pigeon shooting and in the afternoon went flying with Peter, Lloyd's brother, in his light aircraft, over Althorp Estate where Lady Di is buried. As we banked in the plane, I felt that I might fall out! And then when coming in to land it felt as if we just missed the fence but landed beautifully smoothly on his field.

Heading back north, we went to stay with Geoff and Joyce in New Mills, Derbyshire. Here we met up with other friends John and Margaret Richies, as well as Colin and Pat, and went walking and exploring old haunts of my youth. Sam Evans' house and farm land including where our famous 'cabin' had been and despite its extraordinarily rickety appearance sheltered us on many an occasion. I was able to show Else where I tickled trout and passed days of my misspent youth. We walked along the Goyt Valley Reservoir. After a very short while Geoff fell and was unable to feel his feet and I think we then realised how unwell he actually was.

We then drove to the Oswestry area meeting up with many of Else's colleagues and friends, having a meal at Dougie and Margaret's with Ian and Beryl and went out for a meal at the Cross Keys, Kinnerley with Roy and Kim, Kevin and Ness. We stayed with a long time friend Mona Mills, enjoying a meal at Jugs, and as always having a great time. We miss our good friends as we live in Scotland but still manage to see them but obviously not as often. We like to suddenly arrive without notice or make a phone call and say we are only ten minutes away. "Can we pop in to see you?"

In July we were booked to go south for Mark's cap and gowning, celebrating his finishing his university degree. However, I ended up in Ward B, Lorne and Islands Hospital, with tachycardia and was advised not to travel. I was very proud of him and sorry not to be able to celebrate with him and my family. At the end of July, our good friend Roy Simmister died. He was Vanessa's step Dad. We did go down to his funeral, which was extremely well attended in Welshpool, staying with Tim and Max Hall at Bogmarch Cottage in Pennerley.

The mackerel fishing was good with catches of seventy-one in July and ninety-one in August, so plenty to give away to friends and smoke for the freezer. We found that fresh mackerel did not keep as well in the freezer. I put forty pheasants down at Jimmie's for the coming season.

In August we were invited to Derbyshire to stay with Geoff and Joyce and to attend a Gilbert and Sullivan show at Buxton Opera House. Always a favourite of mine, the catchy, pithy political comedy of HMS Pinafore, was well enjoyed by all of us. From here we picked up my brother Michael and went to Cambridgeshire for his son Nicholas's wedding. Then back to Poynton to stay with Bob and Mary for a night and up to the borders where we stayed with Richard and Elke before heading home.

We liked to stay in touch with our many friends, so often travelled south half a dozen times a year and in return enjoyed their company, often when there was likely to be better weather than in Scotland and fewer midges!

I was trying to interest Else in a bit of salmon and sea trout fishing and set her up with a rod and waders. She already had the wellies for our wet garden and walking the dogs over the countryside. I enjoyed fishing the Euchar, at Kilninver, where Else would drop me off and return some hours later. She did have a few casts at the mouth of the river but I think she found fishing on the Orchy, near Dalmally, a bit easier. She caught her first salmon par, all of six inches. While she was in midstream casting, some people driving past stopped to watch her fish, I was quite proud of my wife that day. Later she said that she felt very self-conscious.

Towards the end of August, I noticed that I was unable to see very well and had appointments with Dr Webb and in October with

Dr Murdoch. Then in November, I saw Dr Barrie at Gartnaval Hospital. In the meantime we had visitations from Sue and Sal, Pat and Col, Mark, Becky and Erin, and Ian and Beryl all in September. In October, Oz and Kerry came with Annabel, George, Arthur (my grandchildren) and the Alsatian Ruby.

In November, we headed to Shropshire staying with George and Julia near Wrexham, when we had rented a van in Oban in order to empty the garage at Monkmoor as I had sold the house. There was a clutter of stuff that I felt I wanted to keep such as antlers, life jackets, oars and many planks of wood of different varieties, collected over many years.

Early December brought the arrival of Richard, Elke, Katie and Sarah for a visit. We had a good walk over Jimmy's ground and had a few birds with the black powder guns. We enjoyed canoeing and rowing in reasonably mild weather and had a good walk from Barnacarry along the shoreline, scrambling up a rock face and then onto a stone strewn beach collecting interesting specimens and resting for a coffee break. Then on along the slate paths to Seil Sound and up the Bridge Over The Atlantic and along the road to the house. We would then go and collect the car left at Barnacarry where we had paid one pound for the privilege of parking.

This Christmas our visitors were George and Julia who stayed until the beginning of January, going home after George's birthday.

Bird table with visiting ducks, some of which nest in the garden

Arthur at the helm of Colisa

Family on the 'wishing tree' walk at Ardmaddy – Arthur, Jim, George, Kerry, Annabel and Else

Jim with our first Black Rock hens

Keeping Saddleback pigs

Our vegetable garden and green house

Jim with our home cured bacon

Else with our home cured hams on the drying rack

Home cured salmon – gravadlax

Decorated salmon for Rob and Michelle's wedding

Christmas game pie baking session

Jim in the 'work shed' making benches

Jim enjoying the garden with Grouse and Kate

Chapter 22

Life's Like That Sometimes

2004 was a reasonably quiet year because of my eye problems and I was admitted for surgery on Friday 13th February. Well someone's got to get the short straw! Else stayed at Jury's Hotel otherwise known as The Pond. The dogs stayed in the car as always and were walked regularly round the pond! I had rented some specialist equipment, as I needed to sleep prone, on my tummy. So I had an extension for the bottom of the bed and also a special chair so that as I sat I leaned forward and rested my head on a pad horizontal with the floor. I was allowed to raise my head long enough to eat or drink. Else had bought in a good supply of straws. This follow up treatment allowed the bubble holding my new lens in place to gradually dissipate as everything healed. We had borrowed a good supply of talking books from the library and sought out some of my favourite music. Obviously I could not watch TV, but could listen to the news etc.

Else's cousin Sandy, living in Surrey, also had problems. She was very ill in hospital with an aneurism affecting her optic nerve. A worrying time for all of her family. It took many months for her recovery. Then in mid February, my son Jon fell and was in the High Dependency Unit at The Royal Shrewsbury Hospital with a head injury. That's three and hopefully all of our problems.

We decided to have some chickens, as we would be at home a fair amount. These came in March and were nine to ten weeks old. We initially had an arc which was moved round the garden, then a pen was made around some pine trees which would give them good shelter. They are a joy, running up to us for food and quite happy to sit with us on the steps at the front of the house. And of course, they lay the best eggs.

In August, we went with Jimmy and Doreen to the Edinburgh Tattoo for the first time. An excellent night out and as my Dad would have said about the marching military men, that they had, "Bags of swank!"

In September we went to a funeral in Leeds. My cousin Dorothy's husband Rex had passed away. He had been a rear gunner in a Halifax bomber, I think. I would have dearly loved to ask him questions about his part in the war, if I had only known.

Also this month, we had an open meeting for the public at the Tigh an Truish Inn, the pub next to the bridge as you come onto the island, about the proposed public sewage system. The more I heard about it, the more worried I became that it was not the right system for the island. Individual septic tanks would be better or groups of houses served with one system. They would have had to dig a trench eighteen feet deep in our garden to link the pipes from one neighbour to the other either side of us. We fiercely objected and after a meeting with the powers that be, eventually did not get connected.

In December I was given a six-month follow up appointment to attend Gartnaval Hospital, as the Consultants were happy with my progress.

This year we thought we would try our baking skills at game pie making. We had a supply of pheasants and venison, could get a few rabbits or other game birds and found hands of pork the best cut with a good amount of fat to meat ratio. Delia's hot water pastry recipe, we found the tastiest. Making this pastry also leaves your hands feeling wonderfully warm and supple as you work the pastry when it is still warm. Our output on one particular day was seventy-four pies. These we would give as Christmas presents along with Else's homemade chutneys. Some would also be offered to the guns and helpers on shoot days at Ardmaddy and Ardencaple.

In 2005, we went to Trinidad for Else's sister Lill's 50th birthday. A big party held in their garden near to the huge avocado tree. These avocado pears are at least four times the size of the ones you can buy in the UK, sometimes weighing up to two and three pounds.

Our Baltic Pine conservatory was delivered, flat pack, in March. This would keep us busy for some time. We had some help from our builder Roy Feakes, who put down the base, made a doorway from where a window had previously been and set the roof joists into the existing outside wall and when the roof was finished put in the lead flashing.

I also had a meeting with a Lochgilphead Forestry ranger about renting some land for stalking on the far side of Loch Awe. This I had for several years and was able to invite occasional friends and family to stalk and enjoy the area with me. There was also an osprey's nest in the trees and we were privileged to see the young birds being ringed by the RSPB officer one year. To our absolute horror, as we crouched waiting, the heavens opened and hordes of midges descended and ascended on to us. One of the others had Skin So Soft, a spray-on oil that the midges do not like, which saved our sanity!

In April we drove down to visit Simon and Jeannie in Somerset to see their new house and to stay with brother Bryan and Joyce in their new house. While we were away Else developed toothache and needed an appointment when back in Oban. To cut a long story short, driving back from the dentist, I drove straight to our surgery as Else was in distress. They treated her with aspirin as she may have been suffering from a heart attack. Then she was sent off to Oban hospital by ambulance, had treatment for a possible heart attack and where she stayed for a week. In the meanwhile, Colin came up to stay and helped me finish off the conservatory roof. The day I went to pick Else up to come home I fell off the ladder onto my shoulder. Nothing broken, just a painful shoulder. We couldn't have had two of us off sick! So Else was to take things easy. She helped with painting the wood inside and outside the conservatory, light gardening and housework and attended cardiac rehab at the hospital. She was told not to drive for six weeks.

A dog had dispatched our first lot of hens, not ours I hasten to add, so we had six new hens, Borais Black, eighteen weeks old. Luckily we have very good neighbours, so that if we ever wish to go away, they will look after the hens keeping any eggs laid and water in the greenhouse. We did have another funeral in Leeds. This time it was for my cousin Dorothy whose husband died last year. Another opportunity to meet up with family and friends. Again we stayed with Bob and Mary, with Mona and then with Richard and Elke on the way back up.

Else then had an appointment for her angiogram at the Glasgow Royal Infirmary. She arranged for me to stay the few nights at the Nurses Home next to the hospital. It was a real rabbit warren of a place and I never found the same way to my room! I managed to park the car very close as I had been told when the staff change over, so we were able to keep an eye on the dogs. Opposite the hospital is a huge graveyard called the Glasgow Necropolis. It is a Victorian Cemetery with some fifty thousand burials and three and a half thousand monuments. It is laid out as an informal park, the paths meandering uphill to the summit, an enjoyable walk and profoundly interesting. I would like to spend a whole day walking through and observing more but less keen on spending the night there. On one occasion, a gentleman said to me, "Morning." I replied, "No, just walking the dogs!"

In July, Else was driving again and off all medication, it was my turn to be hospitalised and have a ride in an ambulance. I had a stroke affecting my right side. I was home again a few days later and Else purchased a second hand wheel chair, which helped to keep me active in the house and out of doors. We saw an advert in the local paper for an exercise bicycle and a rowing machine so duly went and bought them to try and build up my fitness. They were put in the spare bedroom and initially were well used, as one does, then gradually forgotten about.

Again we had our summer visitors, Kerry and her friend Jean with the grandchildren, Simon and Jeannie who went on to Mull, son Jon with his children Alicia and Jordan, all growing up, Colin and Pat, and Lynn a colleague of Else's with her husband Brian. Unfortunately while they were here, our dog Glen was very ill and died. So he is now in the garden under snowdrops and daffodils. While we were at the vets, we noticed some pups being advertised and promptly went to see them. Not many days later we had a new addition to our family, a liver and white spaniel called Katie.

And it was, what did Katie chew next? One of Else's brand new shoes, or her purse or even less funny, one of my shoes! We have since kept in touch with Archie and Gail Cameron who bred her.

Graham, my first cousin and his wife Jennifer, visited for a few days before Christmas, and Christmas day we were invited for lunch to Rob and Michelle's. Always a top class meal. This year we invited my three brothers with their other halves for New Year. To spread the load of cooking an evening meal, we arranged that each couple would take a turn in the kitchen. We would cook the first meal, as everyone would be travelling up, venison casserole with herb dumplings. Mike and Pat cooked a delicious lamb roast which they had brought up with them, Bob and Mary did a roast goose with all the trimmings and on the last night Bryan and Joyce cooked roast partridges. Else had made desserts and organised breakfast in general. With our own baked bread, we had smoked a salmon and baked game pies in preparation for lazy lunches. The boys tossed to see who would sleep in the double bed, the single beds or the camper van! A good time was had by all with lots of jolly banter and Jimmy and Doreen joined us for the bells on New Year's Eve.

We enjoyed some good walks, to the wishing tree on the Ardmaddy road to Degnish and over to Puilladobhrain with its magnificent views of Mull and of course a quick stop at the Tigh-an-Truish on our way home!

In 2006 I was still attending the gym at the hospital following my stroke and improving so that I could still do some stalking. In February with the help of some friends, Rob, Bill and Pete, we had five beasts. I also had a follow up appointment with Mr Webb, the eye specialist and would not be seen again for nine months.

In May, Else was invited to a reunion in Bergen with the girls that she did her nursing course with. So we decided to visit family, her mother was Norwegian, and also try some fishing on the west coast not far from Bergen. We took the overnight ferry from Newcastle and cousin Knut was at the harbour to meet us and remind Else of the way to his house on the mountainside. We timed it perfectly, for the 17th May is a holiday, Constitution

Day when Norway became independent from Sweden in 1814. The processions last for hours on the main streets in Bergen, and other towns, children, students and adults dressed mostly in their national costumes waving flags and wearing their rosettes in red, white and blue, the colour of the Norwegian flag. There are big celebrations, special foods and lots of gaiety.

The next day Knut drove us through 'Gamle Bergen' or old Bergen, a conservation area of how things were, beautifully kept painted wooden houses on cobbled roads. Then we went on an island hopping post ferry, its engine sounding very much like that of *Ospray* bringing back memories of being at sea nearly fifteen years ago. Else was picked up by one of her colleagues and enjoyed her reunion though I think found it difficult to keep up with the conversation, as it was mainly in Norwegian. Thirty-five years is a long time to remember a language when she only lived in the country for a year.

The next day we visited cousin Karen and her family for lunch, and out in the country to see her Icelandic horse. That evening cousin Sverre-Jacob drove us up to his house for supper and to meet his family. Else was named after his mother.

Then we drove out to Hellesoy where we rented a 'fiske hutte,' fishing hut for four days. This was on the sea, protected by a breakwater where the rental boats were tied up. It was the first time I felt under floor heating in the bathroom. What a luxury. We had been to the fishing tackle shop in Bergen and bought a variety of colourful lures and then on the way stopped at a supermarket to buy mussels for bait. Rods and other fishing gear we had brought with us in the car. Else had invited one of her nursing colleagues, Eldbjorg, and her husband Ronald to stay with us for several days. We caught a variety of cod, haddock and ling and had delicious Norwegian 'fiske suppe' made by Eldbjorg.

We put the bagged mussels in the sea to keep them fresh. Then, later on, I spied a black animal swimming for the rocks not far away. I went to investigate. Mr Mink had bitten a hole in our bag of mussels and was sneaking off with some of the shells. I wonder how often he had done that before?

LIFE'S LIKE THAT SOMETIMES

A very pleasant fortnight away, celebrating with family, with good sea crossings on the ferry and some frozen fish in the back of the car.

My son Robert and Michelle got married in June at Shrewsbury Castle. We had a good get together with the family and met Michelle's mother and some of their friends. We stayed with George and Julia, also with Mona. Always nice to meet and greet with old friends.

We went to Scone Palace Game Fair and camped at Dunkeld with Colin and Pat. We ate well as the restaurant fare was excellent and enjoyed meeting up with friends at the Fair. We visited the Beatrix Potter Museum, which was not far away.

Our visitors in July and August were Ruth's brother Norman and his wife Kim, then my brother Mike. We went stalking one day and Mike shot a spiker of eighty-five pounds. Our dogs at this time were Gypsy and Katie. All aboard we headed home but to our great consternation, when we got there, Gypsy was nowhere to be found. Mike drove us back, quicker that I would have. And there she was, a very tired dog, very glad to see us and us even happier to see her!

I had some good fishing in Scammerdale River in September. I noted in the diary that on the 22nd, I had a grilse of five and a half pounds and two trout and the next day a grilse of five pounds. On the 30th, I had a hen fish of fourteen pounds, which I released.

Else flew to Trinidad in the beginning of October as her Uncle Ian had recently undergone bypass surgery and was due to go home. She had looked after me after my surgery so had some idea of what was entailed. She stayed for a fortnight, and though it is a very hot time of year, I think enjoyed the change and of course loved being with her family.

In 2007 we were making a few changes to our kitchen, building a breakfast bar and selling a gate-leg round table at the cattle market auction, Oban. I made my best buy ever, a chimney pot for £1, plus 10p commission, which Seumas Anderson brought home for us. It now stands in front of the house surrounded by lavender plants and has a seasonal display of flowers in the top.

I was in the throes of selling my business in Shrewsbury, which had fallen through at Christmas, so we were travelling down to Shropshire to meet prospective buyers and to see Alister who was managing it locally for me. On one of the visits we stayed with George and Julia then went to Rhyl to Pat and Colin. Here we went to see Blazing Fiddles who hail from the north, home from home. On the way north we stayed with Bob and Mary in Poynton and went to a surprise 70th birthday party for my friend John Richies. It was good to chat with long lost friends from my youth.

Bob was doing a repossession job and took Else and I to see what was in the shop. Well I fell in love with several articles. An Easter Island head made of grey stone, concrete frogs, two statues which I think are Indian Buddhas, four to five foot tall, and an elephant to use as a table in the conservatory. I managed to fit the head and the elephant in the back of the car and the rest were delivered two weeks later by a contact of Geoff's, Alan and Anne Stringer. Alan had a flat bed lorry with a hiab so that he could lift the statues into place. He had packed them in straw and covered them with a tarpaulin. Just as well, because a few drivers' heads would have turned seeing the statues and frogs being transported up the motorway!

So the Buddhas, Sam and Janet (some enchanted evening) repose amongst some rhododendrons, Easter Island man stands near our bar-b-cue area, Rivet Rivet, the frogs, one on top of the other, peep out from the bamboo nearby and the elephant gives good service for coffee cups etc. in the conservatory. Alan and his wife stayed the night before heading back. He left his boots in the kitchen where the dogs sleep. And yes, Katie was still a young pup with a healthy appetite for leather. Thank goodness she only chewed the tab out of the back of one boot. Alan had no other shoes with him.

In April, I was down the road again to Gartnavel hospital to have my other eye operated on. Ten days lying prone or sitting with my head bent forward again. Up and down to Glasgow, so we know the route quite well, about one hundred miles from home one way.

LIFE'S LIKE THAT SOMETIMES

Spring heralding a busy time in the garden; we planted potatoes, corn, peas, runner beans and broad beans. Else cut the lawn for the first time at the end of the month. On 18 May, we celebrated our 10th anniversary at Innishail. Time to bring *Fiola* up from the boat yard after the antifouling and varnishing was finished and onto her mooring in front of the house. Ian and Beryl were visiting and helped to bring her up. We are lucky to have our dinghy at the bottom of the garden, a short pull across the beach, and a few minutes row to *Fiola* in the bay. So if we see that the mackerel might be biting, it takes a very short time to be kitted up, rowing out, all aboard including dogs, engine on, steaming out to Balvicar bay and rods in the water with multicoloured mackerel flies. A fish box at the ready for the catch and a board ready for the gutting. The gulls soon know when it is their turn for a treat of mackerel heads when we are returning home perhaps an hour later.

Cutting down the pine trees, lunch break – Jim, Lorne, Martin, Rob and Doreen

Cousin Graham at the helm of Fiola

Putting finishing touches to the 'Drill Hall Bird Café'

Glen and Gypsy mackerel fishing with Jonah and Michelle

Ruth with some of her mackerel catch

Bryan and Jim walking at Raera

At Simon and Nicola's wedding, the brothers- Bob, Mike, Bryan and Jim

Chapter 23

A New Decade

To celebrate my 70th birthday, we went to stay with Mona in Llansantffraid, Powys. It is easier to get family and friends together if we travel south. Else had arranged a surprise lunchtime party to be held in Mona's garden, weather permitting. Along with Else and I, Bryan and Joyce and Bob and Mary would stay at Mona's as she did bed and breakfast. My brothers and I were sent off to watch a display by birds of prey nearby. The wives set to busily making sandwiches, a multitude of cakes being collected the day before from Oswestry. We were twenty or thirty and the sun shone. Friends, children and grandchildren made it a real family occasion.

Our next mammoth cook-up was for Rob and Michelle's wedding at Dunmor on the first weekend in July. I had boldly said that I would do their wedding breakfast. The number of guests increased so that it took us several days to make one hundred and fifty game pies, as there was that many guests, plus a large one as a centrepiece decorated with their initials. We also sliced and plated various roasts and smoked or cooked salmon. Making the garnishes from tomato, radish, lettuce etc. took several days. Else had emptied our fridge at home to store the appetising platters. It was a long evening, slicing more salmon and replating the pies as the trays emptied. When we returned next morning to help clear up, most of the work had already been done.

The following weekend was Ardmaddy fete. Else had made carrot cakes by the dozen for the tea stall, tuna sandwiches and baked bread to sell. I had a display of my antique guns sheltered under a gazebo tied onto the roof rack of my car in the hope that it would not blow away especially if there was any rain. Our one worry was Katie; our Springer spaniel was due to pup imminently. Our neighbour Ann was on maternity duty, keeping a very wary eye on events in the conservatory. Towards the end of the day, Stuart arrived to say that she had her first pup and drove me home to attend the maternity matters. Ann had become quite worried as she felt Katie needed help and was unsure of what to do. Else was left to pack up the car and take down the gazebo with Adam, her godson, who had come to stay for a couple of weeks. As we have no mobile phone reception, Stuart could not phone to give us the news. Katie was soon the proud mother of six pups. The date was the 12th of August, the opening of the grouse season, hence the name of the beautiful liver and white pup that we kept.

In November we had some trees felled by Lorne and Rob. They were very close to the house and conservatory and took most of the light from the south especially in winter. They could have been a danger to our house and our neighbour's house. I was most impressed by Lorne's skill in felling these huge spruce trees. They had to fall within a restricted space, difficult angles to work out, without causing grievous damage to the house. Else was amazed at how quietly the tree, weighing many tons, had fallen. Luckily a few friends arrived to help and as quickly as the boughs were cut, they were taken down the garden and put on a huge fire at the waters edge. Five trees were cut down over the weekend. A continuous supply of coffee, tea, bacon butties and carrot cake were on the go.

In November we had very bad news. My son Andrew had been unwell and then we learned that he had fallen and sustained a brain haemmhorage and was on a life support system. In the meantime Ruth and Mark had travelled to Australia only to find that he was in hospital. I was contacted by the medical staff as to my wishes but advised that he would never make an acceptable recovery. It was very hard for Ruth, Mark and I to make the decision that was ahead of us. With heavy heart we decided to follow the medical advice. A few weeks later after Andrew had been cremated, Ruth and Mark returned home with Andrew's ashes. They met many of his friends as there had been a birthday party arranged as Andrew would have been forty-six that month.

A NEW DECADE

Else's niece Emily was studying in London and came for Christmas. She was due to arrive at Glasgow airport before 10am. She missed her flight and instead arrived after 7pm. It was a long wait in the airport car park along with the dogs, even though we had bought ourselves a book each to read. However we had a lovely Christmas together, invited to Rob and Michelle's for Christmas dinner along with Carl and Jennie Banner. She returned to London three days later on the sleeper from Crainlarich. For New Year we had my brother Mike and his girlfriend Julia arrive for a few days. They brought a present of antler cutlery and some delicious lamb, which was very much appreciated.

In 2008 Gypsy was unwell, having various tests and scans, on antibiotics and pain relieving medicine. She was such a lovely dog, full of fun and totally loyal. She lived until May and then our vet came to inject her while she lay on my lap. She has now joined Glen, her good mate, in the garden.

There were plans being made to put in a new sewage system from the Tigh an Truish pub to Balvicar. The roads had only just settled following the upheaval of the new water pipes being laid. There were places where raw sewage was emptying into the sea and this was not acceptable. This saga went on with general meetings, house meetings, and newspaper articles and was eventually started and finished with many millions of pounds spent. I was against the installation planned as I thought individual plants per house or small systems to serve several houses would be ideal. One local man could then service these or with some systems a contract is signed and that firm would do the servicing for a small fee. There possibly would be a small increase in each electricity bill understandably. I, along with a few other households, was allowed to keep our septic tanks in situ and in working order and not go onto the scheme.

Our first visitors were John and Margaret who brought Joyce with them. Geoff did not come, as he could not face the long drive. They did not stay long as Joyce was worried about her husband but we still had good weather and some walking with the dogs and plenty of catch up on news type chats.

In June, Rob, Michelle, Jonah and Ruth came up by car and we picked up Jon and Oscar from the train station in Oban. It was planned to go out in *Fiola* with Andrew's ashes and spread them into the sea on the way to Shuna along with some flowers picked in our garden. It was a very sad occasion, many tears but lovely words spoken. We all threw our handful of ashes and said our own little prayers. On our way back in we caught a few mackerel and thought how he might have cooked them, Andrew being a chef. May he rest in peace.

At this time of year we have a wonderful assortment of birds visiting our bird table. One of them we had to look up. We had a visit from two rose coloured starlings that attempted to land for seed. Else managed to photograph them so we were able to identify them. Other birds there that day were black birds, robins, blue tits, yellow hammers and siskins. There were starlings about, collared doves and finches. The bird table is in front of a large window in our sitting room that looks down the garden towards the sea. The dining table stands in front of the window so all that sit at it have a wonderful view. Depending on the time of day, one may see roe deer in the early morning, pheasants, rabbits, on the rare occasion partridge, woodcock, water rails at any time of day, and of course bats at night. On very special occasions, we may see otters at the water's edge, often landing on the island to eat their catch of eel or fish or whatever. The binoculars are always at the ready on the window seats, one pair for Else, the other pair is mine.

To celebrate Ruth's 70th birthday, which is in late April, we booked the Red Lion House in Hartington, Derbyshire for one week in mid August. As a surprise I invited her brother Norman and his wife Kim to stay with us for the weekend. Ruth entered the house and commented on the nice floor tiles and to her astonishment a voice recognised as her brother's said, "Yes, they are a lovely colour." I had bought tickets for the Sunday through to Wednesday Gilbert and Sullivan operas, at Buxton opera house, inviting family and friends to stay with us in the house and attend on various nights. Norman and Kim just wanted to stay for the weekend.

A NEW DECADE

Bob and Mary came on Sunday; we dined at a restaurant before attending the show of Pirates of Penzance. Colin and Pat came on Monday; we ate at home before the half hour drive to Buxton to watch The Mikado. Graham and Jennifer joined us on Tuesday to see HMS Pinafore and then John, Margaret and Joyce came with us to see Yeoman of the Guard on Wednesday. We had time to explore the area, the dogs enjoyed new walks and I found a very nice antique shop. This had a very nice davenport, which I decided I must have. I really fell for it, especially after being shown several secret drawers, pull out leaves on which to put candelabra and the amazing carved dragons and intricate inlaid wood. I will treasure this always. We vacated the holiday house on Friday and went to stay with Bob and Mary and were joined by Bryan and Joyce. Then home on Sunday.

Back at home I had been asked to take a girl salmon fishing on the Euchar over three days. Whole days, so I included lunch, coffee and tea in the quote. Her father would be stalking with Rob Cameron. Unfortunately on the second day, her rod tip broke. It was tied to the roof rack and got caught in some roadside bushes. I lent her a rod that I had given to Andrew to fish with in New Zealand and following his death the rod was brought back for me to have. We were lucky with the weather, no foul thunderstorms, but also no large salmon. Dinner at Rob and Michelle's rounded the week off, a happy table full of contented guests. That Christmas we had a lovely present of wine, a thermos flask and hand warmers from Jenny. She returned my rod when hers had been fixed.

Brother Bob's 60th birthday in September was celebrated at Beck Hall, Malham near Skipton. We were there for a long weekend enjoying the Yorkshire countryside, and little did Bob know that there was a lot of family turning up, not just he and Mary. We all hid in our rooms and then joined him for afternoon tea on the Friday. It was a very well appointed hotel, lots of artefacts to talk about, four-poster beds, country views with the sound of water and car parking not far away. We had to cross a little bridge with our suitcases in tow to get to the front door. One night we went out for a special restaurant meal but unfortunately I felt unwell, so Else and I left before the end of the meal. On the Saturday, we boys went to Conniston Hotel and did some clay shooting while the girls went shopping, as is the want of girls, and a canal boat ride.

Towards the end of September we had family arriving from Trinidad, Paul and Lill, family arriving from Denmark, Annette, Stephanie and Jennifer, and family coming up from London, Emily and Sean. So we had a hectic houseful for a week and a bit of driving to and from Glasgow. And doing what one does in the highlands; walking with the dogs, mackerel fishing, canoeing and rowing the dinghy, shopping in Oban, lighting the fire in the evenings, sitting and chatting and laughing, cooking something special and having a few drinks. It was very quiet when they left. The family said that we must know a lot of people on the island noticing the hand signals as we passed other cars. A one-finger salute is an acknowledgement that you have waited at a 'pull in' for a car to go past, a raised hand is a thank you to someone that you might know, however a vigorous wave is someone that you definitely know and the drivers of both cars exchange large smiles! If there are no other cars on the road, then often the two drivers switch off their engines and pass the time with a chat until a car has been noticed ahead or in the rear view mirror!

In October we went to stay with John and Margaret and then went to Colin and Pat's Golden Wedding Anniversary at Rhuddlan Golf Club staying at the Premier Inn hotel. Else refrained from drinking as she was the driver and looked forward to a nightcap when we got back only to find that the bar was closed. You can't win them all. We then went on to Bob and Mary before driving north.

Towards the end of the year, Else looks through our photographs to find some suitable for a calendar. They usually are of the garden, the dogs, perhaps chickens, in the boat with visitors or occasionally of us in the garden and with the dogs. These we like to send to family and friends that have been to stay with us and know a bit about the area. In November, we are busy picking up on the two local shoots at Ardmaddy and Ardencaple. We always appreciate the game given us of pheasant, possibly partridge, a favourite, and occasionally duck. So we always have something to put into our game pies which we make every Christmastime.

At the beginning of 2009 Rob, Michelle and Jonah with their dog Lucy returned home after spending New Year with us. Then it was the time for making Seville marmalade as the oranges became available usually mid January. Else would make at least two dozen jars of marmalade, so the day would be spent juicing and preparing the oranges and lemons and an endless finely slicing of softened peel. Well worth it in the end for a year's supply of delicious marmalade. Of course, some would be given away to friends who did not have the time to make the marmalade. Or exchanged with those that did!

This year we had a fair amount of snow in February and March, something we seldom experienced being so close to the Gulf Stream. Because of our sloping garden, compacted snow makes for dangerous icy treading under foot, so I would not venture out very often as I was beginning to feel unsteady and that I could easily lose my balance and fall.

Mark and Erin visited in mid February and then drove south with us to Poynton to take the train to Shrewsbury. We were invited to a family get together at the 'Moorside' hotel above Disley where Simon and my niece, Nicola's wedding had taken place previously. It is a grand place with lots of moorland for walking the dogs and enjoying the outdoors. We then stayed with cousin Graham and Jennifer for a few days and were driven around to see Bakewell, Tideswell and of course the beautiful grounds of Chatsworth. Of course, we brought back some bakewell tarts for our neighbours as a thank you for looking after the house and garden.

Our cooker decided to do the dirty on us and give up the ghost, just when Bob and Mary were about to arrive for a short stay. We managed to keep fixing this Belling when its door hinges kept breaking. I just ordered more and we put them on until they decided to stop making hinges for that particular model. And so a new one was decided upon. The new cooker fitted the space perfectly but it is not a good design. The knobs that one rotates to turn on the oven or grill are smooth. Therefore if one has wet fingers the knob goes nowhere and is very frustrating. One learns with time that wet hands will not do and dry hands are a must.

In July, our village hall garden was going to be on television, on the Beechgrove Garden programme. The garden had been designed and a few of the presenters came to advise and help with the planting. Locals were asked to donate some of their suitable plants and to help in the kitchen providing food and drink for the workers. I made a bird table for the garden and a bench, which was put on the side of the hall facing one of the slate quarry pools. Else was busy in the kitchen. It was a grand day chatting to other folk, especially those who did the woodcarving. A ceilidh was enjoyed by all that evening in the big hall.

Kevin and Vanessa sold their house and moved to a larger property with several acres of ground in Llandrinio, Powys. They were living in two caravans with their children and assorted Labradors. So we decided to make them a surprise visit in our campervan, having a roof over our heads and a bed to sleep in. They told us their plans for the house and many outbuildings and for the ground. Kev would use a building for storing his tools, as he is a carpenter, Ness wanted to build dog kennels as she trained as a vetinary nurse and Kev could build them. The land, they might rent to the neighbouring farmer, plant Christmas trees to sell at a later date and they wished to keep chickens. It was good to see them so happy and excited about their new venture.

In the meantime, we arranged for the loft to be insulated, an iniative from Argyll and Bute Council and thought about putting photovoltaic panels on the roof. As the roof does not face south, it was decided to put eight panels on the east-facing roof and the same on the west-facing roof. The other energy saving item to do was to measure up for a new double glazed window in our sitting room, which was single glazed. These changes made a huge difference in wintertime and over the next twenty-five years we would be getting money back on our PV panels on the roof.

I was enjoying making benches for our garden out of the wood brought up from Shropshire and some sourced from nearby.

I found out about Oronsay wood mill, not far from Tarbert. I think the mill may have been closing down. We came back with an assortment in the boot and on the roof rack, as much as the car would carry. My other contact was near Appin, a source of kiln dried oak and planks of beautiful burr oak. With some of this Else and I made a coffee table for my niece Michelle and her husband to be Carl. The feet were in the shape of whale's tails and underneath I had cut out a heart, which I hollowed, to hold a special wedding message.

The message read. *This table was made by the two of us for the marriage of Carl and Michelle on July 3rd 2010. The top is of oak, legendary for strength and durability. It is figured with Cat's-paw Burr as if a playful kitten had wandered on to it! The legs and knees are of elm noted for its stolid resistance to splitting. We feel these qualities are reflected in your union. The whale-tail legs indicate you are lovers of the sea and wild things. We saw many of these on our voyage to the West Indies and round the Atlantic. It is mostly sperm whales and humpbacks that throw their flukes in the air as they dive. The old whalers called it 'the hand of God.' Most impressive! The oak was felled in Argyll about 1990; the elm was felled in Shropshire circa 1970 when Dutch elm disease ravaged the country. We wish your voyage through life to have fair winds and calm seas with any storms being short and soon weathered! If black clouds appear, best advice, 'Reef down and sail on!' Best wishes and Bon Voyage. Jim and Else Mellor*

In September, we went to Derbyshire to celebrate Graham and Jennifer's Golden Wedding Anniversary at Chapel-en-le-Frith Golf Course. Else was in charge of Graham's video camera so that they would have a record of the evening party and guest's best wishes. The next night we stayed with Bob and Mary along with Bryan and Joyce.

Back at home there was a meeting at Seil Hall with regard to the proposed wind farm to which there was huge opposition. This certainly was the topic of conversation for many 'Seilites' and kept the Oban Times 'letters' column full. This would continue grumbling on for some while.

A QUIET DAWDLE THROUGH LIFE

In November, Katie managed to cut herself on barbed wire on one of the shoot days, so away we went to the vets for stitches and antibiotics and a lampshade. Later in the month, we heard that Joyce had a stroke and was in hospital and then Geoff had been admitted to hospital, as he was not coping at home. So in December we drove down to Shropshire initially staying with Ruth, visiting Kev and Ness and Mona with Ruth and then to Bob and Mary's, when we visited my old friend Joyce in Stepping Hill hospital, who had suffered a severe stroke, and was unable to talk and walk. As Geoff had returned home we visited him the next day with Bob. It is so sad seeing my old friends having problems. Unfortunately we are all ageing. Tempus fugit.

In 2010 we decided to have a couple of gilts (female pigs). I chose females because, young boar pigs can carry a slight taint called boar taint when butchered. We fell in love with them on sight. They were Saddlebacks and we kept them until they were six months old. The trouble with keeping pigs, they are such loveable creatures, one inevitably acquires a distinct fondness for them. Else would sit in the pen with them, stroke a tummy and then the pig would lie down and turn over to have her upturned tummy tickled. They loved it. We had no problems in containing them although the fence needed strengthening by and by. They had greens fresh from the garden, loved treats of apples and sweet corn, as well as their proprietary pig food.

All of this care and attention meant that our pigs lived and ate like kings, or in our case queens, and the dreaded day came all too soon but they were then at bacon size and our intention was not to breed them.

I bought a book titled 'Manual Of A Traditional Bacon Curer' by Maynard Davies, Master Curer. An excellent book, with all of the recipes that we would need for using every bit of our pigs. I already had a vac-packing machine and bags but we needed and therefore ordered a sausage making gadget, casings, stockinet, string, yeastless rusk and a variety of herbs and seasonings.

The pigs were dispatched humanely and the blood collected. They were butchered and cut up into hams, sides of bacon, streaky

A NEW DECADE

and back, chops, joints, hocks and mince for sausage making. The head was cut in half for ease of boiling, getting at the tongue and head meat.

Then followed a very busy week. Making up a quantity of brine for the hams and some bacon sides that would be wet cured with water, salt, sugar, saltpetre and seasonings. Also making up a dry cure for some of the bacon that would be kept in the fridge with salt, sugar and seasonings. It is well worth writing these times down as the processes vary and the amounts used in case we should do something like this again.

We made our own black pudding with the four and a half pounds of blood collected. To this was added beef suet, pearl barley, oatmeal, onion, rice and seasonings. Then carefully filling the natural beef casing with the mixture through a funnel and tying it into a loop. Gently steaming these puddings so that they did not split and therefore we could try one for our supper that night. Delicious.

Next we made faggots with the head meat, the meat gleaned off the bones, the hearts, livers and kidneys and the hocks. To this was added medium grade rusk, onions and caul fat with seasonings. These were then wrapped in the cleaned caul taken from round the stomach and roasted. Nearly fourteen pounds of meat made forty delicious faggots.

Sausage making was next on the list. We used seven pounds of lean meat to three pounds of fat and half an ounce of seasoning to each pound of meat. We decided on Cumberland spice mix with yeast-less bread rusk and natural hog casings. If you have never made sausages before, there is an art to filling the machine so that there are no air pockets, putting the casing onto the nozzle, filling the casings evenly, and stopping when the casing has finished. Then to top it all, try linking the sausages as butchers do when they are displayed in their shops! Not that easy I can assure you!

We bought a new fridge-freezer in which to hold all of our bounty, some being given away to friends to taste. Nicely vacuum-packed and labelled, they kept well, the hams cured and in the fridge; the bacon sliced and bagged and frozen. This was so successful that we decided the following year to have another two gilts, this time Gloucestershire Old Spot cross Large Whites. Unfortunately, this year (2011) there was a lot of rain. Their house was lovely and warm, cosy in their straw, but outside became quite a quagmire. I know the saying goes, "happy as pigs in muck," but we didn't like the sight of them in all this mud, however much the pigs seemed to enjoy it. These butchered out much heavier that the first two. And again we used everything that we could from the pigs, bar the squeak!

Kate, Else and Jim with the wedding present for Carl and Michelle

Else holding the burred oak table showing the heart feature underneath with a secret message

Chapter 24

A Voyage Through The Land Of The Vikings

In 2011 there were many changes. My friend Geoff was living in a Care Home in Marple, my sister-in-law Mary was admitted for serious surgery and in a high dependency ward. Thank goodness her recovery was slow but steady. Then we decided to have a holiday in Norway and do a voyage on some of the Hurtigruten fleet. We drove to Aberdeen and flew over to Bergen arriving in time to celebrate the 17th May, Norway's Constitution Day, with Else's family.

This is the article entitled, – *To The Arctic – A Voyage Through The Land Of The Vikings*

My wife Else and I have recently returned from a trip to the Arctic. She is of Viking descent and although she does hardly any pillaging these days and hasn't raped anyone for years, she was keen on the trip.

I treat my wife with respect as one should, but with someone who could be related, however distantly, to a chap who rejoiced in the name of Erik Bloodaxe, it seems to make no more than basic common sense!

We soon abandoned the idea of doing the voyage in a galley or long ship. Not only are they scarce and hard to come by but also one has to be so careful with the crew!

Instead we chose, along with many other passengers, to embark on one of the Hurtigruten fleet of vessels. These set sail daily from Bergen, on a six day voyage up the west coast of Norway to Kirkeness on the Russian border, delivering post and supplies to thirty-four settlements on the way, a distance of some two thousand kilometres. The Arctic Circle is crossed on day four at sixty-six degrees thirty-three minutes north just south of the pleasant town of Bodo. From here northwards the Midnight Sun shines twenty-four hours a day at Midsummer Night's eve. From early winter the Aurora Borealis flood the scene with their enchanting display over the dazzling white peaks of the Northland.

The Polar Circle having been crossed, the Captain, who is all heart, had arranged a special treat on the after deck at 9.30am. Else and I arrived to find the 'treat' being administered by the Captain resplendent in full braided uniform, ably assisted by a strikingly ugly King Neptune, who had apparently been dragged up from his kelpie kingdom for this event. They took turns in serving this 'delight' to each person in the queue, as they filed past. The celebration treat consisted in having a large ladle full of ice and water poured down one's neck. Reactions varied, from the strong silent types came a very sharp intake of breath. However, one game old girl in her eighties gave a lusty shriek, which, like John Peel's 'View Halloo would have wakened the dead, or the fox from his lair in the morning.' I would have put a bob or two on a bet that her husband would have rarely been late for his dinner! Out of shame I tagged on to the end of the queue and was rewarded for being last by an extra ladle full. Certificate and hot toddy in hand we lost no time in dashing below to our warm cabin for dry clothes. As I removed my dripping shirt a shower of ice fell out of my underpants. Happy Days! I did catch a cynical remark from a bystander that anyone who volunteered for a cup of ice and water to be poured down his neck in the Arctic hardly needs to be certified. He could have a point!

I had fancied I glimpsed briefly a savage gleam in the Captain's eye at the shuddering groan of a husky volunteer. I pondered on this and a crazy thought flickered into my mind. Could the Captain have a few drops of Viking blood coursing through his veins? Not that long ago such devices using cold water and rolling naked in the snow etc. were used to build strength of character and resistance or even immunity to discomfort; a huge advantage to men who spent much of their lives voyaging in open boats often in vile weather. I just hope Else doesn't get any ideas. The thought of a cold bath on a winter's night does not delight me and would meet with strong resistance! As for me rolling naked in the snow, I have been told that this image may be counter productive to the 'Visit Scotland' campaign. I doubt they could afford my fee anyway!

Whether the cold-water treatment resulted in any greater immunity to discomfort is a matter of speculation, but the general impression was of everyone having a whale of a time, which will be recalled and recounted with hilarity. Long may it continue!

On the hill above Harstad is the gigantic Adolf Gun, a relic of the Nazi occupation during the Second World War. This monstrous weapon was installed as a shore defence against invasion. It weighed over one thousand metric tons with a barrel length of sixty-six feet and a bore of sixteen inches. The largest calibre of any land based gun in the world! Big enough for a child to fit down! This monster could fire shells packed with high explosive weighing up to a ton, at the rate of one every two minutes, to a distance of up to thirty-five miles, with the barrel cranked up to a maximum of fifty-two degrees. At this elevation the apex of the trajectory would be fourteen miles high. Some lob! When a shell of this size landed it would undoubtedly scare the living daylights out of anyone in the area. Fortunately it was never fired in anger. Krupp made this gun and others like it, well known for fooling around with weapons of mass destruction. This gun and three others were installed by three thousand Russian prisoners of war of whom eight hundred died during the construction.

I was puzzled regarding reasons for installing such gigantic and vastly expensive weapons on a sparsely populated coastline. One reason was to safeguard the supply of iron ore from northern Norway, which was vital to the Nazis in wartime.

Another possible reason presented itself in a very odd fashion! It came from the obituary column in the British press, (November 2012) which announced the death of Birgin Stromsheim at the ripe old age of 101 years named as the greatest of the 'Heroes of Telemark.'

This was a team of British trained Norwegian saboteurs, who in 1943 were dropped into the remote Telemark region of Nazi occupied Norway to destroy the Norsk Hydro plant, which produced the heavy water crucial to creating plutonium vital for developing the atomic bomb. This top-secret heavy water plant was sited on a cliff above a 600-foot ravine. The approach to the plant was via a floodlit bridge seething with Nazis. Stromsheim was from Alesund, a small port on the nearby coast. He was regarded as a man of unflappable calm! Stromsheim had escaped from Norway in a boat with his wife Aase to Scotland. He and three Norwegian colleagues, after British training, were dropped 18 miles from the plant on the 16 February 1943. For five days they skied through snowstorms to the ravine, which they scaled to arrive at the plant, finding it only guarded by a Norwegian.

The four then set off on a 400-kilometre ski trek to the safety of Sweden, leaving an upturned hive of Nazi soldiers and a world temporarily safe from the atomic bomb.

During the War my family lived in Derbyshire, twenty miles from Manchester. We would often hear the bombs falling on the city and would be told that Mr Krupp was at it again! Funnily enough as a little lad I fancied that this was the sound of bombs falling in the distance, *krupp, krupp, and krupp.*

And now from devices for dealing death and destruction to a matter at the opposite end of the tranquillity scale. Near Kvaefjord strawberries are grown! These are amongst the most northerly strawberry fields in the world. Close by is the world's most northerly horticultural college. Certainly this is a land of superlatives! The strawberries find a ready market, being harvested when all those further south are finished. Imagine growing strawberries further north than Iceland!

The Lofoten islands are impressive! They are largely guarded by The Lofotveggen a one hundred-kilometre wall of granite towering over the fishing villages that it shelters. This wall rose up out of the Gulf Stream after the last Ice Age and this feature attracts huge numbers of cod, which arrive to spawn from January to April. In the post war years up to twenty thousand fishermen arrived to reap a massive harvest of cod, which were dried on huge wooden racks. The fishermen in those days often slept beneath their upturned boats, which in temperatures of one or two degrees centigrade, one cannot imagine was a snug experience. Maybe the immunity to discomfort training is the answer! These days there are still three thousand fishermen coming to harvest the cod, which they do at the rate of some twenty-five thousand tons per annum. The fishermen no longer sleep beneath their boats but in sturdy cabins which are mostly beautifully maintained and many of which are available to rent in the summer months. The villages are extremely attractive with brightly painted houses and lots of fish drying racks giving an atmosphere of a thriving industry.

Steaming northwards we passed range upon range of dog-toothed peaks, each pinnacle gleaming with a mantle of snow. This spectacle extended as far as the eye could see broken occasionally by a massif of greater bulk, often a weird shape from some of which a fertile imagination could and did produce grotesque monsters peering down at us with evil intent.

The M/S *Richard With* slid gently to a halt in the fishing harbour of Skjervoy where we were shortly to spend a week at the 'Fiske Camp' cod fishing. We were met by Balasz from the fishing camp in whose charge we left some rods and other tackle pending our return in a few days' time.

The furthest point of our northbound leg was Kirkeness near the Russian border in the Barents Sea, which we reached after rounding the North Cape, the most northerly point of the continent at seventy-four degrees north. Kirkeness being on the border betrayed this by the presence of several Russian ships with unpronounceable names moored cheek by jowl with Norwegian vessels.

We had arranged to spend one night at the Arctic hotel about which I had entertained various hopes and fears. My most fervent hope was closely related to a secret dread. I had hoped for weeks that the beds would be fitted with electric blankets. What a wimp I hear you say! But the word Arctic conjures up visions of a couple of dead seals and half a walrus hanging up for dinner. What a pleasant surprise. The whole hotel was beautifully and tastefully appointed, the staff were polite, friendly and multi-lingual. The food was imaginative, presented and served with flair and panache. Impeccable! The finest I have seen anywhere. In our bedroom, my pathetic worries were equally groundless. The room was pleasantly airy but cosy and warm with fluffy duvets folded in the Nordic fashion to keep the warmth in. The window was half open and remained so all night. And this deep into the Arctic, amazing! We left next day vastly impressed.

Next day we board another of Hurtigruten's fleet for the one-day trip back to Skjervoy. This vessel was the *Nordstjernen* (*Northstar*), the oldest and smallest of the fleet, slightly old fashioned and delightfully shippy with lots of polished brass. She was small enough for us to just feel the faint throb of the engines that lulled us quickly to sleep. The following evening we arrived in Skjervoy to be met at the boat by Balasz who spoke seven languages fluently. He took us to our apartment a short distance away where we were shortly to be joined by Colin, an old pal. We had met at school when we were twelve and are now seventy-four! He had flown up from Gatwick to Tromso to share the week with us, after a gentle shove from his wife. Banter and insults flew thick and fast.

We were then taken down to the jetty a short walk away to be shown the facilities. A freezer room, a filleting area and of course the boats, small diesel powered vessels just large enough for four anglers. Several fishermen had just come in and were busy filleting some cod, which were, by far, the biggest I had ever seen. This was 9pm but in the land of the midnight sun, light is no problem. Each angler is allowed by law to take home fifteen kilos of fillets. Norway is one of very few nations that have sustainable fisheries due to rigid adherence to quotas etc. Next day a few short exploratory trips to get the feel of the boat that handled predictably. We caught a few fish for supper and were content. In the evening we were invited by Torlief, one of the camp managers, to be shown the hill, which overlooks the town. I was not walking well so I deemed it best not to go. Else and Colin came back bubbling with enthusiasm. The hill, they said, was alive with grouse and ptarmigan and they had watched a cock ptarmigan calling to a hen from his perch in a tree. The hen trudged up the snow apparently in response. I was amazed at this as the ptarmigan in Scotland dwell normally well above the tree line. The grouse, meanwhile, all around expressed their resentment at intrusion with their usual *go back, go back*. Whilst on the subject of birdlife we saw eagles every day. One day counting seven. Our week at Skjervoy passed all too quickly and we came in each day with fish. Our biggest cod was one of Colin's, a fish of twenty-two pounds; we also caught wolffish, delightful to eat but hideous to behold. A self-respecting wolf would resent the comparison.

Each evening in the filleting room others would come in with enormous cod up to sixty pounds. Towards the end of the week curiosity overcame reticence and we spoke to some of the other chaps. Some had been coming to Skjervoy for up to eight years and had learned many of the best spots and times to fish in the many square miles of available fishing.

One day we were fishing some five miles off shore when I realised it was pleasantly warm, there was no wind and the sea was like a millpond. Naturally venturing deep into the Arctic we had come supplied with long johns, thick sweaters and several pairs of gloves. We never wore our long johns and the only time I wore gloves was to handle wolffish for which I do not apologise.

Our return from Skjervoy to Bergen was on yet another ship, the *M/S Nordkapp*. Same excellent service, part of which was to carry our box of frozen fish in their freezer at no charge. Hurtigruten makes the point as far as possible of visiting settlements called on at night on the northward leg during the day on the southward journey. So that each may be seen without loss of sleep.

A party of school children joined the ship and travelled to Bodo, presumably as part of an educational trip. Excited but well behaved their antics caused many a smile amongst the adult passengers.

Our trip to the Arctic Polar regions left me, strangely enough, with a very warm feeling. We shall return!

Jim has just had ice blocks down the back of his shirt, celebrating crossing the Arctic Circle

Else with her big cod off Skjervoy

Chapter 25

Why We Love Living In The Hebrides

We continue to visit Trinidad, last going for Emily's wedding in September 2011, driving south to visit family, Bryan's 70th birthday in 2012, and friends either in the car or a camper van and of course taking our dogs. Else's Uncle Ian stayed with us for a short while following his brother's funeral in 2012 and was hopefully less sad as this visit coincided with Grouse having a litter of seven healthy pups. These delightful little ones would brighten up anyone's day.

Else cut down the pine tree in front of our bedroom, Lorne helped to take out the stump, to make way for firstly putting down a concrete pad and then for an Arctic Spa. I was being investigated with scans and hospital admission into the lack of my mobility, and the possibility of spinal surgery. We thought being able to relax and exercise in this tub would help my walking and general fitness. Else had also bought a manual wheelchair for use in the house or for out and about.

I decided to sell *Fiola*, as I felt unsafe with Else rowing out to the boat on the mooring even though it was a short distance. Luckily there was a local person interested, Graham Bruce and his wife. Another end of an era. We still had the canoe and the dinghy but I would not be going out in them.

My son and his wife had opened a café in Shrewsbury, so we did a surprise visit and enjoyed some very delicious coffees. However I was surprised how many cafes there were in the near vicinity and that they would have much competition. I wish them well.

As always, unfortunately there were some ill friends, Oz, Kerry's other half and a few funerals to attend. Geoff slipped his cable late September 2012 and his wife, Joyce, a fortnight after not even aware that her husband had died. Brother Bob was to have further heart surgery, which thank goodness has been successful and I decided to sell my collection of antique guns and accoutrements. This was accomplished in December 2012, but I kept one old gun, a single barrel flintlock by Jover.

I was having physiotherapy at our local hospital to improve my gait and, to keep myself and Else busy, I decided to get on with writing a book started many years ago but put down because of my eye operations and worsening eye sight. It would be titled "A Quiet Dawdle Around The Atlantic," the first part being how it was built using my Practical Boat Owner articles, and the second part being about our adventure sailing Osprey across the north Atlantic and back in 1991-1992. I could not get it finished quickly enough. Eventually it was e-mailed to our publishers, I was going to Self Publish, in April 2013. A finished copy of the book arrived just in time for my birthday to check over. I ordered a thousand books and these arrived in July. I sat in the study while Else posted numerous boxes of books through the window, each box containing twenty-three books. So they were quite heavy. Immediately we started posting them to family and friends and asking local shops if they would like to stock them for sale. I would do book signing at the village hall craft fairs.

We arranged to have an all singing and dancing bath put in to our en suite bathroom so that I could be hoisted in and out and still be able to enjoy a decent bath. I have never liked a shower so this was just perfect. Else redecorated our bedroom as we had moved to another and as one does, kept going, painting the passageway, stripping the wallpaper in the kitchen and painting it. She only stopped because the weather was colder and I liked the doors to be shut.

I had another mild stroke in October 2013, shortly after we had been south for Bob's birthday, this time affecting my left side. We invested in a Rise/Recline chair, which was initially a great help, but lately I try to sit and stand using my leg muscles.

Over the winter of 2014, the old greenhouse took quite a battering from the high winds. I think Else and Doreen helped to push it down! There were four bin loads of glass to go to the tip. The wood has kept us in starter sticks for the fire. This time we arranged for a concrete pad to be put down so that the new greenhouse could be screwed securely in place. Else soon managed to fill it with tomatoes, seedlings to eventually plant out and delicious strawberries.

With us having an open fire, I always like to have the woodshed stacked with dry logs at least six months in advance. Else now does the stacking and takes pride in her work, as I can now no longer help her. She also has a fine pair of biceps!

In August we decided to visit Orkney, a place that we both fancied visiting. It is a long drive in a slow camper van, but so what, we arrived safely and spent the first night at John O'Groats. Else was driving and we had the Tramper on the small trailer at the back. She was worried about having to reverse anywhere, especially on the ferry crossings. She did very well and I was therefore able to get about to see the gun emplacements near Scapa Flow. We camped in different places each night. I was amazed at the fertility of the land expecting it to be full of heather, scrub trees and poor grass. On our arrival back home our neighbours, Stuart and Ann, joined us in a Highland Park snifter that finished the holiday very nicely.

The stack of boxes of books is slowly diminishing and as we now have more space, I decided to write another book. This time it will be about my life starting in Derbyshire, moving to Shropshire and then retiring to Argyll. I find that I have great difficulty even to read and my writing has suddenly deteriorated, so I will depend heavily on Else for her support, typing ability and great patience. And again I cannot get this book finished quickly enough. But just to keep us on our toes, we had our youngest dog mated in January 2015 near Kendall, staying with Richard and Elke on the Borders. And now we are kept busy with seven pups and Gypsy is kept even busier feeding seven pups. The most important thing is to find good loving homes for the little tykes. One of the boys is to be called Jim, after myself and Jimmy Gilbert who had been a very good friend. This couple, Ian and Ann are also having two bitches from the same litter. Do they know what they are really letting themselves in for?

We initially decided to move to Innishail permanently as we found that we were happier here and had often taken several holidays in Scotland every year. We were involved in hobbies that we enjoyed and the dogs loved. Our friends and family were prepared to drive for many hours to visit and stay with us and so were we to visit in England. Driving up here is a pleasure as there is scant traffic and wonderful scenery. There are dreich days and there are short daylight hours over winter but a sparkler of a day more than makes up for them. There is little light pollution and peace and quiet although sometimes the dawn and dusk chorus is amazingly loud. We never fail to say out loud, "that's the geese going over," or, "that's an owl calling."

A picture that I have in my head that I will never forget is of a roebuck looking at me one morning, not far away from the road in the long grass, chewing on some meadow sweet. He held the white flowers in his mouth as if it were the most delicious of white posies.

Bill, Rob, Jim and Pete in stalking gear by Loch Awe

Jim relaxing on holiday in Tobago

Our first Glen

Our first Gypsy

Jim on the front steps with Gypsylou, Grouse and Kate

Family birthdays,
Back row – Jennifer, Graham, Bob, Mary, Joyce and Bryan
Front row – Jim and Else

Bryan, Bob and Jim with some of Grouse's litter

Jim on his Tramper at Raera with Kate, Grouse and Gypsy

Annabel, Phoebe, Great granddad Jim and Eloise

Gypsy and her pup Glen, so we now have four dogs!

Jim

Else